· FOOD FOR FRIENDS ·

FOOD FOR FRIENDS

BARBARA KAFKA

PERENNIAL LIBRARY

Harper & Row, Publishers, New York
Cambridge, Grand Rapids, Philadelphia, St. Louis
San Francisco, London, Singapore, Sydney, Tokyo

Portions of this book previously appeared in *Vogue, Bon Appétit, The Pleasures of Cooking,* and *House & Garden.* Color photographs © The Condé Nast Publications, Inc.

Acknowledgment is made for permission to reprint the recipe "Zucchini Custard" from *American Food and California Wine* by Barbara Kafka. Copyright © 1981 by Barbara Kafka. Reprinted by permission of Harper & Row, Publishers, Inc.

A hardcover edition of this book was published in 1984 by Harper & Row, Publishers.

First PERENNIAL LIBRARY edition published 1989.

Designed by Helene Berinsky
Photographs by Susan Wood
Drawings by Susan Gaber

Library of Congress Cataloging in Publication Data

Kafka, Barbara.
  Food for friends.

  "Perennial Library."

  Includes index.
  1. Cookery. I. Title.
TX715.K127 1989   641.5   84-47582
ISBN 0-06-091591-9

89 90 91 92 93 RRD 10 9 8 7 6 5 4 3 2 1

CONTENTS

FOREWORD

———————•———————

Barbara Kafka is one of the most individual, creative and many-faceted members of the New York "food fraternity," and her new book, *Food for Friends,* has the mark of her personality and talents all through it.

I have lunched and dined at Barbara's house many times, and I've never been let down. Oh, not that every meal there is absolute perfection: that would be boring. But when you go there you know you are getting food that she likes and thinks you will like. Something genuine, something that says she's glad you're there and hopes you will like what she's provided for you, because she likes it. This is a rare, rare gift.

Now, in *Food for Friends,* Barbara has described how she does it, and mapped out a series of entertainments for close friends, each one with the stamp of her personality and taste on it.

The first thing you are aware of is that Barbara loves to entertain. The second is that she doesn't believe in making it a week-long experience to have a few people for dinner. She tells you she sometimes stops on her way home from a busy day at work and decides what she's going to have while she stands in the market.

You see that she ponders about the wine and consults her palate very seriously before deciding what to have. You see that she cares about the service and the flowers, never being overly careful about "having company," but always paying heartwarming attention to detail.

Some of her dishes are quite simple. Others are more complicated, but always with a reason behind the complication. This is not just another new cookbook, not just a lot of things jotted down because they seem to go together. Barbara's taste is elegantly casual, and her balance of food and wine quite extraordinary.

I've traveled with Barbara, taught with her, talked with her endlessly about food and wine. I know that we can be on tour together for weeks, and yet at the end of that time, if we each had to come up with a meal made from the same foods, they would be completely different. But we would both admire and enjoy the other's work.

Keep her book on your reference shelf. You will take it down for ideas when you're entertaining, and lean on it for support and verification of your own ideas. I recommend it highly. It is a most endearing book on first reading, one that's going to last as a little treasure to amuse us, reassure us and inspire us.

JAMES BEARD

· FOOD FOR FRIENDS ·

INTRODUCTION

———————————•———————————

Food for Friends is not just the name of this book. For me, it is the essence of cooking. I learned to cook because I wanted to do something nice for my friends. To bring them together over a meal seemed to me the nicest thing of all.

At first I was clumsy. My friends seemed to understand and enjoy the evening anyhow. As I got to be a better cook, I retained the clumsiness of trying too hard, of making the evening too much about the food, too little about the experience. Even so my friends seemed to forgive me as they ate their way through ornate course after ornate course: too much food, too many sauces.

By now, I seem to have relaxed. I entertain as much; we eat as much; I have more things to do; the meals still get made. If anything, I think my friends and I eat better and have more fun with less-demanding meals. No longer does each course require, as it appears at table, that conversation stop and the food be admired.

My cooking is different. I don't know if my taste has changed with the times, if I have simply gotten older, more rushed, more desirous of clearly defined tastes and textures, if I have become newly aware of the rich diversity available with the increase in ethnic supplies and fresh foods from around the globe and my garden. I use less cream and make fewer complicated sauces. The colors on my plates tend to be clearer, as do the tastes. Those long hours spent in previous kitchens taught me to make the classic sauces, understand the classic techniques and the richness and complications in levels of taste that those sauces provided. I am glad I know those things. When confronted by young cooks who really want to know it all as well as make dinner, I still tell them to buy an *Ali Bab* (the first of the orderly and comprehensive French cookbooks and still the best) and cook their way through it. I have learned to get the richness of taste, generally, in simpler ways.

The lack of available time has changed my cooking the most. I do what can be done at the last minute, what can be done ahead, and what requires little shopping.

I'd found myself slipping into the trap of eating in restaurants, meeting friends for a drink or losing people altogether. I missed them and the leisurely evenings of food and conversation. People talk differently in restaurants, with less intimacy, less self-revelation. I can laugh more boisterously and tuck my feet up on my chair at home. Deep friendships thin in restaurants. When I was a girl, the rule of thumb was to meet new men for lunch or a drink out—to minimize the risk. That's fine for beginnings; but no guts no glory. So, for me, it has been back to entertaining at home.

WHO'S COMING
TO DINNER?

———————•———————

Planning a Meal

Most of the time I don't consciously plan a meal. It just happens. Particularly when I am in my habitual hurry, a series of automatic questions seems to pop into my head followed by answers and summed up with the beginnings of work to get dinner on the table. Correction occurs only when I am set back by a sudden sense of distaste: "that's really awful" or "creamed chicken after crème Germiny, yuck." However, the internal computer was not always so efficient and, for those of you for whom it is not automatic as yet, here goes the basic list:

Was it really tonight I invited the X's?
What's the date anyhow?
Did I invite anybody else?
That makes ten, right?
Did I include us when I counted?
Now I only get eight. Whom did I leave out?
It is eight. Eight's a terrible number; the man/woman thing never works.
Should I invite another couple? Remember: six or ten. Never mind, Anne will just have to sit next to me and the other end of the table will work out somehow.
When can I get home to cook?
Is there anything in the house?
Who is allergic to what? Didn't he say his wife couldn't even eat mussels she was so allergic? I wonder if that means lobster too? Better play safe.

Do I have any money with me? Anyhow, I have a supermarket check-cashing card.

Maybe there's some bread in the freezer.

Is it hot because I've been running around like a nut, or is it just hot? Hot! Well, then, who wants a great hot soup? Who said I was making a soup? Well, it is always easy. Just think of something else. Cold soup's nice. If I don't get home until six, it won't be cold.

What else can we start with? Have I seen anything recently that was nice? Asparagus. Everybody likes asparagus. If I just get a few sea scallops and sauté them with the asparagus, some butter, lemon, and some parsley, that should be light, not too hot, and even slimming.

What will we drink? A gewürztraminer should hold up to the scallops.

Booze first? I hate it when they get to the table drunk. Does that mean another wine first? After all, unless you're German, gewürztraminer is a little weird all by itself. I don't have enough wine glasses for a wine before dinner, a wine with scallops, and something with the main course. I won't wash glasses in the middle of dinner.

Well, if I start with the Chandon—I think there are three bottles left—that can go with the scallops as well. If there's any left, it can go with dessert.

Are there eight unbroken Champagne glasses left? How Herman managed to break three the last time he was over I will never know. If there aren't, it will just have to go in goodness knows what glasses.

I guess that takes care of the first course. It should be fancy enough—so that I don't have to have a fancy main course, just a roast. It can be cooking while we're eating; nice and easy; my favorite kind of meal.

Can I get away with a chicken? I love a good roast chicken, lemon and garlic inside. The Thatchers have never been to the house before. Maybe they will think I'm being cheap. I'd better stick with a leg of lamb. Then I can do some of my potatoes in olive oil and garlic that everybody loves. They go in the oven at the same time as the lamb. That will be perfect. Salad and cheese plus a simple dessert and I'm home free.

Now let's see. What do I have to get: red wine for the meat and cheese, asparagus, lettuce for salad, the meat, bread, new potatoes, lemon and scallops. Oh, good heavens, do you think mussels means scallops? Too bad, I can't go through it again. If she can't eat it, she can't eat it.

Now, what about dessert? I'm so tired. I'll buy some cookies and hope they have some good fresh raspberries. Nobody can be insulted by raspberries and cream.

Do I have coffee? I must. If not we'll do without.

All I have to do is run into the house, turn on the oven to 450°, set the table, put the wine in the fridge and start to cook. It will be quick and easy, about a half hour's time before the guests arrive. If I remember to pick up flowers on the way and I want to change, I'll need another half hour.

Setting a Table

One of the reasons I love designing restaurants and giving dinner parties is that I cherish that moment when the candles are lit and the people arrive. It's my own private curtain going up. I like the sparkle and the drama. To me food and its surroundings must be beautiful. They can be informal and direct but they should seduce.

I hate tomato roses, parsley on plates where no one will ever eat it, and any food gotten up to look like something else. I think good food well cooked should look beautiful on its own without meringue swans. I have a friend who is a restaurant owner, and in all his restaurants the butter is molded into the form of little birds. When I go to butter my bread, I have to decapitate, an off-putting sensation.

There is almost no limit, on the other hand, to how fine a table can look—not formal necessarily but lovely. I am a sucker for fresh flowers. In the summer, I raid the garden. In the winter, I envy my California, Florida, and Texas friends the inexpensive flowers in their shops. When I have the time, I descend on the flower markets and buy more armfuls than I can afford.

If the beauty of flowers is partly in their evanescence, fruits and vegetables as centerpieces appeal because they can turn up the following day in salad or a soup. Besides, the forms are wonderful. The

rich glossy black of eggplants set off by the spiky dull green of artichokes is only rivaled by cherimoyas mysteriously lurking behind mangoes and papayas.

And, oh, the delight of candlelight. I have always timidly stuck with white—unscented, of course—but last summer I had dinner in Geneva on the terrace of my most creative entertaining friend's home, and she used pale blue candles in profusion, set off by white linen and pale roses and bachelor's buttons and gentle eighteenth-century blue-sprigged plates. It was ravishing.

I collect odds and ends of dishes: five garlanded dessert plates, eight fiery orange-and-blue bedragoned rim soups deep enough for an entire meal, seven clear-green-glass salad plates with hints of blue, nine majolica plates in a strange bisque which almost match in pattern the three green plates bought years ago in a country store. I mix and match and make do and delight in the variety. No course matches the previous one. If the table gets too crowded, I switch to butter chips (miniature plates just big enough for a dollop of butter) and let the crumbs fall where they may. The real problem is space for storage and the regret for bulky earthenware unpurchased in Siena because I could not bear coping for another month with the awkward fragile package.

Matching food and dishes is part of the game. Occasionally, I will put a robust country stew in an elegant porcelain rim soup; but, more normally, I let the style of the food dictate the style of the dish. Always, one must think about how the colors go or set each other off. Remember, if the dish isn't going to be on the table without food, no one will see the beautiful flowers in the center. Stick to designs on the rim; they are safer. In the days before I collected my cache of plates, I would often pick the food to go with the available dishes. Even today, I will sometimes feel I want to use a certain plate and find a food that seems to match.

Cooking from This Book

Like all cooks, I am idiosyncratic. Like all recipes, these are guidelines. They are guidelines to the way I prepare certain foods. As you try them, I hope that you will feel free to vary them, to make them your own. All recipes vary with the ingredients. Even baking recipes, thought to be scientific formulas, vary with the age of the eggs—old eggs have less viscosity, won't beat up as high to incorporate air—and the humidity retained by the flour. Recipes dependent upon the flavor of ingredients are even more sensitive to variation. One lemon or tomato will be more sweet or more acid than another. The pepper you buy one day will be more pungent than that you bought under the same trademark another day. I can only encourage you to taste your ingredients as you use them.

However, there are certain consistent attitudes toward ingredients, tools, and methods that are expressed in these recipes. For those of you who are interested—why, for goodness sake, does she always use kosher salt?—there is more information in the last chapter of the book (page 321).

I am also a little odd in the way I choose foods to eat both at home and abroad. I have been known to go to a restaurant and order nothing but a succession of first courses, appetizers, entrees or hors d'oeuvre—however they are known. In many kinds of cooking—Greek with its meze (those delicious bits of food served in a staggering variety: stuffed grape leaves, mussels with pine nuts, tarama, and the like)—these are my favorite dishes. It must be admitted that, even in Italian food, by the time I have been through the antipasto and the pasta, I have eaten what often seems to me to be the best part of the meal. While I do try to cook marvelous roasts and stews for main courses, I pay more attention to the first courses. It is simple common sense, or, at least, my kind of sense. I am least tired at the beginning of the meal, most likely to turn out a well-made dish. My guests are most attentive and hungriest. A good first course, well prepared, will always get the most attention. After that, conversation becomes more intense, my guests and I have had a glass or two of good wine. The meal relaxes.

Perhaps my strangest eating habit is the way I devour books. I have a particular appetite for reference books and have been known to go to bed with a new dictionary the way other people take bowls of soup, for comfort. This taste has led, I hope, to a particularly complete Index (page 329). There, for instance, you will find all the sauces in this book listed not only alphabetically and as they occur, as parts of other recipes, but also by type: Tomato-based Sauces, Egg-bound Sauces, etc.

Generally, I have tried to give technical descriptions in the recipes as they are needed. If something isn't clear, or you simply want more information, look in the Index. It may refer you to other recipes where the technique is more clearly described. We have all become so much more sophisticated in our cooking that it is very hard to know what can be taken for granted and what still needs to be described. The one word I use repeatedly that may not be familiar is *reduce*. It simply means that a quantity of liquid should be simmered or boiled to evaporate some of the water, leaving a thicker and more intense residue.

Remember, most of all, to have fun. If you do, your guests will.

COLD
FIRST COURSES

———————•———————

Roasted Red Pepper Spread

Simple Potted Mushrooms

Spiced Olives

White Bean Salad

Chopped Chicken Livers

Tapenade

Tabbouleh

Guacamole

Eggplant Orientale

Eggplant Caviar

Taramasalata with Red Caviar

Hummus

Party Shrimp and Chili Mayonnaise

Asparagus with Ham and Vinaigrette

Raw Scallops with Avocado

Smoked Salmon with Pink Peppercorns

Orange and Onion Salad with Cumin Vinaigrette

Roasted Yellow Bell Peppers and Tomatoes

Warm Vegetable Compote

Prosciutto, Smoked Mozzarella and Celery Root Salad

Julienne of Chicken Salad

Poached Chicken and Cucumber Salad with
Pomegranate Seeds
Duck Breast Salad
Smoked Whitefish Mousse
Mussels Ravigote
Mosaic of Eel and Green Herbs

S ome cold first courses take time to make, though generally they can be made ahead so you are not hurried at dinnertime. Others are last-minute lifesavers—quickly assembled, often from staple ingredients. All depends on when you want to do the work. Many of the dishes listed under Pasta and Side Dishes can be served in smaller portions as first courses. Since many cold things keep a day or so, I have been known to cheat and make enough of a cold first course to serve at two dinners.

Cold first courses can be classically elegant: smoked trout, oysters, and smoked salmon; some can be hearty and peasanty: Hummus, Eggplant Orientale, and Roasted Red Pepper Spread. They can be served in weather hot or cold. They are most interesting before a hot main course.

As They Come from the Store—or Almost

As with many foods, the simplest first courses to serve are the most expensive. If time is money or at least in short supply, expensive may be worth thinking about. A few simple techniques and a handful of on-the-shelf garnishes can turn your bought indulgence into a first course for little but the shopping time.

CAVIAR

Of bought indulgences the most glorious is caviar, particularly big, plump, grayly black eggs. Beyond enough money, all you need is lemons cut in half and some thinly sliced white bread toasted. I collect shells and bone spoons, because silver interacts with caviar as with any eggs. If these or their more elegant vermeil cousins are beyond reach, try for stainless steel egg spoons. Even collect the small plastic spoons given with espresso on European airlines. The size of these spoons also slows down consumption. In a more elegant era, kilo cans of caviar came with mother-of-pearl spoons crossed, in pairs, on top of the rubber-band-sealed cans.

If fresh beluga malassol or sevruga or oestetra is definitely out of the question, a good-quality salmon caviar or the more exotic, recently available, golden (whitefish) caviar is a less expensive and very good alternative. (Beluga is the largest species of sturgeon with the largest egg; malassol is from Russian "malo," meaning "little," and "ssoleny," "salted." Sevruga and oestetra are smaller sturgeon with smaller eggs.) I think lumpfish caviar isn't worth buying, especially if you are going to cook with it, as its black dye leaks all over.

Unfortunately, as the price goes down, the work quotient goes up. While I like my beluga ungilded, I like the lesser caviars with a little gold leaf.

GILDING THE LILY: If you have the time, a baked Idaho potato—at least an hour in a 450°F. oven without butter or foil to soften the skin—slashed and crushed open, filled with sweet butter, dolloped with sour cream, and topped with caviar, makes a fabulous and filling first course.

Small red new potatoes may be baked in a hot oven for twenty minutes, cut in half, and the insides scooped out with a small spoon. Brush shells with melted butter and bake until sizzling, or deep-fat-fry, to serve as edible cups for sour cream topped with caviar. Both the Stanford Court in San Francisco and the Four Seasons in New York serve these at posh cocktail parties. Tiny blini (see the recipe for Basic Blini in the *Art of Russian Cuisine* by Anne Volokh) can be topped with caviar and sour cream, as can miniature Potato Pancakes (page 258). Quicker to make is scrambled eggs, with a little dill or chopped chives stirred in and served spooned on top of a slice of toast, as a soft (not overcooked) yellow frame for caviar. Easier yet is the conventional garnish of hard-boiled eggs with yolks and white chopped separately and chopped onion—my least favorite.

I keep a bottle of good akvavit and a bottle of Polish vodka in the freezer and have an assortment of tiny glasses, some Russian in silver, in which to serve the syrupy liquor. If there is going to be a lot of wine during the evening, I serve American bubbly instead, to reduce the number of hangovers.

▪ ▪ ▪

SMOKED FISH

Smoked salmon, smoked sturgeon, smoked trout, and smoked eel are equally easy. All smoked fish should be taken out of the refrigerator about a half hour before it is to be served. This allows the rich fat that makes these fish so succulent to be at the right, ready-to-melt temperature. I usually arrange individual plates as soon as I take the fish out of the refrigerator; it is easier to separate the slices or skin the fish when it's cold. These delicacies don't do well on a platter. If you are going to serve them as cocktail hors d'oeuvre, cut the fish in small pieces and place on small slices of the Herb-Buttered Bread (page 14). Put wedges of lemon in the middle of the plate. This is a time when napkins are essential.

I don't buy Scotch salmon. It is too expensive and seldom of really superb quality. If I can get it, I buy excellent Northwest or Nova Scotia salmon. Most importantly, buy the salmon from a store that sells a lot and where someone knows how to slice it in broad, thin slices. The best slices come from the center of the salmon, which leads to the classic story of the little old lady who went to the delicatessen and said she wanted some salmon. "How much?" the counterman wanted to know. "Just start slicing." "Is that enough?" "Keep slicing." "Now?" "Keep slicing." "Enough?" "I'll take those two slices." Poor counterman; but she was right. I buy about three large slices per person so as to have seconds for those who want them; but two good-size slices make a serving. All I put on the plate with the salmon is half of a lemon. On the table I usually have a nice small decanter of a light olive oil, a peppermill, some capers in a shallow dish, and a plate piled with thinly sliced wholewheat or German pumpernickel bread buttered and cut in two.

Sturgeon is a little more unusual and a little more expensive. It needs no help beyond lemon and plain buttered bread. Do remember that sturgeon is white, and choose a colored plate. For ultimate luxury, serve each slice with a small spoonful of caviar on top. One slice of salmon and one slice of sturgeon also make an attractive plate.

To serve smoked eel, cut it in three- to four-inch lengths. Slit the skin down the backbone and peel off. Do not attempt to fillet. Serve two pieces per person with Horseradish Whipped Cream (page 14) and a half lemon. Be sure to provide fish or other small knives.

One half of a skinned and boned trout per person should do the trick, again with the whipped cream and the lemon. Feathers of fresh dill or snips of chives look well on the white flesh. Both eels and

1. With the tip of a sharp knife make an incision all along the dorsal spine. Working the tip gently against the bones, free a fillet from the frame.

2. Cut the skin at the tail and below the head to free the fillets.

3. With the fillet skin side down remove any remaining small bones. Watch for those encased in a fine membrane on the stomach side.

4. With the fillet skin side up gently peel back the skin. Repeat steps 3–4 for the second fillet.

FILLETING AND SKINNING SMOKED TROUT

trout can be ordered from a fish store, and, if the store is nice, it will skin and bone the trout for you.

• • •

HORSERADISH WHIPPED CREAM: For a change, if I have a few extra minutes, I shake a bottle of prepared horseradish into a tea strainer to drain. While it is draining, I whip a half pint of heavy or whipping cream (not ultra-pasteurized). Then I mix the two together with a fork and either spoon some onto each plate or pile it gently into a small glass serving bowl.

HERB-BUTTERED BREAD: A stick of unsalted butter can be cut into a food processor bowl and then whirled with two tablespoons of coarsely cut chives, a teaspoon of lemon juice, and a grinding of black pepper. Spread this on the bread. Make extra quantities and freeze for future use.

GRAVLAX SAUCE: An eight-ounce jar of ordinary American brown mustard can be emptied into a bowl, mixed with three-quarters of a cup of sugar, three tablespoons of lemon juice, one tablespoon of white vinegar, and three-quarters of a cup of chopped dill. This is my basic Gravlax Sauce. It is very pretty served in half of the hollowed-out shell of a lemon, as it is at The Four Seasons restaurant in New York: cut the lemon in half between stem and stern; scoop out the pulp with a teaspoon, saving the pulp to squeeze for juice.

OYSTERS AND CLAMS

Although oysters and clams can be ordered opened or shucked, it is a good idea to take a quiet afternoon, proper knives, a preventive supply of Band-aids, and a stiff drink to learn how to open them. It is a skill, like swimming, that, once acquired, is learned forever. The next time your firehouse has a bash, you can be the glory of the evening, opening clams two a minute.

Before you open, or, for that matter, cook clams and oysters, they should be thoroughly scrubbed under cold running water (drawing 1). This will eliminate the two gravest errors in bivalve service: grit between the teeth and plump bodies washed after opening of all natural juices. If your hands are sensitive to the cold, rubber gloves are a good investment. They also provide traction like sand on the ice. A very stiff brush or a heavy-duty plastic scrubbing pad is an ideal tool. Don't use a metal scouring pad; the animals love to eat the particles and then spit them back at you when you think you're swallowing only a plump and succulent body.

A clam knife should be stainless steel, rather long, with a rounded tip that is sharpened on both sides. In the hand with which you do not hold a knife—how's that for avoiding left-right discrimination?—place a cloth in the space formed by your thumb and forefinger. Wedge a clam against the cloth, the hinge toward your forefinger. The clam should have its rounder shell toward the ground (drawing

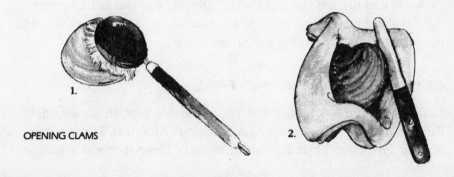

OPENING CLAMS

1.

2.

OPENING CLAMS

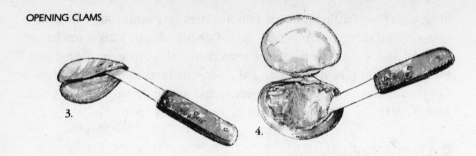

3.

4.

2). Carefully and gently, wiggle the edge of a clam knife in between the top and bottom shells (drawing 3). As soon as you feel the knife slip between the shells, twist it sharply to separate them. Now press the tip of the knife against the top shell and cut the two muscles (one on either side of the shell) that hold the shell halves together. The object is to separate the shells without cutting through the clam itself. Twist off and discard the top shell. Run the knife underneath the clam, pressing the knife close to the bottom shell to prevent cutting the clam (drawing 4). This will separate the muscles from the bottom shell, leaving the clam intact and ready to be eaten on the half-shell.

Oysters are somewhat more difficult than clams to open, which is why a good oyster knife with a hand guard is a worthy investment. The principle is the same: separate the two shells slightly, then free the meat without cutting into it.

Oysters have one deep side and one flat side. The bottom shell is the deeper and more curved. Hold the oyster, flat side up, with the curved side of the shell nestled in the crook between your thumb and forefinger. The tapered end of the oyster should extend out from your hand. With the sharp tip of the oyster knife, search along the back of the shell for the small opening between the shells. Insert the tip of the knife and firmly push and wiggle it to separate the shells. Twist off and discard the top shell. Carefully run the knife between the flesh and the bottom shell to separate them. Serve the oyster on the bottom shell, reserving the juices.

OF HAMS AND SAUSAGES AND PÂTÉS

Good prosciutto is a classic first course, as are jambon de Bayonne, Parma ham, and Westphalian ham. Owing to American sanitary para-noia or agricultural protectionism, none of these meats is available from the appropriate national source. All that we get are American cured. This does not prevent me from shopping until I find the brands that I like and stores that will cut them properly. I look for hams that are not too darkly red—dried out—with plenty of good white fat and a healthy shine. They should be sliced extremely thin, as should Smithfield or, even better, Kentucky ham that is to be served raw as a first course.

While ham may be served alone with several grindings of fresh black pepper on top and a good, thick-crusted peasant loaf on the side, it is often accompanied by thin slices of peeled melon or whole ripe fresh figs. Slices of early fall pears, crisply ripe slices of peeled kiwi, or peeled and sliced cucumbers are less conventional interleavings.

Before dinner, I usually prefer to set up individual plates with the ham. When informal and rushed, I put the sliced ham on a board (a little less than when served plated) and have around crocks of black Nice olives and small salty green Spanish olives, a crock of good butter, a bowl of iced, round, red radishes, a basket of bread, and a dish of chunks of aged Parmesan cheese. A variety of sliced hard salamis and chorizos can replace the ham or be added to it. If I keep going with Italian pickled peppers, slices of fire-roasted red pepper, drained, straight from the jar except for a lashing of olive oil, along with some sliced tomatoes, a can of good tuna or sardines, and possibly a green salad, I have a red-wine meal for great pleasure and little labor. Earthenware crocks and small plates or country pottery look best with this essentially rustic fare.

Increasingly, specialty shops are preparing take-out foods that are edible. Finding one that provides a good pâté is a worthwhile way to pass a cool fall afternoon. Take several good bets home. Serve the assorted finds for dinner with cornichons, pickled onions, an assortment of mustards, a hot soup, bread, and a salad. Complete with fruit and cheese. Remember which was your favorite pâté. Then you are all set for the first course for your next dinner. You can buy the pâté several days ahead—especially if you buy a block rather than slices.

ASSORTED LIFESAVERS FROM CANS

Aside from the mustards, olives, cornichons, pickled onions, canned fish, jarred pickled hot peppers, fire-roasted red peppers, capers, olive oil, vinegar, and good pepper that we already know should be waiting on the shelf, there are several other in-case-of-need emergency rations. The Greeks, Russians, and Scandinavians love small bits of salty foods to spice the evening's ouzo, vodka, and akvavit.

INSTANT GREEK: I always have at least one can of stuffed vine leaves, dolmas, on the shelf. If people are coming for drinks, I zoom home, squeeze a quarter of a cup of lemon juice, open the canned dolmas, put them and their oil into an attractive bowl, and pour over the lemon juice. As I get out the glasses, plates, forks, ice, mixers, and napkins, I gently stir from time to time. I serve, or let people serve themselves, onto small plates and add a few calamata olives hastily emptied from their jar or Spiced Olives (page 21) if I have them on hand. If I have time, I stick some frozen pita bread in the oven and make some Taramasalata with a jar of red caviar or from fresh cod roe—unbelievably inexpensive at a fish store—or jarred tarama (salted cod roe) (see page 28). Good with this is White Bean Salad (page 22).

INSTANT RUSSIAN: In addition to the smoked fish and caviars, there are jarred creamed herrings that are inexpensive and, if one shops brands, quite good. They should be doctored with extra, thinly sliced mild onions, sour cream, and a little chopped fresh dill. Cream cheese is a simple base for variation. Mix it with a little sour cream and some finely chopped scallion tops or chives. If there is a little leftover smoked salmon, it can be put in a blender or food processor with cream cheese and sour cream to form a lightly salty, pale pink spread for dark pumpernickel bread.

INSTANT SCANDINAVIAN: These items are not so different from the foods suggested for Instant Russian because the countries are neighbors and have similar styles of cooking. Yet, Scandinavian has its own twists. There are more kinds of fish from cans that can be added to the Russian selections: different herrings, sprats, and anchovies; or you can buy some matjes herring, cut it in one-inch strips, and place it in the Gravlax Sauce (page 14). Canned or freshly cooked beets can be sliced and tossed with lemon juice, sour cream, and freshly chopped dill. Tiny shrimp, frozen or canned, can be mixed with the omnipresent dill and sour cream, zapped up with a little mustard or turned in a lemony vinaigrette. Stemmed mushrooms or the whites of hard-boiled eggs make good containers for serving the shrimp. Look also at the Simple Potted Mushrooms (page 20).

Eating Before the Meal

I almost never serve hors d'oeuvre with drinks. Why should people get filled up on odds and ends before a good meal? In addition, I eat late since I need time to recover from the day. I figure that this gives most of my guests time to be on time. Therefore, there's no need for a long drink hour and its sobriety snacks. However, the cocktail party arrives for all of us at some point in the best-managed of lives. The first thirteen foods in this chapter can come off their plates and lettuce leaves and function out of crocks or be spread on neat, small pieces of bread as cocktail-party foods.

• • •

ROASTED RED PEPPER SPREAD

There is absolutely no tradition behind this brightly red and rich-tasting spread. Serve it alone or on sesame crackers or as a sauce for steamed white vegetables or steamed fish. I like it so much I always make a triple quantity.

• • •

1 seven-ounce jar roasted red peppers, drained
3 large black olives, pitted
4 flat, oil-packed anchovy fillets
1 tablespoon parsley sprigs
2 teaspoons olive oil
1½ teaspoons fresh lemon juice
Salt
Freshly ground black pepper

Place the peppers, olives, anchovies, and parsley on a cutting board. Using a large chef's knife and working with a rocking motion, chop the ingredients until minced. Make sure as you chop to distribute the ingredients evenly so that they are not chopped too fine—the mixture shouldn't be puréed.

Transfer the pepper mixture to a small bowl and beat in the olive oil and lemon juice. Add salt and pepper to taste. The amount of salt will vary, depending on the olives and anchovies that are used.

This spread can also be made in a food processor by placing the peppers, olives, anchovies, and parsley in the work bowl and processing with very quick on-off motions until the ingredients are finely minced. Do not overprocess. Add the lemon juice and olive oil and process until barely incorporated. Add salt and pepper to taste. Serve alone on a lettuce leaf.

MAKES ABOUT ⅔ CUP; SERVES 4 AS A FIRST COURSE

SIMPLE POTTED MUSHROOMS

·

This is as close to instant food preparation as you can get. Don't use those strangely white, packaged mushrooms, chemically treated, that have appeared on the market. Look for medium-size, firm mushrooms. If you have the time, make them about one-half hour before you want to serve. Otherwise, increase the seasonings slightly. There is no salt, since the mustard has plenty. These will keep for about three days in the refrigerator.

...

12 large firm white mushrooms, trimmed and
  cleaned
4 teaspoons lemon juice
⅓ cup sour cream
⅓ cup Dijon mustard
2 tablespoons coarsely chopped fresh dill
Freshly ground black pepper

Slice the mushrooms very thin. As you work, place them in a bowl containing the lemon juice. When the mushrooms have all been sliced, toss them in the lemon juice to coat. Blend in the sour cream, mustard, and dill. Season to taste with pepper. Serve at room temperature.

SERVES 4 AS A FIRST COURSE, 8 AT COCKTAILS

SPICED OLIVES

Most American olives aren't worth eating. They taste like oversize pieces of water-logged vulcanized rubber. On the other hand, Graber olives, russet-speckled and ripe, need only a little doctoring to be personalized and luscious, also beautiful to look at. I usually make multiple quantities to have on hand or give as gifts. Just don't try to start at the last minute or the taste won't come through.

...

1 seven-and-a-half-ounce can green Graber olives,
with pits, or good Spanish green olives with pits
or even black Italian olives
1 tablespoon olive oil
10 cloves garlic, peeled, bruised
2 three-by-one-inch strips orange zest
2 three-by-one-inch strips lemon zest
½ teaspoon cumin seeds
½ teaspoon coriander seeds
½ teaspoon lemon juice

Rinse the olives briefly and pinch each one gently to bruise. Mix the olive oil, garlic, orange and lemon zests, cumin and coriander seeds, and lemon juice in a small bowl and pour over the olives. Toss to coat evenly, and transfer to a jar with a tight-fitting lid. Cover and store in the refrigerator, shaking them whenever you think of it, until they become flavorful, 5 to 7 days.

MAKES ABOUT 2 CUPS

WHITE BEAN SALAD

This is a fearfully simple last-minute ration. It is also good with cold poached fish or leftover cold sliced lamb.

• • •

3 twenty-ounce cans white cannellini
⅔ cup good olive oil
1½ cups chopped yellow onions (use medium-size onions)
¼ packed cup finely chopped mint leaves
¼ packed cup finely chopped Italian parsley leaves

Pour all 3 cans of beans into a large sieve or colander. Rinse well under warm running water. Drain. One hour before you plan to serve the salad, place the drained beans, olive oil, chopped onions, mint, and parsley in a large glass bowl. Use two forks to toss.

Let the salad stand at room temperature for an hour before serving. For a first course, serve with bowls of Tapenade (page 24) and Roasted Red Pepper Spread (page 19) and crisp sections of raw fennel for dipping.

MAKES 4½ CUPS, TO SERVE 12

CHOPPED CHICKEN LIVERS

This is a classic. If you are saving up chicken livers, cover them with milk and freeze. Keep adding livers and milk until ready to use. Defrost in the refrigerator. Drain before using. Milk removes any bitterness from livers, whether fresh or frozen.

• • •

¼ cup chicken fat (see note)
2 medium onions, coarsely chopped
Salt
Freshly ground black pepper

1 pound chicken livers, soaked overnight in milk,
drained, and cut in halves with connecting
membranes removed
2 peeled hard-boiled eggs

Heat the fat in a large sauté pan over medium-high heat. Add the onions, 1 tablespoon salt, and 1 teaspoon pepper. Cook until nicely browned. Transfer to the work bowl of a food processor.

Add the livers to the pan and adjust the heat to medium. Sauté, turning frequently, for 3 to 4 minutes, until cooked through. Test the livers by cutting one with a sharp knife. The center should be just slightly pink. When they are cooked, transfer the livers to the food processor.

Add the eggs. Process in 3 or 4 very quick pulses, so that the mixture is coarsely chopped. Transfer to a clean bowl, taste, and season with additional salt and pepper, if needed.

Serves as many as 10 cocktail-party snackers, or makes, on crusty rye bread, substantial sandwiches.

MAKES ABOUT 2 CUPS

NOTE ON RENDERING CHICKEN FAT:
You can buy rendered chicken fat at supermarkets. It is expensive and not very good. Rendering your own is easy and cheap. When you are preparing chickens, before roasting or cutting up, it is necessary to pull out the large pieces of fat inside the tail opening. They will come out in your hands in one piece. Cut them up and put them in a freezer container. Add to them as you do more chickens until you have enough fat to make it worth rendering—at least two pounds.

Place frozen or fresh fat in a deep, heavy pan with a shallow layer of water on the bottom. Cook over low heat. It will boil and sizzle, evaporating all the water; but the initial water will keep the fat from sticking to the pan and burning. Keep the fat just at the boiling point of water. This way it will not darken and will render out the maximum amount of liquid fat.

Pour through a cloth-lined sieve. Refrigerate or freeze until needed. The cracklings left in the cloth make delicious snacks served hot or reheated and sprinkled with kosher salt. The very best cracklings come from duck or goose fat that has been prepared in the same way.

TAPENADE

———————————— • ————————————

This black spread is a Provençal classic that keeps well. Rich in taste, it is addictive. It is beautiful on a plate with Roasted Red Pepper Spread (page 19) and crunches of white vegetables. The spread is supposed to be spicy; let it ripen for half an hour before final seasoning, if possible, as it takes time for the spiciness to develop. The salt comes from the anchovies and the richness from the oil and the olives.

• • •

½ cup pitted black olives (weighing about 2 ounces
*   unpitted, see note)*
1 large clove garlic
Small handful fresh basil leaves
6 canned oil-packed anchovy fillets
1½ tablespoons capers, drained
1 tablespoon lemon juice
4 tablespoons green olive oil
Freshly ground black pepper

If you are using unpitted olives, pit them as described in the note below. With a large, heavy pot or the flat side of a large knife, smash the garlic clove. This will break and loosen the peel, which you can then easily remove with your fingers.

Place all the ingredients in a food processor and, using the metal blade, process until finely puréed but not mush. You can also chop the olives, garlic, basil leaves, anchovies, and capers fine by hand.

Place the chopped ingredients in a large bowl and beat in the lemon juice, olive oil, and pepper.

Serve the tapenade with sliced raw vegetables. I particularly like thinly sliced fennel or daikon radish.

MAKES ¾ CUP

NOTE: Use Nice olives or oil-cured Moroccan or Greek olives, as they impart the most flavor. Oil-cured olives are soft, and you can pit them yourself quite easily. With your thumbnail, split each olive lengthwise. Pull apart the halves and the pit will slip out. To pit Nice olives, set them on a counter, smash them with the heel of your hand, and remove the pits with your fingers.

TABBOULEH

———————— • ————————

Tabbouleh, made with bulgur—processed cracked wheat—is instantaneous and fresh tasting. It can be served with chicken or fish but is delicious on its own served with raw vegetables or leftover cooked vegetables on the side.

• • •

7 cups water
1½ cups bulgur
¼ cup olive oil
½ cup chopped fresh mint leaves
3 cloves garlic, smashed, peeled, and minced
2 red bell peppers, stemmed, seeded, deribbed, and
   cut into ¼-inch dice
2 hot green peppers, stemmed, seeded and thinly
   sliced
1 bunch scallions (green and white parts), thinly
   sliced
1 tablespoon kosher salt
Juice of 2 lemons

Bring the water to a simmer. Place the bulgur in a bowl and add 4 cups of the simmering water. Let sit for 15 minutes. Drain. Return the bulgur to the bowl and add the remaining 3 cups of simmering water. Let sit for 10 minutes. Drain well.

Toss the bulgur with the olive oil to coat, then stir in the remaining ingredients. Let sit at room temperature for at least 30 minutes.

Serve as a first course with sliced tomatoes and watercress sprigs or fresh coriander. Cucumber strips, red radishes, slices of raw, variously colored peppers, carrots sticks, and raw mushroom slices also are good accompaniments. When asparagus is in season, serve Tabbouleh with the cooked tips sprinkled with olive oil and lemon juice.

SERVES 6 AS A FIRST COURSE, 8 AS A SIDE DISH

NOTE: If you want to serve this before it rests 30 minutes, increase the seasonings. If you like it spicier, leave in the seeds from the hot peppers.

GUACAMOLE

———————— • ————————

This is a guacamole with which I have always had a lot of success. It can be served with taco chips and raw vegetables. It's also a terrific topping for chili.

...

1 medium avocado
1 teaspoon kosher salt
1 tablespoon lime juice
1¼ teaspoons finely minced fresh green chili pepper
1 tablespoon finely minced onion
⅓ cup finely chopped peeled and seeded tomato
1 tightly packed teaspoon chopped fresh coriander leaves

Halve and pit the avocado. Hold one half in the palm of your hand and slice the flesh of the avocado lengthwise through to the skin every quarter inch. Then slice crosswise every quarter inch. Repeat for the second half-avocado. With a spoon, scrape the avocado cubes into a bowl. Stir in the salt, lime juice, chili pepper, onion, tomato, and coriander.

MAKES 1½ CUPS

VARIATION

Follow the above recipe, using only the avocado, salt, and lime juice plus an additional tablespoon of lime juice. This will make only 1 cup.

EGGPLANT ORIENTALE

———————— • ————————

This unlikely version of eggplant caviar, containing both ketchup and chili sauce, was given to me years ago and is deliciously sweet and sour as well as colorful. At risk of my reputation, I pass it on to you. Also, as it does not call for the usual prebaking of the eggplant, it is most untraditional and rapid. Serve with halved lemons, Russian pumpernickel, and crisp lettuce. You can add wedges of tomato if you find good ones. Ice-cold vodka is better with this than wine. If you want to stick to wine, choose a chilled Beaujolais Villages or a California zinfandel. I always make the whole recipe, as later-day dividends taste even better than the original servings. It makes a delicious late-summer accompaniment to a main course as well.

• • •

3 one-pound eggplants, peeled
1 large onion
2 green bell peppers, stemmed, seeded, and
    deribbed
1 cup vegetable oil
1 one-pound can whole tomatoes, drained and
    chopped
1 large clove garlic, finely minced
2 tablespoons tomato purée
2 tablespoons ketchup
2 tablespoons chili sauce
2 tablespoons tomato paste
5½ teaspoons kosher salt
Pinch cayenne pepper
Freshly ground black pepper
1 tablespoon fresh lemon juice

Finely chop the eggplants, onion, and peppers. Keep them separate.

In a heavy-bottomed 3-quart non-aluminum saucepan, heat ⅓ cup oil over medium heat. Add the onions and cook, without browning, until they are translucent. Add the green peppers and continue stirring and cooking until the peppers have the same texture as the onions. Add the remaining ⅔ cup oil and the eggplant and continue cooking over medium heat, stirring occasionally, for 30 minutes. Add the tomatoes and garlic to the saucepan, along with the tomato purée, ketchup, chili sauce, and tomato paste. Cook, stirring well, for another 10 minutes. Add the salt, cayenne and black pepper, and lemon juice. Refrigerate until chilled.

SERVES 12 AS A FIRST COURSE OR MANY AT A BUFFET

EGGPLANT CAVIAR

———•———

Here's a much simpler, more usual eggplant caviar. It is known properly as Baba Ghanouj. Serve with warm pita bread and raw, fresh vegetables or, simply, on a leaf of ruby lettuce with an extra wedge of lemon. Give this to friends who love garlic.

• • •

*2 medium-size eggplants (about 1 to 1¼ pounds
    each), with no holes in the skin
¼ cup olive oil
2 tablespoons lemon juice
1 to 2 teaspoons minced garlic (1 to 2 medium-size
    cloves), depending on freshness
2 teaspoons salt
Freshly ground black pepper to taste*

Place the oven rack in the center position. Heat oven to 400° F. Roast the eggplants on a heavy, ungreased baking sheet until they burst and the centers become very tender. This will take about 1½ hours.

Remove from the oven. Using two forks, immediately tear each eggplant open. Scrape out the pulp onto the hot baking sheet. Let it sizzle and brown. This will help some of the liquid to evaporate. Discard the dry skins.

Transfer the pulp to a bowl. Continue to pull it apart with the two forks until it is very finely shredded. Beat in the olive oil in a thin, steady stream until well blended. Beat in the lemon juice, garlic, salt, and pepper to taste. Chill, covered, in refrigerator until serving. The tastes develop over a few days.

MAKES ABOUT 3 CUPS

TARAMASALATA WITH RED CAVIAR

———•———

I love taramasalata, which is nothing but a mayonnaise made with fish eggs rather than chicken eggs. Traditionally tarama, a bought paste of salted cod eggs, is used as a base. The only trouble with tarama is that it can be very salty in one batch and mild in another. Although I give a traditional version at the end of the recipe, I prefer this somewhat more elegant version made with salmon roe—red caviar. You can use the kind that is vacuum-packed, which will be less expensive than fresh.

This is another of those lifesaver first courses made with on-the-shelf ingredients and staples. Make sure that the lemon balances the salt. The onion and garlic are meant to be background tastes, so, if the garlic has a large germ, remove it. This is good for last-minute preparation, or make ahead; the salt and lemon will preserve this in the refrigerator for a week.

• • •

3 slices firm white bread, crusts removed
1 small onion
2 cloves garlic
1 four-ounce jar red salmon caviar
¼ cup fresh lemon juice
1 cup light olive oil

Tear the bread into pieces. Soak it in water for about 3 minutes; then squeeze out the water. Place the bread, onion, and garlic in the work bowl of a food processor and purée. Add the caviar and lemon juice. Process for 10 seconds.

With the machine running, gradually add the oil, beginning with drops. Then pour in a steady stream. Transfer the mixture to a bowl. Keep refrigerated until you are ready to serve.

Serve with toasted pita wedges, extra pieces of lemon, and some good Greek olives or raw vegetables.

MAKES ABOUT 2 CUPS

VARIATION WITH TARAMA

Follow the above recipe, using 5 slices bread, 1 small onion, one 4-ounce jar tarama, ½ cup lemon juice, 1⅓ cups olive oil and 2 garlic cloves. This makes about 3 cups.

HUMMUS

———————•———————

A Middle Eastern specialty that is given depth of flavor by the toasted sesame oil and freshness by the mint. If mint is unavailable, substitute two tablespoons of chopped parsley. Serve on a lettuce leaf and top, untraditionally, with thinly sliced red onion for color. A clear yellow plate makes a lovely background. As a drink with this, you might try Greek ouzo or Turkish raki on the rocks with a splash of water to turn it milky.

• • •

1 can (20 ounces) whole chickpeas, drained
2 tablespoons lemon juice
2 whole cloves garlic, peeled
1¼ teaspoons salt
½ teaspoon oriental (toasted) sesame oil
⅓ cup olive oil
2 teaspoons sesame seeds
1 tablespoon chopped fresh mint

Rinse the chickpeas, drain thoroughly, and place in the food processor. Process, stopping occasionally to scrape down the sides, until the peas are coarsely mashed. Add the lemon juice, garlic, salt, and sesame oil, and continue processing until the mixture is smooth. With the motor running, pour the olive oil into the hummus and process until incorporated.

Remove the hummus to a bowl and stir in the sesame seeds and the mint. Serve as above or as a dip for pita bread or vegetables.

MAKES ABOUT 1½ CUPS

PARTY SHRIMP AND CHILI MAYONNAISE

———————•———————

This is a simple and lightly spicy version of that ubiquitous favorite, boiled shrimp. The important thing is not to overcook the shrimp and not to add salt to the cooking water, which will toughen them. The sauce is equally good with broiled fish. This will serve 12 people as a sit-down first course but should do for considerably more if added to other things at a buffet or cocktail party. You never can tell with shrimp. People are greedy.

• • •

SHRIMP

4 dried small hot red peppers, or 1 teaspoon red-
pepper flakes
6 medium cloves garlic
2 teaspoons celery seeds
3 quarts water
4 cups dry white wine
5 pounds medium shrimp

CHILI MAYONNAISE

3 egg yolks
1 tablespoon chili powder
1 teaspoon dry mustard
1½ teaspoons kosher salt
¼ cup fresh lemon juice
4 medium cloves garlic, crushed and peeled
1½ cups light olive oil
1 seven-ounce can Mexican tomatoes with hot
peppers, or 1 seven-ounce can salsa verde, or ¾
cup drained canned tomatoes and 2 canned
jalapeños

Bring the hot peppers, garlic, celery seeds, water, and wine to a boil. Peel the shrimp (use the shells for Shrimp Butter, page 146). Allow the spiced water to boil for 20 minutes. Add the shrimp; stir; turn off the heat. Allow the shrimp to remain in the water for about 5 minutes or until one when tested is barely cooked. Drain. Do not refrigerate.

Place egg yolks, chili powder, mustard, salt, 2 tablespoons of the lemon juice, and the garlic in a food processor. Process for 2 minutes, scraping down the sides of the bowl from time to time if necessary. With the machine running, add the olive oil in a steady stream. If the mayonnaise gets too thick, add a little lemon juice as you go. When all the oil has been added, with the machine still running, add your canned Mexican ingredients. Process until well blended. Taste. Add more lemon juice and salt if you want. Serve with the shrimp, at room temperature.

SERVES 12 AS A FIRST COURSE

ASPARAGUS WITH HAM AND VINAIGRETTE

In their increasingly long season, asparagus make a perfect first course, cold or warm. They can be served with Mayonnaise (page 312); with a vinaigrette (page 316) enriched with hard-boiled eggs, capers, parsley, and dill; with Hollandaise (page 310); with brown butter and capers lightened with a touch of vinegar; or with the somewhat unusual sauce below. With a poached egg on top, this also makes a good, light main course.

Asparagus come in every size from pencil-thin grass to obscenely thick. It is also available (fresh and American) in the pale lavender-tipped cream color that is called white; it needs to be cooked longer than the green. Aside from the grass, I snap off the woody ends of the asparagus (see page 131 for a soup using these ends). Then I peel them with a potato peeler from about an inch below the tip to the end. With white string, I tie them into even bunches, and boil them uncovered in lots of salted water until the point of a knife just slips into the fat end.

Pick them up by the strings; lay on a clean cloth with all the tips pointing in the same direction; cut the strings. Remove from the cloth when completely drained. Serve with sauce over middle of asparagus. If you need to keep them warm for a while, cover with a cloth. I don't like to serve them hot or ice-cold.

• • •

1½ pounds asparagus
Soy-Sesame Vinaigrette or Everyday Vinaigrette
   (pages 266 and 316)
¼ pound thinly sliced smoked ham

Clean and cook the asparagus as above until tender but still firm. This will take 3 to 8 minutes, depending on the thickness of the asparagus. Place in a colander and rinse very briefly under cold running water. Drain well. Arrange on a serving platter.

While the asparagus is cooking, stir the sliced ham into the vinaigrette. Spoon the dressing and ham over the center of the asparagus, leaving the tips and ends exposed. Serve at room temperature.

SERVES 6

RAW SCALLOPS WITH AVOCADO

———————————•———————————

This is a particularly delicious seviche. Don't substitute the more expensive bay scallops for the sea scallops; they are too sweet. If you like your Mexican food sharp, use about one inch of fresh jalapeño pepper, finely chopped, instead of the hot pepper sauce. A strange but interesting substitution is one teaspoon of tamari soy sauce instead of the salt.

This is attractive served in a scallop shell. A dry gewürztraminer thoroughly chilled holds up to this dish.

• • •

¾ pound sea scallops
½ cup lime juice
2 tablespoons chopped scallions
2 tablespoons chopped coriander leaves or parsley
1 small tomato, peeled, seeded, finely chopped
1 small garlic clove, finely chopped
½ teaspoon kosher salt
½ teaspoon freshly ground black pepper
Dash hot red-pepper sauce
¼ cup olive oil
½ avocado, peeled and cut into thin wedges

Cut the scallops into quarters and place them in a container in which they will just fit comfortably in one layer. Pour the lime juice over the scallops and toss to coat. Refrigerate for an hour, by which time the citrus juice will have turned the scallops opaque and made them firm—in effect, cooked them.

When the scallops have finished "cooking," drain them. Combine the remaining ingredients, except the avocado, and pour them over the scallops, tossing gently to mix. Chill for 30 minutes. Garnish with the avocado wedges before serving.

SERVES 4

NOTE: The scallops can marinate for up to four hours, but after that they will have exuded too much liquid and will start to shrivel.

SMOKED SALMON WITH PINK PEPPERCORNS

•

Recently, there has been a big brouhaha about pink peppercorns. They don't seem to bother me. I like the way they look and taste. If they bother you, avoid this recipe. I originally tasted a similar dish at the Hôtel des Bergues in Geneva.

• • •

3 tablespoons olive oil
4½ teaspoons raspberry vinegar
1 tablespoon fresh lemon juice
1 tablespoon crushed pink peppercorns
1 tablespoon finely sliced chives
8 slices smoked salmon

Mix together the oil, vinegar, lemon juice, peppercorns, and chives. Arrange a slice of salmon on each of 8 salad plates. About 30 minutes before serving, dribble some of the dressing in a wide band across the middle of each salmon slice.

SERVES 8

ORANGE AND ONION SALAD WITH CUMIN VINAIGRETTE

•

In Morocco and Algeria, they eat salads with these brilliant colors and the mysterious background flavor of cumin. This and prosciutto with melon or figs are virtually the only primarily fruit first courses I can tolerate, let alone like. It is a marvelous meal introduction on a gray winter night, bringing hints of warmth and tropical vacations just when I need them most.

• • •

2 thin-skinned juice oranges (ask store for
    uncoated oranges)
¼ cup olive oil
1½ tablespoons fresh lemon juice
½ teaspoon kosher salt
¼ teaspoon packed ground cumin

    1½ to 2 red onions, sliced very thin in rounds
    ¼ cup Nice olives

Slice the oranges crosswise into thin even rounds. Discard the seeds but do not remove skins. Squeeze the juice from the ends. You should have about 2 tablespoons.

In a small bowl, mix the orange juice with the olive oil, lemon juice, salt, and cumin. Let stand about 10 minutes to develop flavor.

Meanwhile, arrange alternate orange and onion slices, overlapping, on a platter. Sprinkle the olives around. Pour the dressing over the oranges and onions. Let marinate at room temperature for 30 minutes. From time to time, spoon some of the dressing that accumulates in the bottom over the slices.

SERVES 4 TO 6

ROASTED YELLOW BELL PEPPERS AND TOMATOES

With the new ready availability of yellow peppers, I have been having a wonderful time creating new recipes and adapting old ones. They have a rich, fleshy sweetness that is positively voluptuous. Eat this tepid. If you make it ahead, allow enough time for it to come back to room temperature. If you bake it in an attractive earthenware dish, it can be served as is.

• • •

    3 medium-size yellow bell peppers
    3 medium-size ripe tomatoes
    ¼ cup olive oil
    2 teaspoons minced garlic
    2 teaspoons minced fresh thyme or 1/2 teaspoon
       dried thyme, crumbled
    1 teaspoon salt
    ¼ teaspoon freshly ground black pepper

Heat the oven to 400° F.

Cut the yellow peppers in half lengthwise. Remove the cores and seeds. Then cut the peppers into strips 1½ inches wide. Core the tomatoes. Cut them into slices ½ inch thick. Arrange the peppers and tomatoes, overlappping, in an oval baking dish.

In a small bowl, blend the oil, garlic, thyme, salt, and pepper. Pour over the tomatoes and peppers. Bake for 1 hour and 15 minutes, until the peppers are tender. Baste occasionally with the pan juices during baking. Cool to room temperature before serving.

SERVES 6

WARM VEGETABLE COMPOTE

This is a quick sort of vegetables à la grecque. It is very pretty because of the pink color lent by the beets. Either make three or four days ahead and refrigerate or make early on the day you wish to serve it. Either way, serve at room temperature, not too warm and not chilled. This is great to keep on hand in case company drops in unannounced.

. . .

1 cup sliced peeled seedless cucumbers (preferably, English or hothouse variety) (¼-inch-thick rounds)
2 teaspoons kosher salt
8 small red radishes
4 small leeks, trimmed just to where root joins white and only 2 inches of greens removed, with a ½-inch-deep cross cut into the bottom
2 cups Chicken Stock (page 110)
½ cup olive oil
Freshly ground black pepper
1 small beet, peeled and sliced into ¼-inch-thick rounds (¾ cup)
2 small red new potatoes, peeled and sliced into ¼-inch-thick rounds (½ cup)
¾ cup shelled fresh peas or defrosted frozen peas
3 small carrots, peeled and sliced into ¼-inch-thick rounds (¼ cup)
12 small string beans, topped and tailed

½ cup peeled and sliced daikon or other white
* radishes, cut lengthwise ¼ inch thick*
2 small white turnips, peeled and cut into ¼-inch-
* thick rounds (½ cup)*
¾ cup red onion rounds (¼ inch thick)
1 packed cup fennel slices (¼ inch thick)
½ cup fresh lemon juice

Put the cucumbers in a bowl with 1 teaspoon salt. Toss to mix and set aside.

Bring a large pot of water to a boil. Add the red radishes and cook for a minute. Remove with a slotted spoon and plunge immediately into ice water. Set aside. In the same boiling water, blanch the leeks for 3 minutes. Remove with a slotted spoon and plunge into ice water. Set aside.

Meanwhile, bring the chicken stock to a boil in a 4-quart pot. Add the olive oil and black pepper. Add the beet and let the liquid maintain a rolling boil. Let cook for 1½ minutes, then add the potatoes. Let cook for a minute, then add the shelled peas, if using fresh. After another minute, add the carrots.

As the vegetables cook, skim off any scum that rises to the top. Let the carrots cook for 2 minutes, then add the string beans. Let cook for a minute, then add the white radishes, turnips, onions, fennel, lemon juice, and frozen peas, if using. Drain and rinse the cucumbers, and add to the pot. Let everything boil 1 minute longer. Taste the liquid. Season with about 1 teaspoon salt, and pepper to taste.

Drain the leeks and red radishes and arrange them in a large serving bowl. Pour the other vegetables and their liquid over the leeks and radishes and stir slightly. Let come to room temperature.

SERVES 4 AMPLY. TO SERVE 6, ADD 2 MORE LEEKS.

NOTE: Seedless cucumbers are firmer than the varieties with seeds. However, if you can't find them, use the usual seeded variety, cut them in half lengthwise, and remove all the seeds with a spoon or small knife; then slice as before.

PROSCIUTTO, SMOKED MOZZARELLA, AND CELERY ROOT SALAD

Insalata Caprese, interspersed slices of mozzarella and tomato, dribbled with basil vinaigrette, is a classic of summer. This is a similar invention for winter.

• • •

2 tablespoons Dijon mustard
3 tablespoons red wine vinegar
½ cup olive oil
Pinch kosher salt
Freshly ground black pepper
⅓ cup peeled, julienned celery root
24 very thin slices prosciutto
24 very thin slices smoked mozzarella
2 tablespoons chopped Italian parsley

Place the mustard in a bowl and whisk in the vinegar. Gradually whisk in the oil, beginning with drops and then increasing to a steady stream. Season with salt and pepper. Fold in the celery root.

Overlap 4 mozzarella and 4 prosciutto slices across each of 6 salad plates.

Strew the celery root and dressing over the middle. Sprinkle with parsley.

SERVES 6

JULIENNE OF CHICKEN SALAD

This is one of my most glamorous first courses. It is a pain because it requires a lot of slicing and, about a half hour before dinner, hot quick cooking; but the splendid tastes and enthusiastic reception make it all worthwhile. The salad is not truly Chinese, what with endives and so forth, but it is certainly deeply reminiscent of things Chinese.

A garland even more glamorous than sautéed spinach with

which to surround this salad is made with the deep-fried leaves of spinach, celery, flat-leaf parsley, and coriander. Wash the leaves well and then dry them scrupulously. Fill a clean wok halfway with vegetable oil and heat to the temperature for deep fat frying. You can test the temperature with a thermometer or, when the oil has become bluish and shimmery, you can insert a clean wooden chopstick or spoon. Lots of good-size bubbles should froth up around the bottom of the chopstick. Wood always absorbs some moisture from the air, and this is what is bubbling furiously when the temperature is right—old Chinese chefs' trick. Drop the leaves into the fat in batches about the size that you can hold in two hands. Step back rapidly so that you are not spattered by sizzling oil. When the leaves are crisp, remove with a skimmer to brown paper bags. Continue with the remaining leaves.

Whichever garland you use, mound the salad in the center of a deep round or oval platter, and surround with the greenery.

• • •

1 cup dry Chinese mushrooms
3 chicken breasts, skinned and boned
3 heads Belgian endive
1 bunch scallions
3 cups Chicken Stock (page 110)
1 teaspoon Chinese hot oil (see note)
4 large slices ginger
2 tablespoons oriental (toasted) sesame oil
2 tablespoons sesame seeds
½ cup pecans
3 cloves garlic, smashed and peeled
1 cup drained canned straw mushrooms
2 to 3 tablespoons soy sauce
¼ cup plus 2 tablespoons untoasted sesame oil or
*   plain vegetable oil, such as peanut*
2 tablespoons tarragon vinegar
3 pounds fresh spinach, stems removed, washed
*   and dried (4 pounds if serving for lunch)*
Fresh coriander leaves

Cover the mushrooms with hot water and soak until they are soft, about 20 minutes. Squeeze dry. Remove and discard the stems, then slice the mushrooms into ⅛-inch-wide strips.

With your knife parallel to the work surface, cut each chicken breast into 2 even slices. Cut the slices lengthwise into strips about ¼ inch wide.

Trim the base of the endives. Cut them in half lengthwise, then cut each half into long strips about ⅛ inch wide.

Cut the greens off the scallions. The greens should be as long as the endive strips. Reserve the whites for another use. If the greens are thick, cut them lengthwise into quarters. If thin, cut them lengthwise in half.

Heat the chicken stock, 1 teaspoon hot oil, and ginger in a wok. Bring to a boil, lower the heat, and simmer for 4 minutes. Add the chicken and stir vigorously so the pieces do not stick together. Cook just until the meat is white on the outside, about 30 seconds. With a skimmer, remove the chicken to a bowl. Let cool.

Pour the cooking liquid into a bowl to cool. When the liquid is cool, remove the ginger slices and cut them into julienne strips. Reserve cooking liquid.

The rest of the cooking is done quickly over high heat so have everything measured and handy before you begin.

Place the wok over high heat until it is dry. Add the sesame oil. When it is hot, add the sesame seeds and cook until lightly toasted. Then stir in the pecans and cook until brown.

Next, add the garlic and cook until it begins to brown. Add the mushroom strips and toss to mix. Add the reserved ginger and toss again. Stir in the straw mushrooms and toss. Add 1 tablespoon soy sauce and ¼ cup reserved cooking liquid. Cook until almost dry.

Turn off the heat, but leave the mixture in the wok. Toss in the scallion greens. When they begin to wilt, add the endives and toss. Then toss in the chicken, ¼ cup untoasted sesame oil, another ¼ cup reserved cooking liquid, and the vinegar. (The remaining cooking liquid is the cook's bonus. Drink as you toss.) Toss well and remove to a bowl. At this point, the mixture can wait at room temperature for an hour or more.

Just before you are ready to serve, wipe out the wok and place it over high heat. Add the remaining 2 tablespoons untoasted sesame oil. When it is hot, add the spinach and toss quickly to wilt. Do not let the spinach cook to nothing. Toss in 1 or 2 tablespoons soy sauce, or to taste.

Arrange the spinach in a ring on the plate and put the chicken mixture in the center. Top with some fresh coriander leaves.

SERVES 8 AS A FIRST COURSE, 4 FOR LUNCH

NOTE: For a spicier salad, add another ½ teaspoon hot oil to the finished chicken mixture.

POACHED CHICKEN AND CUCUMBER SALAD WITH POMEGRANATE SEEDS

———————————— • ————————————

This is another spectacularly beautiful first-course salad, brightened and given an acid crunch by the pomegranate.

• • •

2 whole boned chicken breasts, cut in half and
  skinned
3 cups Chicken Stock (page 110)
1 large pomegranate
10 ounces màche (field salad), carefully rinsed
  and dried
1 small English (hothouse or seedless) cucumber,
  cut into very thin, almost transparent slices (if
  cucumber is long, use only about 10 inches)
6 tablespoons light virgin olive oil
Salt and freshly ground black pepper to taste

With a small, sharp knife separate the thin fillets from the underside of each chicken breast. Remove the tendons and discard. Cut the remaining pieces of breast into 3 equal strips.

In a medium-size saucepan, bring the stock to a boil over high heat. Add the chicken and remove the pan from the heat. Allow the chicken to cool in the stock for 10 to 12 minutes. When the chicken is cool enough to handle, remove it from the stock. Pat dry. Holding your knife at a 45-degree angle, slice each strip into long, slender, ¼-inch slices. Put the slices on a plate, cover, and set aside.

With a sharp knife, quarter the pomegranate. Use your fingers to detach the seeds from the fruit. Measure 4 tablespoons pomegranate seeds and set them aside for garnish. Put the remaining seeds in a strainer set over a bowl. With your fingers, press the seeds firmly back and forth against the mesh to break the skin and release the juice. You will have at least 6 tablespoons of juice.

Make a bed of mâche on each of four serving plates. Alternate chicken and cucumber slices in a circular wreath on the mâche. Sprinkle 1 tablespoon pomegranate seeds over each salad. In a small bowl, whisk together the olive oil and 6 tablespoons pomegranate juice. Season with salt and pepper. Spoon 3 tablespoons dressing over each serving. Serve.

SERVES 4

NOTE: You may poach the chicken strips a day ahead, leaving them to cool in the chicken stock. Refrigerate the chicken in the stock. Bring to room temperature before drying and slicing.

DUCK BREAST SALAD

•

This is a simpler version of a cold fowl salad than the chicken salad above. It is both pretty and good. Use the remaining carcass for more stock and the legs for Duck Burgers (see page 210).

•••

Duck or Chicken Stock (page 112 or 110)
2 boneless duck breasts, skinned and trimmed
3 tablespoons olive oil
2 tablespoons tarragon vinegar
1 tablespoon lemon juice
1 tablespoon vegetable oil
1½ teaspoons celery seed
1 teaspoon salt
8 medium radishes, trimmed, finely julienned
½ cup whole celery leaves
4 medium-size mushrooms, trimmed, halved, thinly sliced
1 one-and-a-half-inch piece parsley root or parsnip, peeled, finely julienned
1 one-and-a-half-inch piece Kirby (pickling) cucumber, finely julienned
3 scallions, trimmed, slivered (use 5 scallions if making this as a main course)

In a medium-size saucepan, bring the stock to a slow simmer. Poach

the duck breasts in the simmering stock about 8 minutes. Only occa-
sional bubbles should break the surface of the stock. The meat will
be rare. Remove from the stock and cool to room temperature. Keep
enriched stock for tomorrow's soup.

In a small bowl, blend the olive oil, vinegar, lemon juice, vegetable oil, celery seed, and salt. In a larger bowl, toss all the vegetables, except the scallions, with the dressing. Let stand for 30 minutes. Place the slivered scallions in a bowl of ice water. Store in the
refrigerator until needed.

Cut the cooled duck breasts into julienne strips (2 inches by ¼
inch by ¼ inch). Stir into the bowl with the vegetables.

Just before serving, drain the scallions thoroughly. Arrange in a
ring around the outside edge of each of 4 plates. Toss the salad well.
Place a scoop of salad in the center of each plate.

SERVES 4, OR 2 AS A MAIN COURSE

SMOKED WHITEFISH MOUSSE

———————————•———————————

For those days when you need a pâté try this unusual smoked-fish
event . . . light, unusual, and not expensive. Serve this with a bit of
green around it.

▪ ▪ ▪

3 quarter-ounce packages unflavored gelatin
½ cup cold water
2 tablespoons dry white wine
1 pound boned, skinned smoked whitefish (2 cups
  fish pieces)
2 tablespoons fresh lemon juice
Kosher salt
Freshly ground white pepper
Cayenne pepper
2 cups heavy cream

Oil a 6-cup mold and set aside.

Sprinkle the gelatin over the cold water in a small skillet. Set
aside until it is absorbed. Place over low heat until the gelatin is
completely dissolved. Set aside until cool. Then stir in the wine.

Place the fish in the work bowl of a food processor; process until it is a rough purée. Stir in the cooled gelatin mixture, lemon juice, ½ teaspoon salt, and white and cayenne pepper to taste. Add more lemon, salt, and peppers as needed, remembering that the intensity will be diluted when you add the cream. Put the mixture in a bowl.

Whip the cream until soft peaks form. Stir some of the cream into the fish to lighten it, then fold in the rest. Spoon the mixture into the prepared mold and tap firmly against the work surface to settle the mixture and eliminate air bubbles.

Chill to set, about 3 hours. Unmold (page 58) to serve.

SERVES 12

MUSSELS RAVIGOTE

I often serve mussels as a hot first course. If I have some left over I make this dish, though it's good enough to be worth making from scratch. It is a kind of opulent surprise to find two mussels in each shell.

When picking mussels be sure not to get an extra-heavy one; it is bound to be full of black muck. Make sure all the mussels you choose are tightly closed. When you are washing them, if any are open, press edges lightly together or run under very cold water. If the mussels don't shut up, discard them. For more mussel notes see page 61.

• • •

RAVIGOTE SAUCE

1¼ cups olive oil
¼ cup vegetable oil
¾ cup red wine vinegar
1 cup chopped fresh parsley
3 hard-boiled eggs, whites chopped, yolks sieved
3 tablespoons minced shallots
2½ tablespoons minced chervil
1½ tablespoons each minced tarragon and chives

¼ cup drained, minced capers
2 teaspoons dry mustard
2 teaspoons salt
⅛ teaspoon freshly ground black pepper

MUSSELS
8 dozen mussels
1 cup white wine

RAVIGOTE SAUCE

In a large mixing bowl, blend the oils. Slowly whisk in the vinegar until well blended. Whisk in the remaining ingredients. Cover and store in the refrigerator until needed. Before using, whisk thoroughly.

MUSSELS

Scrub and debeard the mussels. Place them in a shallow stainless-steel sauté pan. Add the wine. Heat over medium heat until the liquid is steaming. Cover and steam the mussels about 4 minutes, just until they open. With a slotted spoon, remove the mussels immediately from the pan. Set them aside to cool.

Whisk ¼ cup of the mussel liquid into the Ravigote Sauce. Reserve the rest of the liquid for another use; for instance, as part of the fish stock called for in the recipes for seafood stews and soups (pages 147–151).

When the mussels are cool enough to handle, remove them from the shells. Place in the bowl with the Ravigote Sauce. They will marinate in the sauce and, by the time you are ready to serve, will have cooled to room temperature.

Set aside half of the mussel half-shells and discard the rest. Scrub the half-shells thoroughly. Set one or two marinated mussels in each half-shell. Arrange several shells in a flower pattern on each of eight plates. Spoon the Ravigote Sauce over the mussels.

SERVES 8

MOSAIC OF EEL AND GREEN HERBS

This is an unusual and complicated recipe with results worth the effort. Technically and in the selection of herbs it is a variation of the Belgian classic anguilles au vert. It is easier to eat and prettier to look at. The herbs should be very fresh-tasting and no one herb should dominate. The lemon juice should sing through. If you want to you can serve a little fresh Mayonnaise with this (page 312); but I really don't think it's necessary.

...

> 1½ to 2 pounds skinned, gutted eel
> 1 quart dry white wine
> 4 cups water
> 1 medium onion, cut into chunks
> 1 carrot, peeled, cut into chunks
> 1 celery rib, cut into chunks
> ½ bay leaf
> 5 cracked black peppercorns
> 3 to 4 teaspoons kosher salt
> 2½ tablespoons unflavored gelatin
> 2 to 3 tablespoons fresh lemon juice
> Few drops hot red-pepper sauce
> 4 cups packed spinach leaves, blanched 1 minute
>   in boiling salted water, drained, squeezed, and
>   chopped
> 7 tablespoons chopped fresh dill
> 5 tablespoons chopped fresh mint

Carefully, remove the bones from the eel, keeping the meat intact. With scissors, cut down the back on either side of the fin; remove and discard. Cut the eel into 3½- to 4-inch pieces.

Put the wine, water, onion, carrot, celery, bay leaf, peppercorns, and ½ teaspoon salt in a large saucepan. Bring to a boil over high heat, reduce the heat, and simmer 15 to 20 minutes.

Add the eel to the simmering liquid and poach 3 to 5 minutes, or until tender. With a slotted spoon remove the eel to a plate. Let cool.

Strain the liquid into a clean saucepan through a sieve lined with a dampened cloth. There should be 4½ cups liquid. If you have more, bring it to a boil and cook until reduced to 4½ cups. If you have less, add water. Let cool.

Gradually whisk in the gelatin. Place over moderate heat and stir until the gelatin is dissolved. Stir in the lemon juice, remaining salt to taste, and red-pepper sauce. Let the liquid cool in the refrigerator until partially set. Stir in the spinach, dill, and mint.

Lightly oil a 6-cup loaf pan.

Pour about 2 cups lightly-set green jelly into the bottom. Cut the cooked eel into pieces ½ to ¾ inch wide. Poke the eel randomly into the jelly. Fill the pan with the remaining jelly, adding more eel here and there. Place in the refrigerator for several hours until firm.

Unmold (page 58). Slice at the table.

SERVES 6 TO 8

HOT FIRST COURSES

Beurre Blanc

Artichokes with Snails and Beurre Blanc

Scallops with Caviar and Saffron Beurre Blanc

Sole Mousse with Grapefruit Sauce

Marinated Shrimp on the Grill

Moules Poulette

Glazed Mussels with Basil and Spinach

Scallops à l'Américaine

Mousses of Broccoli and Acorn Squash

Risotto with Olympia Oysters

Duck Liver, Apple, and Raisin Sauté

Shrimp Quenelles with Watercress Sauce

Shirred Eggs with Herbs, Tomatoes, and Cream

Hot Shrimp and Cabbage Slaw

Mini-Pizza

Cayenne Quail on a Coriander Nest

These are probably more ornate than any other dishes in the book. I find if I am going to spend a lot of time cooking, the first course is the place in the meal to do it. The guests and I are both sober and untired. Exclamations over the food do not interrupt the dinner conversation. Elaborate food has the best chance of coming out of the kitchen in impeccable condition at the start of the meal. The pastas (pages 79–103), soups (pages 105–137), and many of the fish dishes (pages 153–163) can also be hot first courses; and generally those are less finicky. Still and all, it's the dishes in this chapter that let me live up to a reputation as a cook.

Basic Beurre Blanc

A useful tool and one that has been heavily exploited in recent years—placed on everything from the appropriate (fish and chicken) to the inappropriate (sausage, steak, and everything just short of dessert)—is Beurre Blanc. It has an awesome reputation for difficulty that is unwarranted. It can be easily mastered. The only difficult part is excusing yourself from your guests to whisk it up at the last minute. Even here there is a practical alternative, although I don't mind a few minutes of quiet whisking and a chance to check everything out one final time before the guests descend on the table. A really good Thermos will keep the Beurre Blanc and its variations warm for a considerable period of time. If you like this sauce and find it as convenient as I do, multiply the ingredients for the reduction any number of times. Reduce and freeze in two-tablespoon quantities to have on hand for any recipe calling for Beurre Blanc.

Beurre Blanc used to be considered a woman's or home sauce because it did not call for any of the elaborate *fonds de cuisine,* basic chef's sauces, then in vogue. It is convenient for the last-minute cook for just this reason. Most of its ingredients can be kept on hand for pleasurable emergencies. Once you are comfortable making it, it is subject to extensive variation. Change the herbs and use a neutral (white unseasoned) vinegar. At the end, whisk in a little tomato paste or homemade tomato purée (page 82) and finely sliced fresh basil. Use orange juice and Lillet in the original reduction instead of the white wine and vinegar, with a fillip of lemon juice for acidity. To finish, stir in some grated orange zest. Use red wine in the reduction to make southwestern France's beurre rouge. Melt a tablespoon or so of Chicken Glaze (page 309), if you have it, into the finished sauce to make a marvelous sauce for poached chicken. Instead of salt, stir anchovy paste and some capers into a sauce for fish. Add several spoonfuls of Roasted Red Pepper Spread (page 19) for a richly colorful and fresh-tasting sauce, or Tapenade (page 24) for a rather mysterious one. The potential variations are endless.

Beurre Blanc was originally a sauce for fish. It is still good on virtually any poached or steamed fish as a first or main course. It is festive with cooked shelled seafood.

A Shrimp Butter (page 146) or similarly made lobster butter can be used as you would regular butter in a Beurre Blanc. Your final seasonings need to be accentuated—extra lemon juice, hot pepper sauce—to balance the rich shellfish taste.

When served with this sauce, shrimp can be left whole; but lobster should be thinly sliced. If serving with steamed mussels, remove them from the shells and add the steaming liquid, sharply reduced. Make the same addition for steamed scallops.

In my basic reduction, I use tarragon and tarragon vinegar, but the most classic version has neither. When using a white wine instead of vinegar, make sure it is on the acid side like a Loire wine. The French use gray shallots because they are not very sharp. If you are using pink shallots, reduce the quantity slightly. Don't, in any case, increase the amount of shallots unless you want a sweet sauce. After the reduction is made (page 53), some people add crème fraîche, which is also acid, to help stabilize the sauce and give it a creamy texture. I feel it makes the sauce heavier. Now is the time for the cold butter to be whisked in in chunks. The sauce never gets very hot. At the end, adjust the seasonings to your taste. I like a bit of hot pepper sauce, cayenne, salt, pepper, and lemon juice.

As a plain Beurre Blanc is light in color and so are most fish and seafood, plan to garnish the plate with a sprinkling of fresh herbs, some steamed small vegetables or julienne of vegetables, blanched strips of citrus-fruit zest, whole Nice olives, the meat of skinned and seeded tomatoes cut in curbs, or any other colorful garnish that blends well with the flavors you have chosen.

. . .

BEURRE BLANC

¼ cup chopped shallots
¼ cup chopped parsley
1 tablespoon dried tarragon
6 tablespoons tarragon vinegar
6 tablespoons white wine
¾ pound unsalted butter, cut up and firm
¼ teaspoon kosher salt
¼ teaspoon freshly ground black pepper
Cayenne pepper to taste
1 tablespoon fresh tarragon and 2 tablespoons
*   parsley; or 3 tablespoons parsley (optional)*

Place the shallots, ¼ cup parsley, dried tarragon, vinegar, and wine in a non-aluminum pan. Begin reducing over low heat, which will permit some of the sharp odors and tastes of vinegar to escape. After 10 minutes, you can increase the heat and reduce rapidly. When the reduction looks dry, remove it from the heat. By tilting the pan and pressing on the mixture with a spoon, you can see that about 2 tablespoons of liquid still remain.

At this point, the reduction can be put through a sieve into a clean pan or used as is. Unsieved it will be a somewhat textured, rather more peasanty, sauce. Taste the reduction. It should be quite acid. If it isn't, add some extra lemon juice or vinegar and heat for a second or two.

Place the pan over low heat and whisk in the butter, a few pieces at a time, adding more butter as the preceding is absorbed. When all the butter is absorbed, remove the pan from the heat. Stir in the salt, peppers, and fresh herbs, if desired. Use promptly. If you are using this as an ingredient in the Artichokes with Snails and Beurre Blanc (page 54), then chill until firm.

MAKES ABOUT 1½ CUPS

ARTICHOKES WITH SNAILS
AND BEURRE BLANC

———————— • ————————

This is a sensational recipe that requires time. However, it can be made less painful. All the component preparations can be done ahead. Then reheat the artichoke hearts and snails at the end just before beating the cold Beurre Blanc into the cream reduction. I have written this as an elegant meal introduction for four, but the recipe doubles easily. For goodness' sake don't serve any cream or butter later in the meal. After this, just cook a roast meat and a simple vegetable. This is the kind of dish that deserves your best chardonnay or Burgundian Meursault or Montrachet. For all its many glories, this dish is not colorful; try to choose a plate with a flowery elegant rim.

•••

> *28 snails, packed in brine*
> *1 cup dry white wine*
> *Acidulated water*
> *4 medium to large artichokes*
> *2 cups heavy cream*
> *1½ teaspoons Dijon mustard*
> *1 recipe Beurre Blanc, using fresh herbs (page 53),*
>   *chilled, cut into pieces*

Drain the snails and put them in a bowl with the wine for at least an hour. Drain the snails again, reserving wine, and set aside.

Put ¾ cup of the snail-flavored wine in a small saucepan and cook over moderate to high heat until reduced to 4 teaspoons. Set aside.

Have a bowl of acidulated water ready, and bring a pot of acidulated water to boil. ("Acidulated water" is a fancy way of saying water that has either lemon juice or white wine vinegar added to it in sufficient quantity to keep the food in it from discoloring—about the juice of 1 lemon to 1 cup of water.)

With a knife, cut the stems off the artichokes (drawing 1). Cut away all the leaves (drawing 2; and see note below) and the choke (drawing 3). Trim the bottom so that none of the hard green skin remains (drawing 4). As you work, keep dipping the cut edges of the artichoke bottoms into the bowl of acidulated water to keep them from darkening. Put the trimmed bottoms in the boiling acidulated water and cook until done, about 20 minutes. Drain and keep warm.

Place the cream and mustard in a saucepan and cook over medium to high heat until slightly reduced, about 5 minutes. Stir in the reduced wine and raise the temperature to high. Whisk in the pieces of Beurre Blanc until you have a smooth sauce. Lower the heat and add the reserved snails. Cook just to heat through.

Place a warm artichoke bottom, hollow side up, on each of 4 individual plates. Divide the sauce and snails evenly among the plates, pouring them over the artichokes. Serve immediately.

SERVES 4

NOTE: Don't waste the artichoke leaves. Throw them back into the artichoke cooking water and cook for 20 minutes more. Reserve the water. Remove the leaves and put them through a food mill. This will remove all the inedible parts and force through all the nice, tender bits that you generally chew off the leaves. Add enough of the artichoke cooking liquid, some heavy cream if you wish, and a couple of egg yolks to make an unusual soup.

PREPARING ARTICHOKE HEARTS

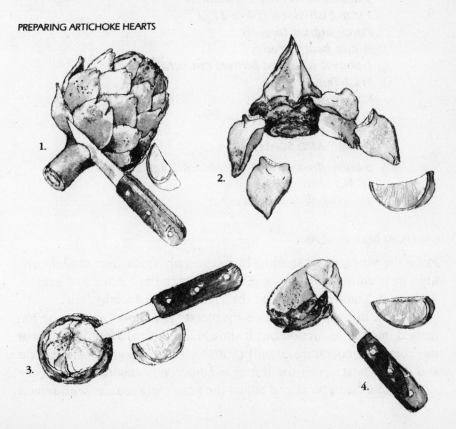

SCALLOPS WITH CAVIAR AND
SAFFRON BEURRE BLANC

———————•———————

This is an expensive, beautiful, and elegant last-minute dish. I find that it makes any dinner party. It was inspired by a recipe of the talented young French chef Gerard Pangaud. Golden caviar (American whitefish roe) instead of black makes a less expensive dish that is almost equally beautiful. The ideal white wine for this dish is an Haut-Brion blanc. To leave the ideal world of dreams and stay festive, consider a good dry bubbly or an excellent Chablis.

Before starting this recipe, you can read the general notes on Beurre Blanc (pages 51–53).

• • •

SAFFRON BEURRE BLANC

1 cup white wine vinegar
3 tablespoons chopped shallots
1 cup Fish Stock (page 113)
Pinch saffron threads
¼ cup heavy cream
1 pound unsalted butter, cut into pieces
Fresh lemon juice
Kosher salt
Freshly ground black pepper

SHRIMP AND SCALLOPS

6 butterflied shrimp, peeled, tails left on (see note)
18 sea scallops
1½ teaspoons black caviar

SAFFRON BEURRE BLANC

Place the vinegar and shallots in a saucepan. Cook over moderately-high heat until reduced to a glaze. Stir in the fish stock and saffron. Reduce to 2 tablespoons. Add the cream and reduce by half.

Whisk in the butter, piece by piece. The butter should be absorbed into the reduction but it should not melt. To keep the pan at the correct temperature, it will probably be necessary to move it on and off the heat. Once the butter is completely absorbed, strain the sauce into a clean bowl and adjust the seasoning to taste with lemon juice, salt, and pepper. Sauce may be kept hotter in a thermos, though it will always be warm rather than hot.

SHRIMP AND SCALLOPS

Bring 1 inch of water to a boil in the bottom of a steamer. Lightly oil the inside of the top section. Place the shrimp and scallops in the top. Place over steam, cover, and cook until they are barely done, about 5 minutes. They are done when the shrimp are pink and the scallops opaque.

TO ASSEMBLE

To serve, spread a layer—about 3 tablespoons—of the sauce in the center of each of 6 simple plates. Place a shrimp in the center. Arrange 3 scallops in a circle around each shrimp. Top each scallop with a little of the caviar.

SERVES 6

NOTE: See page 60 for how to butterfly shrimp. Save the shrimp shells for making Shrimp Butter, page 146, or for flavoring fish sauces that are sieved, such as the one on page 64.

SOLE MOUSSE WITH GRAPEFRUIT SAUCE

This recipe grew from one of the rather strange ideas I get every once in a while: why not a grapefruit beurre blanc with a pleasing hint of bitterness to underline the acidity. It worked out so well I thought you might like to try it. It is very festive indeed. You can serve the mousse cold; but then you might prefer Basil Sauce (page 224) or a Chili Mayonnaise (page 31) with it.

Find a colored platter and plates for this dish because of the very pale colors.

If you are using this warm version, be careful about the wine. It needs to be a really intense chardonnay or Chablis.

• • •

SOLE MOUSSE

3 large egg whites
1½ pounds skinned sole fillets, cut into 1½-inch
  pieces
3½ cups heavy cream
½ teaspoon freshly ground white pepper
½ teaspoon hot red-pepper sauce
2 teaspoons kosher salt
Vegetable oil

Heat the oven to 350° F.

Put the egg whites and the fish into the work bowl of a food processor. Process for 30 seconds. With the machine running, slowly pour the cream through the feed tube. The mousse should start moving from the sides of the work bowl. Season with the pepper, hot pepper sauce, and salt.

Oil an 11-by-4-inch terrine, 3 inches deep. Pour the mousse in. Tap it firmly against the counter a few times to eliminate air bubbles. Smooth out the top. Grease a piece of aluminum foil and place it, greased side down, over the top of the terrine. Place the terrine in a baking pan, and pour boiling water into the pan to come halfway up the sides of the terrine.

Bake for 1 hour and 10 minutes, or until firm to the touch. Remove the foil and raise the temperature to 475° F. Bake 10 minutes longer. Remove from the oven and cool on a rack.

To unmold, dip the terrine for several seconds in boiling water; if necessary, slide a knife between the mousse and the terrine. Place a platter over the terrine, then turn the platter and the terrine over together. Lift off the terrine.

• • •

GRAPEFRUIT SAUCE

7 pink grapefruits
¼ cup fresh lemon juice
7 large shallots, finely chopped
1½ pounds cold unsalted butter, cut into ½-inch
  pieces
Kosher salt to taste
Freshly ground pepper to taste

With a knife, cut away the rind and the thin membrane from all around the grapefruits. Working over a non-aluminum baking pan, cut against the membranes to release the whole sections. Squeeze the juice from the membranes into a saucepan.

Prop up one end of the baking pan so it tilts. Put the grapefruit sections at the top so the juice runs down and collects at the bottom. Add this juice to the juice in the saucepan, along with the lemon juice and shallots. Cook over high heat until reduced to half, skimming the foam from the top.

Whisk in the butter, one or two pieces at a time, adding more butter as the first is absorbed. The butter should be absorbed and foamy but not melted. It may be necessary to move the pan on and off the heat to keep it at the right temperature.

Season the sauce with the salt and pepper to taste. Stir in half the grapefruit sections.

To serve, arrange the remaining grapefruit sections over the mousse. Spoon the warm sauce over the mousse. Serve in slices with some of the sauce. Pass the remaining sauce. (I never have any left.)

SERVES 12

MARINATED SHRIMP ON THE GRILL

This is one of my favorite ways to serve shrimp. Three make a light first course, and six to eight a main course. This should only be served to eaters who don't mind using their hands to pick up the shrimp and who will be happy chewing on the shells and spitting out the indigestible residue. I have had friends eat these with a knife and fork, but they miss a lot of the fun and a good deal of the flavor.

This is a good dish to make on an outdoor grill. The shells help protect the shrimp from drying out.

While these are rewarding with a good chardonnay, out of doors a simpler, less expensive white table wine would be a better idea. Anywhere, provide extra napkins and, if you have them, finger bowls.

• • •

MARINATED SHRIMP ON THE GRILL, CONTINUED

> *30 large shrimp (about 1¼ pounds)*
> *¾ cup lemon juice*
> *1¼ cups olive oil*
> *3 cloves garlic, smashed, peeled, and minced*
> *¼ teaspoon freshly ground black pepper*
> *Salt to taste*

Remove the feelers from the shrimp (drawing 1). Leaving the shells intact, place each shrimp flat on the work surface. Holding the knife parallel to the surface, slice the shrimp in half evenly, starting at the head and stopping when you reach the tail (drawing 2). Do not cut through the tail. The shrimp will be in two even halves attached at the tail (drawing 3).

BUTTERFLYING SHRIMP

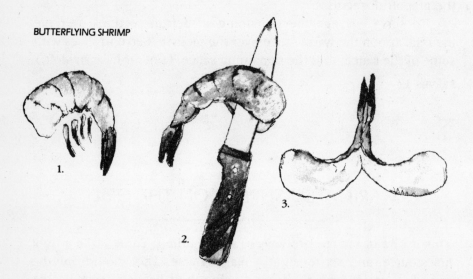

Place the shrimp in a bowl. Whisk together the lemon juice, olive oil, garlic, and pepper. Pour over the shrimp and turn gently to coat without tearing off the shells. Set aside for 30 minutes.

Heat a grill or broiler to very hot. Arrange the shrimp, shell sides down so the sides curve outward, on the grill or broiler. Cook only until the shrimp turn opaque, about 2 minutes.

Arrange 5 shrimp on each of six plates, tails meeting in the center. Add a little salt to the marinade and serve on the side as a sauce.

SERVES 6

MOULES POULETTE

———————•———————

This is a classic variation on a favorite dish of hot mussels marinière. I like the sexiness of the cream. Provide large spoons and good bread to dunk in the sauce. If you don't want the calories, use all the ingredients except the egg yolks and cream and add a large handful of basil leaves to the cooking broth.

Being lazy, I like to use the very clean mussels from Maine that have appeared in fish stores recently. If I need to clean mussels— can't persuade the fish store to clean them—I scrub them under cold running water with a plastic scrubbing pad. Do not store mussels in water; they tend to absorb it.

Years ago, having plucked mussels from seacoast rocks in the South of France and in Maine, I discovered that the largest shells don't necessarily contain the fattest mussels nor are the biggest mussels the best and sweetest. I actually prefer them small and sweet. If they are just snatched from the briny, pack the pot bottom with seaweed wetted down with sea water and steam tightly covered. Eat with inexpensive white wine. It is better if you are in love.

• • •

4 pounds mussels
½ cup dry white wine
¼ cup white-wine tarragon vinegar
1 tablespoon finely minced garlic
2 tablespoons finely chopped parsley
Freshly ground black pepper
2 egg yolks
1 cup heavy cream
Kosher salt (optional)
1 dash hot red-pepper sauce

When you get the mussels, check to make sure they are clean. If not, with a plastic scrubbing pad scrub them well under cold running water. With a sharp knife, remove any pieces of beard and any barnacles that do not come off by scrubbing. When the mussels are clean, drain well and store in a bowl in the refrigerator until needed. Discard any mussels that do not close when the shell is lightly pinched; they are probably dead.

Place the wine, vinegar, garlic, parsley, and pepper in a large pot. Swirl to mix and bring to a boil over medium heat. Add the mussels to the boiling wine mixture. Cover the pot tightly. Cook until all the mussels open, about 5 minutes. Remove the pot from the heat.

Place the egg yolks and cream in a bowl and whisk until smooth. Slowly whisk in the mussel liquid to raise the temperature of the yolks gradually. When all the liquid has been added, taste the sauce. If necessary, add salt. Adjust the pepper and add the hot pepper sauce.

Pour the sauce back into the pot, over the mussels. Place the pot over low heat and cook gently, shaking the pot from time to time, until the mussels are heated through. Be careful not to let the sauce boil or the egg yolk will curdle.

Serve immediately from a tureen or from the pot into deep rim soups. Large spoons are needed for the sauce, but the best tool for extracting mussels from the shell is two half-shells connected at the joint used as tweezers.

SERVES 6, OR 3 AS A MAIN COURSE

GLAZED MUSSELS WITH BASIL AND SPINACH

This is an extremely elegant end-of-summer dish and less fussy than it sounds. The taste of the basil with the spinach is a little surprise.

• • •

1 cup basil leaves plus 36 perfect large leaves, all
   washed
4 cups spinach leaves, washed
36 mussels
⅓ cup dry white wine
3 tablespoons unsalted butter
2 teaspoons flour
1 cup heavy cream
1 tablespoon lemon juice
5 drops hot red-pepper sauce
Kosher salt to taste

Cut the cup of basil leaves and the 4 cups of spinach leaves into a thin chiffonade (⅛-inch shreds cut across the leaf and the leaf-veins.) Set aside.

Thoroughly scrub the mussels and debeard them. Place them in a large, heavy skillet with a tight lid. Add all but 2 tablespoons of the wine. Cover.

Cook over low heat until the liquid in the bottom of the pan is steaming. Increase the heat to medium. Steam about 4 minutes, shaking the pan from time to time—be careful to hold the lid down—until all the mussels have opened. Using a slotted spoon, transfer the mussels to a large bowl. Set aside to cool. Strain the liquid from the skillet through a cheesecloth. Reserve the liquid.

In a large skillet, melt 2 tablespoons of the butter. Add the spinach and basil chiffonade. Sauté about 1 minute, until wilted. Transfer to a bowl to cool.

In a small saucepan, over medium-low heat, make a roux using the remaining butter and flour. Cook for 3 minutes, stirring continuously. Over the heat, whisk in ¼ cup of the mussel liquid, the heavy cream, and the remaining wine. Continue whisking, and simmer about 4 minutes, until the mixture is smooth and thick. Whisk in the lemon juice, hot pepper sauce, and salt. Remove from the heat. Stir 2 tablespoons of the sauce into the spinach and basil. Set remaining sauce aside.

Twist the mussel shells to separate. Discard half the shells. Remove the mussels from the shells. You will need one half-shell for each mussel. Scrub the retained half-shells thoroughly. Place a basil leaf, nice side up, in each shell so that the tip of the leaf extends beyond the pointed end. Spoon ½ teaspoon of the spinach-and-basil mixture over each leaf. Place a mussel on each lump of spinach. Coat each mussel with sauce, about 1 teaspoon.

Just before serving, place the oven rack 4 inches from the broiler. Heat the broiler. Place the mussels, in their shells, on a baking sheet. Broil for 30 seconds, until sauce is browned and mussels are warmed through. Serve hot, 6 to a plate. If you have some extra basil, especially the center flowers, put some in the center of each plate.

SERVES 6

SCALLOPS À L'AMÉRICAINE

This delicious preparation is usually made with expensive lobster. Unfortunately it requires shelling—which is a messy procedure, for either the cook or the guest. I make it with scallops, which sidesteps the whole to-do. I like the way it tastes with scallops and I like the white color peeping through the richly red sauce. Don't clutter up the plate with rice. Provide spoons for the sauce and encourage guests to use them.

...

2 pounds sea scallops
12 tablespoons (1½ sticks) unsalted butter
2 tablespoons olive oil
½ cup Cognac
1 cup Sauternes
1 cup very strong Fish Stock (page 113)
2 tablespoons Meat Glaze (page 309)
2 cups shrimp shells or peelings, roughly ground
  (optional)
1 large tomato, peeled, seeded, and finely chopped
  (about 1 cup)
2½ tablespoons chopped shallots
¼ teaspoon dried tarragon
¼ teaspoon quatre épices (purchased, or see note)
Freshly ground white pepper
Pinch cayenne pepper
Kosher salt
Fresh lemon juice to taste, about 1 tablespoon
Chopped fresh parsley

Pat the scallops dry. In a 12-inch sauté pan, melt about 4 tablespoons butter and the olive oil. Heat until very hot. Add the scallops and sauté for 30 to 60 seconds, just until they become opaque on the outside. Warm Cognac in a small pan, ignite and immediately pour over scallops. When the flames have died down, remove the scallops with a slotted spoon to a dish. Cover and keep warm until the sauce is finished.

To the liquid in the pan, add the wine, stock, meat glaze, shrimp shells, tomato, shallots, tarragon, quatre épices, and peppers. Let cook over moderately high heat until the sauce is reduced by a little more than half, about 10 minutes. From time to time, add any liquid the scallops are giving off. As the sauce reduces, skim off any scum that rises to the surface. The sauce should be slightly thick.

Strain the sauce through a fine sieve into a saucepan. Taste and season with salt, additional peppers, and lemon juice. Cut the remaining 8 tablespoons butter into 1-inch pieces. Over moderate heat, beat in the butter, one piece at a time. Add the scallops, taste again for seasonings, and sprinkle with chopped parsley. Cook until the scallops are just heated through. Divide scallops and sauce onto each of six plates. Give each guest a large spoon and a chunk of bread for the best part, the sauce.

SERVES 6

NOTE: Quatre épices is made by mixing together 1⅛ cup freshly ground white pepper, 1½ tablespoons ground cloves, 3½ tablespoons ground ginger, and 4 tablespoons grated nutmeg. Store in a tightly sealed jar.

MOUSSES OF BROCCOLI AND ACORN SQUASH

A vegetable mousse can be served as a side dish with roasts or other simple main courses, but is good enough to stand alone at the beginning of the meal if accompanied by a light sauce. While you should feel free to substitute any vegetable of your choice, the broccoli and acorn squash contrast beautifully both in taste and in color. The pool of pale yellow sauce flecked with green is a perfect frame.

Squash is particularly American; it is part of the feast of new vegetables that the Europeans found upon landing here and took back to incorporate into their cuisines.

This mousse doesn't need much wine; a little of whatever you are going to use for the main course will be just fine.

• • •

BROCCOLI MOUSSE

1 bunch broccoli
1 tablespoon unsalted butter
¼ cup heavy cream
3 egg yolks, lightly beaten
1¼ teaspoons kosher salt
Freshly ground black pepper
Pinch nutmeg
Pinch cayenne pepper

ACORN-SQUASH MOUSSE

3 pounds acorn squash, peeled and seeded, cut
   into chunks
1 tablespoon unsalted butter
¼ cup heavy cream
3 egg yolks, lightly beaten
1¼ teaspoons kosher salt
Freshly ground black pepper
Pinch cayenne pepper

LEMON-CHIVE SABAYON

8 egg yolks
3 tablespoons fresh lemon juice
1 teaspoon kosher salt
½ cup water
2 tablespoons chopped fresh chives

▪ ▪ ▪

8 blanched chives, for garnish

BROCCOLI MOUSSE

Trim the broccoli, discarding all the leaves. Cut the broccoli head into flowerets. Peel the stem and slice thin. Steam the flowerets and slices for 5 to 10 minutes, or until just tender and bright green. Drain well. Immediately place the broccoli in a food processor with the butter; process until smooth. Remove the purée and cool. You should have about 2½ cups. Stir in the remaining ingredients.

ACORN-SQUASH MOUSSE

Steam the squash pieces for 10 minutes, or until soft. Remove immediately. Place in a food processor with the butter, and process until smooth. Remove the purée from the processor and cool. You should have about 2½ cups purée. Stir in the remaining ingredients.

Preheat the oven to 350°F. Generously butter 8 six-ounce ramekins. Divide the broccoli mousse evenly among the ramekins, keeping the tops smooth. Place equal quantities of acorn-squash mousse over the broccoli. Smooth the tops. Cover the ramekins with buttered wax paper, buttered side down. Place them in a baking pan and add boiling water to come halfway up the sides of the ramekins. Bake for 20 to 30 minutes, or until firm to the touch.

Remove the pan from the oven and the ramekins from the pan. Place them on a rack. Let them cool 20 minutes before unmolding.

LEMON-CHIVE SABAYON

While the mousses are cooling, prepare the sauce. Place the egg yolks in the top of a double boiler over simmering water. Whisking constantly, cook the yolks until very thick. Still whisking, add the lemon juice, salt, and ¼ cup of the water. Cook another 30 to 60 seconds. Stir in the 2 tablespoons chives and enough additional water to make 2 cups.

ASSEMBLY

On each of 8 plates, place a puddle of sauce. Unmold a mousse onto the center of each plate. Decorate with 1 or 2 whole chives if you like. Remember that this is a very colorful dish when choosing plates.

SERVES 8

RISOTTO WITH OLYMPIA OYSTERS

This recipe was originally created for Olympia oysters; but except for those of you who live on the northwest coast, Olympia oysters—less than half a dime in size—will be very hard to find. In any case the recipe seemed worth giving because it is so very good and so nicely illustrates a technique taken from another cuisine and adapted to American ingredients. You can approximate the taste with fresh

RISOTTO WITH OLYMPIA OYSTERS, CONTINUED

shucked oysters in their liquor, available in many parts of the country. Quarter the oysters with large scissors before stirring them in.

Oysters and Champagne—or, in our case, California bubbly—are a proverbial combination. Any good, crisp dry white wine, such as a Johannisberg riesling made without any residual sugar, a sauvignon blanc, a chardonnay made without too much oak, or even a brand-name white that is dry and light would begin any dinner with a bang.

• • •

9 tablespoons unsalted butter
3 tablespoons chopped shallots
1 tablespoon chopped parsley
1 cup arborio rice
1 cup shucked Olympia oysters, with 1 cup oyster liquor
1 cup Chicken Stock (page 110)
1 cup dry white wine
1 cup bottled clam juice
Freshly ground black pepper
¾ cup freshly grated Parmesan cheese

In a 2-quart saucepan melt 3 tablespoons of the butter over medium heat. Add the shallots and cook, stirring once or twice, for 2 minutes. Add the parsley and rice, and stir to coat the rice with the butter. Add the oyster liquor, and shake the pan gently until the liquid begins to simmer. Lower the heat slightly. Using a wooden spoon, stir the rice until the liquid is almost completely absorbed. The rice will form a cohesive mass at this point.

Combine the chicken stock, wine, and clam juice. Add enough liquid to barely cover the rice. Continue cooking and stirring until the liquid is absorbed. Continue adding the liquid and stirring and cooking until all the liquid has been added. The rice should be creamy and firm but not hard. If not yet done, add more liquid. Season to taste with pepper. Whisk in the remaining 6 tablespoons butter with the Parmesan cheese and oysters. Mix thoroughly and serve immediately.

SERVES 6

DUCK LIVER, APPLE, AND RAISIN SAUTÉ

———————————— • ————————————

Duck livers are expensive and hard to find on their own; but they come free when you buy a duck. Accumulate them and keep in milk as you do chicken livers (page 22).

• • •

4 sets duck livers, soaked 24 hours in milk
3 tablespoons unsalted butter
¼ cup chopped shallots
1 cup peeled, cored, and thinly sliced apples (firm-textured apples work best)
½ cup Calvados
2 teaspoons Duck or Meat Glaze (page 309)
⅔ cup golden raisins, soaked in Madeira for at least 15 minutes, drained
¾ cup heavy cream reduced by boiling to ¼ cup
2 teaspoons fresh lemon juice
½ teaspoon kosher salt
Freshly ground black pepper
4 toasted croutons (about 3-inch rounds)
Chopped parsley

Drain the livers and pat dry. Separate lobes and remove connecting membranes.

Melt the butter in a skillet. Add the shallots and cook until softened, about 30 seconds. Do not brown. Add the apples and sauté gently for a minute. Add the livers and gently sauté, about 2 minutes, letting the sides set but not toughen.

Gently heat the Calvados in a small pan. Ignite and pour over the livers. When the flames die down, stir in the glaze, raisins, reduced cream, lemon juice, salt, and pepper. Simmer 1 minute.

Put a crouton in the center of each of 4 salad plates. Spoon a portion of the livers over each crouton. Sprinkle with chopped parsley.

SERVES 4

SHRIMP QUENELLES WITH WATERCRESS SAUCE

This is one of the most spectacularly beautiful dishes I make. The rich green sauce sets off the pale pink and feathery-light quenelles. A sprig of fresh green watercress adds the final note. I serve it on individual black plates. Provide spoons so people can eat every bit of the sauce.

...

QUENELLES

1 pound shrimp, peeled and deveined
2 large egg whites
2 teaspoons kosher salt
1½ cups heavy cream
⅛ teaspoon freshly grated nutmeg
Unsalted butter

WATERCRESS SAUCE

3 bunches watercress
1½ cups heavy cream
1 cup milk
5 egg yolks

QUENELLES

Place shrimp, egg whites, and salt in the work bowl of a food processor. Process until the mixture is fairly smooth. With the machine running, pour in the cream and nutmeg through the feed tube. Process until you have a smooth mixture. Cover and refrigerate for at least 45 minutes.

Bring a large pot of water to a simmer. Butter a flameproof 1-inch-deep baking pan and set on the stove. Shape the quenelles by either piping them out into 1-by-2-inch strips with a pastry bag fitted with a ½-inch tip, or forming them with two soup spoons into elongated ovals (drawings 1 and 2). If using soup spoons, keep them wet so the mixture does not stick to them. Place the formed quenelles on the greased pan, leaving space between them (drawing 3). Pour on the simmering water (drawing 4) until it almost covers the quenelles.

MAKING QUENELLES

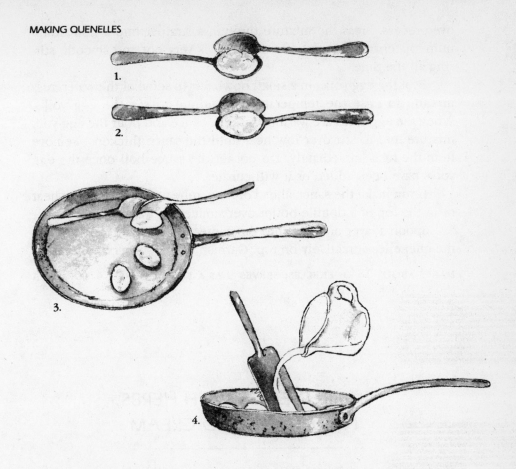

Do not pour the water directly on the quenelles or they will break up at this point. Make sure the quenelles do not stick to the pan. Turn on stove. Keep the heat at a point just high enough so that the water is always barely simmering. After about 3 minutes, turn the quenelles over and cook on the other side for about 2 minutes. Remove with a slotted spoon. Keep warm until ready to serve.

WATERCRESS SAUCE

Bring a large pot of salted water to a boil. Wash the watercress and trim off the leaves. Discard the stems. Add the leaves to the boiling water. Bring the water back to a boil and let boil for 6 minutes, making sure the watercress is always covered with the water.

Drain the watercress and squeeze dry. Chop well in a food processor. Add the cream and milk, and process just until thick. Do not overprocess. Press the mixture through a strainer into a non-aluminum saucepan. Heat the sauce until it is very hot and smooth, stirring all the time.

Beat the egg yolks in a small bowl. Stir in some of the watercress mixture to raise the temperature. Continue to stir the egg yolks. When the egg yolks are warm, whisk the sauce and pour the egg-yolk mixture into it. Stir over low heat until the sauce thickens. Remove from the heat immediately. Do not let the sauce boil once the egg yolks have been added or it will curdle.

If you make the sauce ahead of time, reheat slowly over low heat or in the top of a double boiler over simmering water.

Spoon a layer of sauce into the center of each plate and arrange the quenelles attractively on top. Garnish with a sprig of watercress.

MAKES ABOUT 18 QUENELLES; SERVES 9 AS A FIRST COURSE, 4 TO 6 AS A MAIN COURSE

SHIRRED EGGS WITH HERBS, TOMATOES, AND CREAM

————————————•————————————

When trying to think of a last-minute first course, don't ignore the loyal eggs waiting in the refrigerator. These shirred eggs can be prepared with nothing more exotic than parsley if you don't keep herbs growing on the windowsill all year round. Serve an inexpensive, fresh-tasting wine such as an Alsatian riesling, Italian pinot grigio, or California chenin blanc. Don't overcook the eggs.

• • •

1 teaspoon unsalted butter
8 eggs, at room temperature
¼ cup chopped mixed fresh herbs
¼ to ½ cup peeled, seeded, and chopped fresh
tomatoes
Kosher salt
Freshly ground black pepper
Heavy cream

Heat the oven to 450° F.

Butter 4 small gratin dishes. Into each break 2 eggs. Scatter the chopped herbs and tomatoes over the surface. Season to taste with salt and pepper. Spoon the cream on to cover the surface evenly.

Bake in the preheated oven until set—8 to 10 minutes; don't overcook. Turn on the broiler. Place eggs under it a moment to brown lightly. Serve immediately, setting each gratin dish on a plate or doubled napkin, and providing each guest with a soup-dessert spoon.

SERVES 4

HOT SHRIMP AND CABBAGE SLAW

The barely cooked cabbage wilts to make this colorful slaw, lightly shrimp-tasting throughout. It serves eight people from two pounds of shrimp.

• • •

*1 green cabbage, cored, thinly shredded as for slaw
    (3 cups)*
½ cup good olive oil
*1 red bell pepper, peeled with a vegetable peeler,
    stemmed and seeded, cut lengthwise into ¼-inch-
    wide strips (¾ cup)*
*1 green bell pepper, peeled with a vegetable peeler,
    stemmed and seeded, cut lengthwise into ¼-inch-
    wide strips*
4 strips lemon zest
2 pounds shrimp, peeled
⅓ cup fresh lemon juice
2 teaspoons kosher salt
Freshly ground black pepper

Bring about 6 cups of water to a boil. Place the cabbage in a colander in the sink. Pour the boiling water over the cabbage to wilt it. Set aside.

Heat the oil in a 10- to 12-inch skillet over medium heat. When it is hot, add the red and green pepper strips. Toss to coat with the oil. Add the lemon zest and stir to mix. Add the shrimp and cook, stirring, for 1 minute. Add the lemon juice, salt, and generous amounts of pepper to taste. Continue to cook until the shrimp are barely done. With a slotted spoon or skimmer, remove the shrimp and peppers to a bowl, leaving the liquid in the pan.

With the pan over high heat, add the cabbage, toss to coat, and cook for 30 seconds. With a slotted spoon or skimmer, remove the cabbage from the pan and divide it among 8 serving plates so that there is a neat layer of cabbage on each. In the center of each cabbage layer, arrange an eighth of the shrimp-and-pepper mixture. Divide any liquid remaining in the pan among the 8 plates, pouring it over the shrimp.

The salads may be served immediately or left at room temperature for up to half an hour.

SERVES 8

MINI-PIZZA

This is a sort of nouvelle California stand-up-and-eat pizza. I don't like to eat standing; but the taste is terrific. It goes well with drinks or an outspoken red wine. It can be last-minute food if you follow the freezing instructions in the pizza dough recipe.

• • •

PIZZA DOUGH

¾ cup warm (90° to 100° F.) water
2 teaspoons granulated yeast
2 to 3 tablespoons olive oil
1 teaspoon kosher salt
½ teaspoon freshly ground black pepper
2½ cups bread flour, approximately

PIZZA FILLING

Fruity olive oil
48 basil leaves (about 2 bunches)
1 small green bell pepper, stemmed, seeded, and minced
1 small red bell pepper, stemmed, seeded, and minced
96 small Nice olives, whole (about 1¼ pounds)

8 ounces mild goat cheese, such as Montrachet or
Bouchette, cut into ¾-inch cubes (see note)
Freshly ground black pepper

PIZZA DOUGH

In a large bowl, stir the water, yeast and olive oil until the yeast dissolves. Let stand for 10 minutes. Add the salt and pepper. Stir in enough of the flour to form a stiff dough. Scrape the sides of the bowl as you stir. Turn the dough out onto a lightly floured board. Knead 5 to 10 minutes, adding flour as necessary to prevent sticking. When the dough is smooth, cover it with a clean towel and let it rest 20 minutes.

Divide the dough in half. Roll out each half into a log about 12 inches long and 1 inch in diameter. Cut each log crosswise into 24 equal-sized, coin-shaped pieces. With your fingers, stretch each coin into a 3-inch round. Form the edges slightly thicker than the centers.

The pizza shells can be made in advance to this point and frozen. Arrange the shells in a single layer on a baking sheet. Freeze just until solid, about one hour. Transfer the shells to a plastic freezer bag. Seal tightly. Frozen shells can be stored up to three months.

PIZZA FILLING

Place the dough circles on an oiled baking sheet, one inch apart. Brush lightly with oil and place a basil leaf in the center of each one. Mix the red and green peppers together in a small bowl and sprinkle lightly over the top of each pizza. Place 2 olives and 2 squares of goat cheese in the center of each pizza. Drizzle pizza with olive oil. Sprinkle with pepper.

Bake in a 400° oven until the cheese is melted and the crust is cooked through, about 8 minutes. Cool slightly before eating.

MAKES 48 THREE-INCH PIZZAS

NOTE: Put the cheese in the freezer for 10 minutes before cutting it. Then arrange the cut pieces in a single layer on a baking sheet in the refrigerator for easier handling.

• FOCACCIO •

To make Focaccio—a flat, savory, pizza-like bread—use 3, instead of 2, tablespoons of olive oil. Proceed as for the pizza dough. Divide the dough into two equal portions. Shape each portion into an 8-inch round, leaving the edges slightly thicker than the centers. Place the rounds on a baking sheet. Freeze just until solid, about 1 hour. To bake, heat the oven to 375° F. Place the frozen loaves on an oiled baking sheet. Bake 10 minutes. Remove them from the oven and brush with olive oil and, if desired, sprinkle with salt and dried rosemary. Return the loaves to the oven and continue to bake an additional 10 to 15 minutes, until they are golden brown and crisp.

CAYENNE QUAIL ON A CORIANDER NEST

This is an absolutely smashing first course once you convince guests that fingers are the best tool. It is a close relative of the Spicy Pigeon on page 206. Remember, this needs advance planning because of the marinating.

• • •

⅓ cup cayenne pepper
2 cups vegetable oil
8 fresh quail, 4 ounces each
Kosher salt
Freshly ground black pepper
5 cups loosely packed fresh coriander sprigs
8 lemon wedges

In a heavy saucepan, stir together the cayenne pepper and oil. Heat over medium-low heat for 1 hour. The oil should not get so hot that the cayenne changes color. Remove the pan from the heat and allow the oil to cool to room temperature. Strain through cheesecloth. Let cool.

Cut the quail into quarters. Remove the feet at the ankle joints. Cut away any innards from the body cavity. Remove backbones. Reserve bones, hearts, and gizzards to cook with a chicken or turkey stock (pages 110 and 111). (The livers can be sautéed with a few mushrooms and some sliced shallots, seasoned with salt and pepper, and used to fill an omelet for 4 for another day's first course.)

Place the quail pieces in a large, shallow dish. Cover with the cayenne-oil. Marinate for 2 or 3 days in the refrigerator if you think of it. If you are in a hurry, marinate overnight at room temperature. The pepper acts as a preservative.

When you are ready to cook the quail, remove them from the marinade. Allow the oil to drip off; do not wipe them. This is easily done by placing a cake rack on top of a baking sheet and putting the quail on the rack. Sprinkle with salt and pepper. The oil can be saved in a jar in the refrigerator for another time.

You can cook the marinated birds in two different ways. They can be grilled over charcoal or under the broiler. Either one should be very hot. If cooking over charcoal, lightly grease the grill and, with tongs, arrange the quail pieces in a single layer, bone side down, over the hot coals. If cooking under a broiler, lightly grease the perforated rack and arrange the quail pieces bone side up. In either case, cook for 1 minute. Then turn with the tongs so the skin is toward the heat. Cook for about 2 minutes more, until the skin is crisp. The birds will be crisp on the outside and rare in the center.

While the quail are cooking, make a nest of coriander on each of 8 plates. On each nest neatly arrange two breasts and two legs. Place a lemon wedge in the center of each plate. Make sure guests have large napkins and encourage them to use their hands to eat with. This is a time for finger bowls if you wish.

SERVES 8

• QUAIL WITH GORGONZOLA POLENTA •

There is another nice way to serve quail that is a little more work but is so unusual as to be worth it. Marinate the quail as in this recipe for one or two days before your dinner. An hour before dinnertime, make the Gorgonzola Polenta on page 263. Omit the lemons, and reduce the coriander to one cup of sprigs. When you put the quail on to grill, reheat the polenta, beating like crazy to avoid lumps. Make a circle of polenta on each first-course plate. Arrange four quail pieces on each round of polenta. Place a few coriander sprigs in the center of each plate. I did this for a very fancy charity dinner with great success.

PASTA

———————•———————

• PASTA •

Hot Spaghettini with Raw Tomato Sauce

Linguini with Fried Peppers and Tomatoes

My Spaghetti

White Noodles, Green Cabbage, String Beans, and Cream

Green Pasta with Tomato and Scallops

Penne à la Vodka

San Pietro Lasagne

• STUFFED PASTAS •

Tortellini with Basil, Cream, and Chives

Very Italian Cappelletti

Ravioli Stuffed with Clams and Italian Sausage

Ravioli Stuffed with Duck and Chinese Seasonings

I have never had a guest who didn't like pasta. The more sophisticated the tastes of the friends, the simpler and more direct the pasta I serve. As long as I have a box of pasta on the shelf and the normal staples around, I am never at a loss for a first course or a simple meal. I bring some lightly salted water to a boil. By the time a pound of linguini has cooked—about eight minutes—I have heated three crushed cloves of garlic, a tiny pinch of red pepper, salt, and pepper in a half cup of good olive oil to make a simple sauce to toss with the hot, drained linguini. This is the sauce for those killer, richly fruity green olive oils that I often find too insistent-tasting for salad and always too dominant for mayonnaise. With a bottle of red wine and, if the refrigerator provides, some good Parmesan, fifteen minutes after walking in the door I am ready for dinner, having had time also to put plates, forks, knives, napkins, and lit candles on the table. Give me ten minutes more shopping time and we can have salad, salad dressing, and bread. The evening is complete. It may not be the world's most elegant meal; but, so far, no complaints and lots of good conversation and laughter have gone with it.

Pasta is too good and various to have this be the sum of my repertoire. Pasta is a chameleon that can be as elegant or peasanty as I wish. I steal ideas and seasonings from many of the world's cuisines and improvise on my own, making summer pastas created in response to the marvelous vegetables in season, dreaming up new things to tuck into the middle of fresh tortellini or wonton skins.

I have some pet pasta peeves: pasta that is overcooked and gummy, pasta that is drowning in sauce, pasta indiscriminately sprinkled with grated cheese, dimming the clarity of its flavors. Cheese is wonderful on northern Italian, meat-rich sauces but does less than nothing for clear-tasting seafood sauces or crisp crunches of vegetables.

By now, many of us have one kind of pasta machine or another to make fresh egg noodles, well worth the doing when time is available. As for dry pastas—egg and macaroni types—fancy imported pastas from Italy and Japanese buckwheat udon now vie for space on the grocery shelf; even fresh Chinese and Italian egg noodles can be bought. All are good and worth trying. For most of my harried purposes, good-quality American pasta (made with the same wheat we send to Italy) is sufficient. I always have boxes of linguini or spaghettini on the shelves. They stand up well to the strong flavors of the sauces my friends favor.

COOKING FRESH OR DRIED PASTA: The basic rule for cooking pasta is to use more lightly salted water than you think necessary and to make sure it is at a rolling boil before you add the pasta. If your pasta is dry and too long to fit easily into the pot, don't break it. Ease it into the boiling water as it softens. Stir the pasta until the water returns to the boil. Timing is hard to give accurately since it will vary with the dryness of the pasta and its size. The Italian rule of thumb is that the pasta is ready when a piece flung at the kitchen wall sticks. While I have shown off doing this, I don't really like it. I usually sneak a piece out of the pot and taste. The pasta shouldn't be raw in the center, but it should offer some resistance when you bite in. Fresh pasta that you buy needs cooking; homemade pasta needs virtually none—thirty seconds to one minute. It gets tough if overcooked, like scrambled eggs. Unless the pasta is to be served in soup, a little olive oil should be added to the pot at the last minute, or, if the sauce is creamy or buttery, tossed with a little butter the instant it is drained. Toss drained Chinese noodles with a vegetable oil. The slightly slippery surface keeps the strands of pasta from clinging together in an ungainly mess.

HOMEMADE TOMATO PURÉE: In the winter, if I want tomatoes for sauce, I use canned Italian plum tomatoes or, better yet, tomato purée I put up at the end of the summer. I take a bushel of tomatoes, wash them, chunk them up coarsely, and put them in a heavy-bottomed pot—so they don't scorch—and cook them for about twelve hours over very low heat. This drives out the water without killing the natural acids. Then the whole thing is put through a food mill to remove skins and seeds. I check to see that the purée is thick enough. If it isn't, the pot is put back on the stove and kept cooking. (My purée is more like a sauce than a tomato paste in texture.) I put the cooled purée in 8-ounce freezer containers, freeze, then remove the frozen purée chunks to individual plastic bags. When you use the purée to make a sauce, remember to season it. One version for pasta, pork chops or shrimp follows.

QUICK TOMATO SAUCE: To quickly turn 8 ounces of frozen tomato purée into sauce, I peel and mince 2 cloves of garlic, melt them in 2 tablespoons of olive oil. I add salt and pepper, a shot of red wine and a tiny sprinkling of marjoram or parsley. Then I simmer for 15 minutes. A quarter cup of crumbled, ground meat (pork, beef, veal or sausage) sautéed with the garlic turns this into a simple meat sauce. For more elegance, see Salsa Bolognese, page 90.

FROZEN FRESH BASIL: Similarly, I prepare for winter by buying a case of basil, washing and stemming it, chopping it, and turning it in hot olive oil just until it wilts. I freeze it in ice-cube trays and, when it's frozen, pop the cubes into plastic bags, ready to bring the taste of summer to grim, gray winter days.

An ample, wide earthenware bowl is wonderful for presenting and tossing pastas of the more robust sorts. If I am serving cheese, I generally just put it in a rotary grater and let people grind their own.

The reason most of the pastas that follow are not sauced with meat is that it is easier to precede a meat main course with a non-meat pasta. For American tastes, I think of the San Pietro Lasagne (page 90) as a main course.

▪ ▪ ▪

PASTA

———— • ————

HOT SPAGHETTINI WITH RAW TOMATO SAUCE

———— • ————

This is one of the best and simplest of the pasta recipes. The only problem is that it can be made only at the end of summer, when tomatoes are burstingly ripe, onions are sweet, and there is a plethora of basil. The sauce is almost a salad. With bread, cheese, a bottle of zinfandel, a piece of cheese and a ripe peach this is for me a perfect, complete meal.

> *6 large ripe tomatoes, cored and cut into 1-inch*
> *chunks (about 4 cups)*
> *7 tablespoons kosher salt*
> *1 pound spaghettini*
> *⅓ cup plus ½ cup olive oil*
> *1½ cups coarsely chopped red onions*
> *½ cup firmly packed chopped basil*
> *½ cup fresh lemon juice*
> *Freshly ground black pepper*

Bring 6 quarts of water to a boil.

Place the tomatoes in a non-aluminum bowl. Sprinkle 2 table-spoons salt over them and let sit for 30 minutes.

Add 4 tablespoons salt to the boiling water, then add the pasta. Cook until barely done, about 8 minutes. Add ⅓ cup olive oil to the pot with the cooking pasta, then drain in a colander. Shake to remove all the water and place in a serving bowl.

As the pasta cooks, drain the tomatoes and add the onions, basil, lemon juice, ½ cup olive oil, the remaining tablespoon salt, and freshly ground black pepper to taste. Push the hot pasta to the sides of the bowl and pour the cold sauce into the center.

SERVES 8 AS A FIRST COURSE, 4 AS A MAIN COURSE

LINGUINI WITH FRIED PEPPERS
AND TOMATOES

This is currently my, bar none, hands-down favorite pasta—very Amalfi coast. It is clear in taste, sinus-clearing, and mildly addictive. Make more than you think you will need: people always take seconds. The flavor is a balance of sweet, hot, and fresh-fruit flavors—"a beaker full of the warm south" that gets any meal off to a joyous start. Try it before the Poached Filet of Beef with Basil Sauce (page 224) and follow it with melon. A Morgon or Barbaresco could accompany the pasta and still go with the meat, or be followed by a good St.

Émilion if you are feeling plush. Alternatively, you might want to try the crisp, light Episcopio white wine from Ravello.

Perhaps the best version of this dish is made with sweet, ripe yellow bell peppers, cut in strips, to replace the frying peppers and with three-quarters of the tomatoes being yellow and fleshy sweet. With this version use spaghettini instead of linguini.

• • •

½ cup olive oil
1 pound dry linguini
16 long (4 to 5 inches) hot green peppers, stemmed
3 large sweet frying (Italian) peppers, stemmed,
  seeded, quartered
8 cloves garlic, sliced thin
6 cups cored tomatoes in 1-inch dice (about 5
  medium)
Salt and freshly ground pepper

Bring a large pot of salted water to a boil. Heat the oil in a large, heavy skillet over medium heat until very hot.

While the oil is heating, stir the linguini into the boiling water. Cook, stirring from time to time, until the linguini is tender but firm, about 10 minutes.

Add hot and sweet peppers carefully to the hot oil, shaking the pan to distribute the peppers evenly. Cook until the peppers are wilted, about 4 minutes. Add garlic and fry until fragrant, about 30 seconds. Add tomatoes and cook just until softened, 4 to 6 minutes. Longer cooking will make the sauce watery. Add salt and pepper to taste.

Drain the linguini in a colander, shaking to remove all the water. Transfer it to a deep serving platter or divide among individual plates. Spoon peppers with sauce over the linguini. Serve very hot. Do not top with grated cheese or offer it. Cheese will only kill the wonderful fresh taste.

This dish is as hearty in color as it is in taste. It goes well in a vivid bowl or on colorful plates. I tasted it and got the recipe at the San Pietro Hotel in Positano in an idyllic dining room overlooking the bluest part of the Mediterranean, with vines creeping along the ceiling, stretched inward by the penetrating fingers of the sea-sun. There they use brightly colored patterned local plates that are happiest with the brilliant-colored local food.

SERVES 8 AS A FIRST COURSE, 4 AS A MAIN COURSE

MY SPAGHETTI

This is another fresh, virtually instant pasta. Rich with the taste of basil, it is lighter than a traditional pesto saucing. When the best of the summer tomatoes are just a memory, and I can no longer make my raw tomato sauce, I make this because I can still buy good basil in the stores or I can substitute three of my Frozen Fresh Basil cubes (page 83) for the fresh basil.

• • •

> ¾ cup well-packed fresh basil leaves, washed and dried
> ½ cup well-packed flat-leaf Italian parsley leaves, washed and dried
> 4 cloves garlic
> ½ teaspoon kosher salt
> ¾ cup good olive oil
> Freshly ground black pepper
> 1 pound spaghetti

Bring a large pot of lightly salted water to a boil.

Place the basil and parsley leaves, garlic, salt, ½ cup olive oil, and pepper to taste in the work bowl of a food processor fitted with the metal blade. Turn on and off, scraping down the sides once or twice with a rubber spatula, until you have a medium-smooth mixture. Place it in a small saucepan over low heat. Stir from time to time as the pasta cooks. Keep heat low so that the basil remains fresh-tasting.

When the water comes to a boil, add the pasta and cook at a rolling boil until just done but still firm—about 10 minutes. Pour in the remaining ¼ cup olive oil and stir once. Pour the pasta and water through a colander to drain. While the pasta is still hot, place it in a serving bowl and toss with the basil mixture.

Hope that some will be left over to eat for breakfast—cold, with your fingers.

SERVES 8 AS A FIRST COURSE, 4 AS A MAIN COURSE

WHITE NOODLES, GREEN CABBAGE, STRING BEANS, AND CREAM

This is a wonderfully elegant first-course pasta, simple to make and with an original combination of unexpected ingredients. Be sure the cabbage is young and, if possible, pale green so that it has a delicate taste. This creamy fettuccine is pale but for hints of green beans (the cabbage and onions disappear), so serve it on plates with a colorful rim. A perfect prelude to a Roast Loin of Pork (page 183) with a Montalcino.

...

3 tablespoons unsalted butter
2 cups thinly sliced onions (about ⅛ inch thick)
4 cups (1½ pounds) thinly sliced cabbage (about
   ⅛ inch thick)
1 pound string beans, cut lengthwise into quarters,
   blanched 2 minutes in boiling salted water
½ pound fettuccine (see note)
2½ cups heavy cream
2 tablespoons fresh lemon juice
2¼ teaspoons kosher salt
Freshly ground black pepper to taste
A tiny squeeze of Hungarian paprika paste
   (optional)

Bring a large pot of salted water to a boil.

Heat 2 tablespoons of the butter in a large skillet. Add the sliced onions and cook until soft and translucent but not brown. Add the remaining tablespoon of butter and let melt. Add the cabbage and blanched string beans, and toss to mix with the onions. Remove from the heat.

Place the pasta in the boiling salted water and cook until done but still firm (al dente). Drain and immediately toss with the onion mixture. Place the skillet over moderate heat and add the cream, lemon juice, salt, pepper, and paprika paste, if you want a hint of sharpness. Toss until heated through.

SERVES 8 AS A FIRST COURSE

NOTE: Capelletti pasta dough, pages 94–95, can be cut into thin strips and used in this recipe.

GREEN PASTA WITH TOMATO
AND SCALLOPS

———————•———————

This fresh-tasting first-course pasta makes a small amount of scallops go a long way. I almost never serve lunch, but if I did I'd serve this with a crisp white Mâcon or Corvo.

• • •

1 pound fresh, green linguini (see note)
6 tablespoons olive oil
2 teaspoons minced garlic
1 pound sea scallops, cut into quarters
4 teaspoons fresh lemon juice
2 tablespoons minced fresh chives
2 tablespoons chopped fresh parsley
1½ teaspoons kosher salt
Freshly ground black pepper
1⅓ cups canned Italian plum tomatoes, drained
½ cup tomato purée (page 82)

Bring a large pot of salted water to a boil. Add the linguini and cook until done but still firm (al dente), about 5 minutes. Drain and rinse under cold running water. Toss with 4 tablespoons of the olive oil to keep the pasta from sticking. Set aside.

Heat the remaining 2 tablespoons of olive oil in a large skillet. Add the garlic and scallops, and sauté just until the scallops begin to change color, about a minute. Add the lemon juice, chives, parsley, ½ teaspoon of the salt, and pepper to taste.

Heat the plum tomatoes in a small non-aluminum pot until warmed through. In a separate large non-aluminum skillet heat the tomato purée, the remaining 1 teaspoon salt, and pepper to taste. When hot, add the pasta and toss to heat through.

Place the pasta in a serving bowl or on individual plates; arrange the plum tomatoes on top, leaving a border of green around the red. Then center the red circle with the white scallops.

SERVES 8 AS A FIRST COURSE OR 4 AS A MAIN COURSE FOR LUNCH

NOTE: Broad Green Noodles, pages 90–91, can be cut in thin strips and used in this recipe.

PENNE À LA VODKA

———————•———————

This is a rather trendy recipe in Italy where it's made with red-pepper flakes. I worked out this version using a spicy Hungarian paprika paste. I think it tastes smoother and better. This penne was on the menu of Joanna's Restaurant in New York, and it became very popular.

• • •

½ pound penne
2 tablespoons olive oil
½ cup finely chopped peeled Italian plum tomatoes
3 tablespoons vodka
1 teaspoon Red Gold–brand paprika paste
½ cup heavy cream
½ teaspoon salt
Freshly ground black pepper to taste

Bring a large pot of salted water to a boil. Boil the penne about 12 minutes, until tender but firm. While the pasta is cooking, make the sauce.

In a small skillet, heat the oil over medium heat. Add the tomatoes and stir to coat with oil. Take the skillet off the heat and pour in 2 tablespoons of the vodka. Carefully tilt the pan toward the flame to ignite the vodka. If you prefer, you can light it with a long kitchen match. Shake the pan until the flames subside.

Return the skillet to medium heat. Stir in the paprika paste. Add the remaining tablespoon vodka, the cream, salt, and pepper. Boil until slightly reduced and thickened.

Drain the cooked penne thoroughly in a colander. Rinse briefly under warm water. Transfer it to a serving bowl. Pour the sauce over the penne and toss well. Serve at once.

SERVES 4 AS A FIRST COURSE OR 2 AS A MAIN COURSE

SAN PIETRO LASAGNE

————————————————

The best baked lasagne I ever ate was at the San Pietro Hotel on the cliff rim of Positano. Free-form cook though I am, I decided not to try to improve on perfection. The taste and texture are light. This is not food for a hurry—although it can be made ahead and reheated. It is simple food good enough for any party. I serve it as a main course, particularly at buffets—but not to Italians. To them, pasta is not a main course—it is an essential beginning to a meal. If enough people annoy wine sellers asking for Episcopio red, a wine produced up the Amalfi coast from Positano, maybe some wise soul will import it so we can drink it with our lasagne. In the meantime, try for an energetic red.

SALSA BOLOGNESE (MEAT AND TOMATO SAUCE)

½ ounce dried porcini mushrooms (about ¼ cup)
½ pound ground pork
½ pound ground beef
¼ pound ground veal
1 small carrot, peeled and cut in ¼-inch dice
1 small onion, cut in ¼-inch dice
1 celery stalk, trimmed and cut in ¼-inch dice
2 ounces pancetta or blanched slab bacon, diced
1 can (28 ounces) Italian plum tomatoes, undrained
2 teaspoons salt
¼ teaspoon freshly ground black pepper

SALSA BALSAMELLA (WHITE SAUCE)

2 tablespoons unsalted butter
4 tablespoons all-purpose flour
3 cups milk
3 teaspoons salt
¼ teaspoon freshly ground black pepper

BROAD GREEN NOODLES (LASAGNE VERDE)

*¼ pound fresh spinach, stemmed (about four
    packed cups of leaves)*
*2 cups all-purpose flour, plus additional flour, as
    needed*
3 eggs

• • •

3 cups grated Parmesan cheese

SALSA BOLOGNESE

Soak the mushrooms in warm water to cover about 20 minutes, until softened. Drain the mushrooms. Strain and reserve the liquid to use in a bean dish or a winter soup. Rinse the mushrooms under cold running water to remove sand and grit. Mince.

In a 2-quart skillet, combine the ground meats. Cook and stir over medium heat for about 5 minutes, until the meat crumbles and begins to brown. Stir in the carrot, onion, celery, pancetta, and mushrooms. Increase the heat to high. Cook an additional 5 minutes, until the vegetables are wilted.

Stir in the tomatoes and their liquid, the salt, and pepper. Reduce the heat to very low. Simmer about 1½ hours, until the sauce is thick and well-flavored. Break the tomatoes up with a spoon as the sauce cooks.

SALSA BALSAMELLA

In a small, heavy saucepan, melt the butter over low heat. Whisk in the flour. Cook the roux over medium heat for 4 minutes, stirring constantly. Pour the milk in a thin stream into the roux. Whisk to incorporate and continue whisking until smooth. Stir in the salt and pepper. Reduce the heat to low. Simmer 5 minutes. Store at room temperature, covered with plastic wrap (to avoid having a skin form) until needed.

BROAD GREEN NOODLES

Wash the spinach leaves well in several changes of water. Transfer them to a large pot. Using only the water that clings to the leaves, steam over high heat about 4 minutes, until wilted but still bright green. Drain in a sieve. Rinse under cool running water. Use your hands to squeeze as much water as possible from the spinach. Chop coarse.

Place flour and spinach in the work bowl of a food processor. Process with the metal blade until the spinach is very finely chopped and mixed with the flour. With the motor running, add the eggs all at once through the feed tube. Process until a stiff dough forms.

Transfer the dough to a lightly floured surface. Knead, adding a tablespoon or two more flour as necessary, until dough is smooth and elastic. Wrap the dough in plastic wrap. Let it rest at least 30 minutes.

Divide the dough into 12 equal portions. Roll out each portion with a pasta machine. Start rolling with the machine on the largest setting and work down to the third-smallest setting. As you work, store the rolled sheets of pasta between lightly floured kitchen towels. Cut each sheet of pasta into 4-inch squares. The 12 sheets of pasta will give you about 4 squares each, or 48 squares all together.

ASSEMBLING THE LASAGNE

Bring a large pot of salted water to a boil. Have available a large bowl of ice-cold water. Slip in about 12 squares of the pasta to boil. Cook 1 to 2 minutes, until the pasta is softened but still very firm. Remove with a wire skimmer to the cold water. Repeat with the remaining pasta.

Heat the oven to 350° F. Drain the cooked pasta on kitchen towels. Lightly butter a 12-by-8-inch ovenproof baking dish or lasagne pan at least 2 inches deep. Arrange about one-fifth of the noodles over the bottom of the pan so that it is completely covered. Spoon 1 cup of the Salsa Bolognese over the noodles and dot with ½ cup of the Salsa Balsamella. Sprinkle each layer with ½ cup of the grated Parmesan. Repeat with the remaining noodles and sauces. Spoon the last cup of Salsa Balsamella over the top layer of noodles. Sprinkle with 1 cup Parmesan.

Place the pan on a baking sheet to protect the oven from spills. Place in the oven. Bake about 40 minutes, until the filling is bubbling and the top is a dark golden brown. Let stand 10 minutes before serving.

SERVES 16 AS A FIRST COURSE, 8 AS A MAIN COURSE

STUFFED PASTAS

———————•———————

From Chinese steamed dumplings to kreplach to tortellini, pelmenyi, cappelletti, wontons and Japanese gyoza, there are lots of bits
of noodle dough stuffed with all kinds of filling. Frankly, though I
do give a few recipes for made-from-scratch stuffed pasta, I seldom
have the time or ambition to make it myself. Fortunately, as part of
the great American culinary explosion, an array of frozen pastas of all
nationalities has appeared on the market. Some of them are quite
good. A little experimenting will give you a terrific freezer resource.
There are recipes using bought frozen pasta here and elsewhere in
the book.

...

TORTELLINI WITH BASIL,
CREAM, AND CHIVES

———————•———————

If it is the middle of winter and you are working out of the freezer,
replace the fresh basil with two or three of the Frozen Fresh Basil
cubes (page 83). Sometimes I add tiny frozen peas and flowerets of
fresh broccoli, blanched, for visual allure and texture.

...

> *2 packed cups fresh basil leaves, stems removed*
> *3 cups heavy cream*
> *¼ teaspoon freshly ground black pepper*
> *1 tablespoon kosher salt*
> *5 tablespoons chopped chives (¼-inch pieces)*
> *3 tomatoes, peeled*
> *3 pounds fresh or frozen tortellini*

Bring a large pot of salted water to a boil.

Reserve 16 beautiful basil leaves for the garnish. Finely chop the
rest in a food processor. You should have about 1 cup.

Place the basil in a saucepan with the cream. Bring the liquid to a boil, reduce the heat to a slow simmer, and add the pepper and salt, then 4 tablespoons chives. Let cook over low heat for 10 to 15 minutes.

Meanwhile, remove and discard (or save for a sauce) the core, seeds, juice, and inner pulp of the tomatoes. Cut the outer flesh into ¼-inch-wide strips, then cut these crosswise into squares.

Stir the tortellini into the boiling water and cook just until done, 2 to 3 minutes if fresh, 6 to 8 minutes if frozen.

Just before the tortellini are done, add the tomatoes to the cream sauce to heat through.

Drain the tortellini and toss with the cream. Serve hot, garnished with the reserved basil leaves and remaining tablespoon of chives.

SERVES 8

VERY ITALIAN CAPPELLETTI

I serve these cappelletti lightly sauced with cream and stock or sometimes simply floating in an aromatic broth. They can also masquerade as pelmenyi and turn Russian (page 141).

•••

PASTA DOUGH

2 eggs
1 tablespoon olive oil
1½ cups all-purpose flour

FILLING

2 tablespoons unsalted butter
1 bone-in loin pork chop, about 12 ounces
1 boneless, skinless chicken breast, about 6 ounces
1 cup grated Parmesan cheese
4 egg yolks
½ cup heavy cream
Salt and pepper to taste

SAUCE

2 cups heavy cream
1½ cups Chicken Stock (page 110)
Lemon juice, salt (if needed), and pepper to taste

• • •

Grated Parmesan cheese

PASTA DOUGH

Beat the eggs and oil in a small bowl. Put 1¼ cups of the flour in the work bowl of a food processor with the steel blade in place. Pour the egg and oil through the feed tube while the motor is running. Process until a stiff dough forms. Add 2 to 3 tablespoons more flour if necessary. Remove the dough to a lightly floured board. Knead for about 5 minutes, adding 2 to 3 tablespoons of flour as necessary, until the dough is very smooth and elastic. Wrap the dough in a kitchen towel. Let it rest at room temperature for 15 minutes.

FILLING

Melt the butter in a small, heavy skillet over medium-low heat. Add the pork chop and cook, turning once, until no trace of pink remains in the center. This takes about 12 minutes. Remove the meat from the pan and set aside to cool.

Over medium heat in the unwashed skillet, sauté the chicken breast about 6 minutes. Turn once. The center remains barely pink. Place the chicken with the pork to cool.

Cut the pork away from the bone and trim off the fat. With a large chef's knife, mince the chicken and the pork. Do not use a food processor. In a small bowl, blend together the meat, Parmesan cheese, egg yolks, heavy cream, salt, and pepper. Cover and set aside.

MAKING THE CAPPELLETTI

Divide the dough into sixths. On a lightly floured board, roll each piece out very thin. You should be able to read a magazine—don't use the traditional newspaper; the print will smear onto the dough—through the pasta. With a glass or a sharp cookie cutter, cut pasta into 2-inch circles (drawing 1). Reroll and cut scraps quickly. Place 1 teaspoon of filling in the center of each circle (drawing 2). Brush the edges lightly with water (drawing 3). Fold half of the circle over the filling, forming a half moon (drawing 4). Press the edges together to seal. Pick up the half moon and pinch the enclosed filling lightly between your forefinger and thumb. Bring one end of the half moon around your thumb to meet the other end (drawing 5). You have formed a cappelletti; slip it off your thumb. Firmly pinch the two ends together to seal. Set the finished cappelletti (it should look like a tiny bishop's miter) on a lightly floured kitchen towel (drawing 6). Repeat with the remaining filling and circles of dough.

At this point, the cappelletti may be cooked, put aside uncooked and covered for up to an hour, or frozen (see note).

MAKING CAPPELLETTI

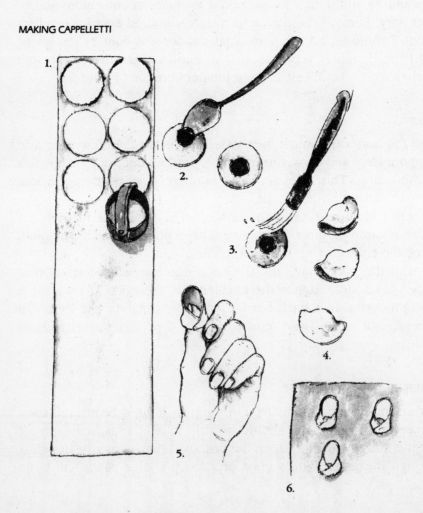

COOKING CAPPELLETTI

Bring a large pot of salted water to a boil. Even if you are serving them in broth, they will need to be blanched first so that the broth doesn't become pasty. Slip the cappelletti into the boiling water a few at a time until all are in the pot. Stir gently until the water returns to the boil. Boil until the pasta is tender but firm, about 3 minutes. Drain thoroughly in a colander.

SAUCE

While you are waiting for the water to boil, combine the heavy cream and chicken broth in a small, heavy saucepan. Bring to a boil over high heat. Boil until the mixture has thickened enough to lightly coat a spoon, about 10 minutes. Add lemon juice, salt, and pepper to taste.

Transfer the cappelletti to a serving bowl. Toss with the cream sauce. Sprinkle with freshly grated Parmesan cheese. Serve immediately.

MAKES 6 DOZEN, ENOUGH FOR 4 AS A FIRST COURSE

NOTE: In order to freeze the cappelletti, place them on a baking sheet in a single layer. Freeze just until solid, about 1 hour. Transfer to plastic freezer bags and seal tightly. Frozen cappelletti can be stored up to 3 months. They can be cooked right out of the freezer, without defrosting. In that case, add about 1 minute to the cooking time.

RAVIOLI STUFFED WITH CLAMS
AND ITALIAN SAUSAGE

———————————•———————————

One of the pleasures of being a cook is playing "what if," and coming up with a recipe like this as a result. Many restaurants, French and American, have been playing the same game with stuffed pastas in recent years. I have found many of their inventions too bland or too expensive to be of interest, but this recipe is worth doing—it's unusual without being freaky. The very light tomato-juice sauce lets the filling flavors and textures sing out. These ravioli positively spurt when bitten.

PASTA DOUGH

3 egg yolks
1 whole egg
1 teaspoon olive oil
1½ cups all-purpose flour

FILLING

6 ounces (about 2 links) sweet Italian sausage
6 littleneck clams, shucked and minced
2 tablespoons minced scallion
⅛ teaspoon freshly ground black pepper

SAUCE

1 cup tomato juice
½ cup bottled clam juice
Salt and freshly ground black pepper to taste
Hot red-pepper sauce to taste

• • •

Whole Italian parsley leaves

PASTA DOUGH

Beat the egg yolks, egg, and olive oil in a small bowl. Place 1¼ cups of the flour in the work bowl of a food processor fitted with the steel blade. With the motor running, pour the eggs and oil through the feed tube of the processor. Process until a stiff dough forms. Add 2 to 3 tablespoons more flour if necessary. Remove the dough to a lightly floured board. Knead, adding 2 to 3 tablespoons more flour as necessary, until the dough is very smooth and elastic. Cover the dough with a kitchen towel and let it rest at room temperature while you prepare the filling.

FILLING

Place the sausages in a small, heavy skillet. Pour in enough water to coat the bottom of the pan. Heat over medium heat until the water is steaming. Cover the skillet. Cook the sausages about 15 minutes, turning occasionally, until no trace of pink remains in the center. Remove to paper towels to drain. When the sausages are cool, remove the casings and crumble the meat fine into a small bowl. Stir in the clams, scallion, and pepper.

MAKING THE RAVIOLI

Divide the pasta dough into sixths. On a lightly floured board or with a pasta machine, roll out two pieces of dough into 16-by-4-inch rectangles. Keep the remaining dough covered. Place level teaspoonfuls of the filling on one sheet of pasta, spacing them 1 inch from the edge of the pasta and 2 inches apart. Lightly brush the pasta with water along the edges and in between the portions of filling (drawing 1). Place the second sheet of pasta over the filling. Press it gently with the sides of your hands to remove any air bubbles and to seal (drawing 2). With a knife or fluted pastry cutter, cut the pasta between the lumps of filling to form 2-inch-square ravioli (drawing 3). Repeat with the remaining pasta and filling. Store the ravioli on a baking sheet lined with lightly floured kitchen towels until ready to serve. Stack the pasta, if necessary, placing a lightly floured kitchen towel between sheets.

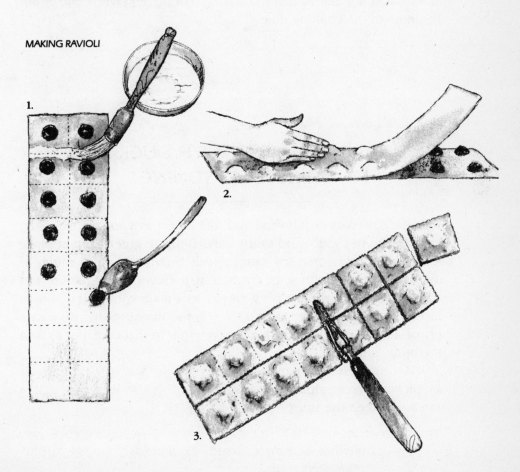

MAKING RAVIOLI

1.

2.

3.

COOKING THE RAVIOLI AND MAKING THE SAUCE

Bring a large pot of salted water to a boil.

While you are waiting for the water to boil, combine the tomato and clam juices in a large skillet. Add salt, pepper, and hot pepper sauce to taste. Heat to simmering.

When the water in the pot is boiling, add the ravioli. Stir until the water returns to the boil. Cook the pasta 2 to 3 minutes, until it is tender but firm. Drain thoroughly. Add the cooked ravioli to the skillet with the sauce, and stir gently until coated. Transfer to a serving bowl. Sprinkle with parsley leaves. Serve immediately.

MAKES 48 RAVIOLI, TO SERVE 6 TO 8 AS A FIRST COURSE

NOTE: To freeze ravioli, place in a single layer on a baking sheet. Freeze about 1 hour, just until solid. Remove from the baking sheet and transfer to plastic freezer bags. They can be stored up to 3 months. Do not defrost before cooking. For frozen ravioli, add about 1 minute to the cooking time.

RAVIOLI STUFFED WITH DUCK AND CHINESE SEASONINGS

This is a delicious ravioli version. I like it best as a first course in the clear broth; but you could sauté some Chinese greens and shiitake mushrooms, add some soy sauce, fresh coriander, and a touch of duck broth mixed with some cornstarch, then cook for a minute and add the cooked ravioli. Serve with rice as a main course. If you have made Crisp Roast Duck, pages 173–175, you may already have a supply of stock and cooked duck meat on hand. In that case, just season the broth and go.

Having these ravioli on hand is my favorite way of giving myself a treat when home alone with a cold. This dish also leaves me with a carcass to keep the stock going.

• • •

*1 medium-size duck (about 4½ pounds),
preferably fresh*

BROTH

8 cups water
2 scallions, trimmed
2 slices (¼-inch thick) fresh ginger, unpeeled
1 small dried red chili pepper
Salt and pepper to taste

FILLING

¼ cup chopped chives
1 tablespoon soy sauce
2 teaspoons rice wine or white wine vinegar
½ teaspoon minced garlic
⅛ teaspoon crushed red pepper
72 coriander leaves

PASTA DOUGH

5 eggs
1 tablespoon olive oil
3 cups all-purpose flour, or as needed

Remove the breasts from the duck; reserve these, along with livers, for another use. (See Duck Breasts with Transparent Noodles, page 211, and Duck Liver, Apple, and Raisin Sauté, page 69).

Remove the legs from the backbone, leaving the rest of the carcass whole. Trim the fat and skin from the legs and carcass. Reserve the trimmings for another use, if desired. With a heavy cleaver, cut the carcass into 2-inch pieces. Cut each leg at the knee joint into 2 pieces.

BROTH

In a large (12-inch or more), heavy skillet, sauté the duck pieces for about 20 minutes over medium-high heat. Pour off the fat and turn the pieces as necessary until they are deep brown. Transfer the sautéed duck to a small stockpot or to a 3-quart saucepan.

Into the unwashed skillet in which the duck was sautéed, pour the 8 cups of water. Bring to a boil over high heat, scraping the sides and bottom of the pan. Pour the hot liquid into the stockpot with the duck. Add scallions, ginger, and chili pepper. Heat over low heat to simmering. Remove the duck legs 30 minutes after the stock begins to simmer. Set them aside for the filling. Simmer the rest about 6 hours, skimming the surface occasionally, until a rich stock is produced. Alternatively, if you have duck stock on hand (see page 112), pour into the skillet enough stock to cover the pieces of duck. Add the scallions, ginger and chili pepper. Simmer 30 minutes. Remove the duck legs and set aside.

When the stock has finished cooking, strain it through a very fine sieve. Skim the fat from the top. Pour the stock into a saucepan and heat over low heat until reduced to 2 cups. Season to taste with salt and pepper. Chill, uncovered, until needed. Remove any solid fat from the surface before reheating.

FILLING

Remove the meat from the duck legs. Mince fine. Transfer to a small bowl. Stir in the chives, soy sauce, vinegar, garlic, and crushed red pepper. Chill, covered, until needed.

PASTA DOUGH

In a small bowl, beat the eggs and oil. Place 2¾ cups of the flour into a food processor fitted with the metal blade. With the motor running, add the egg-and-oil mixture. Process until a stiff dough is formed, adding more flour as necessary. Transfer to a lightly floured surface and knead. Add additional flour by the tablespoonful, as necessary, and knead until the dough is smooth and elastic. Wrap in plastic and let rest at least 30 minutes, or up to 24 hours in the refrigerator.

MAKING THE RAVIOLI

Divide the dough into 12 equal pieces. Roll out each piece, either by hand or with a machine, into a 12-by-4-inch rectangle. (The pasta dough should be so thin you can read a magazine through it.) To store the pasta sheets, stack them—with a lightly floured kitchen towel between each layer—on a baking sheet. Cover with another towel. They can be left at room temperature until you are ready to make the ravioli, up to 2 hours.

Lay one sheet of pasta on the work surface. Imaginarily divide it into twelve 2-inch squares. Place 1 teaspoonful of filling in the center of each square. Lay 1 coriander leaf on each mound of filling. With a pastry brush dipped in cold water, lightly dampen the pasta dough around edges and between spoonfuls of filling. Cover with a second sheet of pasta dough. Press the dough around the filling with your fingers to remove air and to seal together the two sheets of pasta. Using a fluted pastry wheel or sharp knife, cut the pasta into 2-inch ravioli. Store flat in a single layer on a lightly floured kitchen towel until you are ready to cook them. The ravioli can be frozen at this point (see freezing instructions in the note at the end of the preceding recipe).

COOKING THE RAVIOLI

Bring a large pot of salted water to a boil. Drop in the ravioli. Stir gently to separate. Cook 3 to 4 minutes, until tender but firm. If you are cooking frozen ravioli, boil for 5 to 6 minutes.

While the ravioli are cooking, skim any fat from the reduced duck broth. In a saucepan, bring the broth to a simmer over low heat.

When the ravioli are done, remove from the heat and drain in a colander. Rinse briefly under cold running water. Place in the simmering duck broth for just a minute to reheat. Serve in heated shallow soup bowls, dividing broth and ravioli evenly among the bowls.

MAKES 72 RAVIOLI TO SERVE 8 AS A FIRST COURSE OR 4 AS A MAIN COURSE

SOUPS

---·---

· STOCKS ·

Meat Stock

Chicken Stock

Quick Chicken Stock

Quick Beef Stock

Turkey Stock

Duck Stock

Fish Stock

· COLD SOUPS ·

Cucumber Soup

Dilled Chicken Madrilène

Borscht

Cream of Sorrel Soup

Gazpacho

Green Gazpacho with Citrus Fruit and Yellow Squash

· HOT SOUPS ·

Parsley Soup

Scallion and Radish Soup

Julienne of Five-Lettuce Soup

Chicken Soup with Pastina and Greens

Thai Chicken Soup

Basil Consommé with Basil Quenelles

Green Soup

Oyster Soup with Broth

Cannellini Soup

Asparagus Soup

Spring-Vegetable Gumbo

Full-Flavored Tomato Soup

Acorn Squash Soup

Quick Bourride

Along with salads and sauces, soups are my favorite thing to cook. When I have the time, I set large pots of water with bones and meat trimmings—chicken, duck, veal and beef, and fish—on to simmer for long, unattended hours. I make sure that the stock doesn't boil, or the gelatin and protein from the bones will bind in the floating solids and fats and make the stock cloudy. The only drawback is that sometimes in the night I awaken hungry and excited by the rich perfumes from the all-night kitchen. After eighteen hours or so—having topped up the liquid with cold water, if necessary—I strain the stock through a wet-cloth-lined (otherwise the cloth absorbs good broth) colander.

This is not to say that a can of chicken broth isn't the harried cook's best friend. I always have a selection of carefully chosen cans of chicken broth on my shelf. That is why there are so many chicken-broth–based recipes in this chapter. The need for salt will vary between freshly made broth or stock, which contains none, and canned broth or stock, which is variable. The richer the homemade stock, the more seasonings you will need. Otherwise the strength of the stock will overwhelm everything. I have also devised a few very quick stocks that are high-quality compromises, somewhere between the slow-simmered real thing and the handy-dandy cans.

Cold soups are wonderful in summer, but they require more forethought than hot soups. I find that hot soup with aromatic herbs and fresh vegetables is very welcome even on a warm summer night. I have a few favorite soups that must be served cold. Generally I make them in large quantities and leave quart jars in the refrigerator for random snacking. The only thing to be careful about is to have enough soup left for dinner. And then there are the wonderful soups that *are* dinner.

• • •

STOCKS

These are still the basis of the best in cooking—as they are—or turned into glazes (page 309). I make them without any vegetables or seasonings, since those things can always be added later in customized versions for each recipe. In that way you also don't risk clouding, spoilage, or too great a concentration of salt.

To turn two quarts of stock into a flavored soup: Chop one small onion, one small clove garlic, one small carrot or half a normal one, a tomato, one stalk of celery, four sprigs of parsley, and, if the stock is chicken, a few sprigs of dill. Cook the chopped vegetables and herbs in a tablespoon of butter over low heat for twenty minutes. Pour on the stock. Simmer for twenty minutes. Put through a fine sieve. Do not press. Taste; add salt and pepper; serve hot. The addition of a few noodles cooked separately or a few cooked julienned vegetables make these clear soups very festive.

If you are making the stocks to cook with later, divide them into eight-ounce freezer containers. Once they are frozen, you can unmold them and wrap them in aluminum foil. Mark what they are and the date made, and replace them in the freezer. This way you know you have a cup of stock at hand when you need it.

MEAT STOCK

———————•———————

This is the kind of stock I like to make and the quantity I like to make it in. You can make it darker and richer by roasting the bones in the oven at 400°F. for one to two hours or until they are very brown. *Do not burn.* Deglaze the pan. For a less beefy stock, omit the beef bones and double the veal bones. Note the variation if you want to make a flavored stock and see page 309 if you want to make a meat glaze.

• • •

5 pounds beef shin bones
5 pounds veal knuckles, split
10 pounds beef shin, meat only

Place the bones and meat in a tall, narrow stockpot, or divide between two pots. Add just enough water to cover. Bring to a boil over high heat. Skim the surface of any scum that rises. Reduce the temperature and simmer for 4 hours. Remove the shin meat for another use. Continue to cook for 8 more hours. Add water from time to time to keep the contents just barely covered. Strain the stock. Skim off any fat. Reduce if necessary to intensify flavor.

MAKES ABOUT 5 GALLONS STOCK

VARIATION: FLAVORED STOCK

If you wish to use this as a flavored stock or soup, during the last hour of cooking, add the ingredients below.

• • •

2 carrots, trimmed and quartered
2 medium onions, quartered
2 celery ribs, quartered
2 ripe tomatoes
1 head unpeeled garlic
1 bunch parsley stems
2 bay leaves
1 teaspoon dried thyme
1 teaspoon black peppercorns

CHICKEN STOCK

You can buy chicken parts for stock making or store carcasses in the freezer every time you bone a chicken—either the whole bird or parts—but don't use the liver.

• • •

1 five- to six-pound chicken, or 6 pounds chicken bones, necks, and wings

Place the whole chicken or bones and parts in a stockpot with water just to cover. Bring the water to a boil and skim off the fat and scum that rise to the top. Lower the heat so the liquid is just barely simmering, and continue cooking for 8 to 12 hours, skimming from time to time. The more often you skim, the clearer your stock will be.

Pour the stock through a sieve and let cool at room temperature. Discard meat and bones, then refrigerate. Remove the fat from the surface and any sediment from the bottom.

Use as is, refrigerate, freeze, or reduce for Chicken Glaze (page 309).

MAKES ABOUT 3 QUARTS STOCK

QUICK CHICKEN STOCK

This is the expensive way to do it. However, if canned stock is unacceptable and you don't have stock from the previous recipe on hand or don't want to take the time to make it, this will give you a first-rate stock in virtually no time.

• • •

2½ medium carrots, peeled and cut into 1-inch chunks
6 small ribs celery, cut into 1-inch pieces
½ large onion, cut into 1-inch chunks
1 pound boneless, skinless chicken breasts, cut into pieces
1 large (46-ounce) can chicken stock

3 sprigs parsley
1 clove garlic

Place the carrots and celery in the work bowl of a food processor, and process with on and off turns until roughly chopped. Add the onion and process on and off until all the vegetables are finely chopped. Transfer the vegetables to a stockpot.

Place the chicken breast in the processor, and process with on and off turns until finely chopped. Add the chicken to the vegetables. Pour in the stock, parsley, and garlic.

Cover, and bring the liquid to a boil. As the liquid heats, beat the mixture from time to time with a wire whisk so the pieces do not clump together and they release their maximum flavor. Cook at a boil for 20 minutes, stirring from time to time. Strain through a sieve lined with a damp kitchen towel. Discard solids. Skim off any fat.

Use as is or chill until needed up to 5 days.

MAKES 5½ CUPS

QUICK BEEF STOCK

Follow the recipe for Quick Chicken Stock, substituting 1 pound ground lean beef for the chicken breast. Use canned chicken stock rather than beef for this because canned chicken stocks tend to be better than canned beef stock. The beef flavor will still be dominant.

TURKEY STOCK

Although you can make a good turkey stock just using water, it will be richer and fuller if you start with chicken stock. Note the variation for turkey soup.

• • •

TURKEY STOCK, CONTINUED

> *Carcass of a roasted 8- to 15-pound turkey, cut in*
>   *pieces*
> *Gizzard, heart, and neck of the turkey*
> *3 quarts Chicken Stock (page 110) and/or water*

Place the carcass, gizzard, heart, neck, and chicken stock in a stock-pot and bring to a boil. Skim thoroughly. Lower the heat and simmer for 12 hours or longer, skimming from time to time, as needed. The more often you skim, the clearer your stock will be. Add water as needed to keep the level constant.

Strain the stock, discarding the bones. Reduce the liquid to 2½ quarts; leave unseasoned. Cool to room temperature, then refrigerate. Skim off all the fat from the top and remove the sediment from the bottom.

MAKES 2½ QUARTS

VARIATION: FLAVORED TURKEY STOCK

If using this for soup, add the ingredients below before you reduce the liquid. Strain the mixture through a sieve lined with a dampened kitchen towel, pressing on the solids to release all the liquid. Season to taste. Cool and refrigerate or freeze until ready to use.

• • •

> *2 cups coarsely chopped celery, with leaves*
> *2 medium onions, quartered*
> *4 medium carrots, peeled and cut into chunks*
> *4 fresh sage leaves or 4 sprigs parsley*
> *Few sprigs of thyme*

DUCK STOCK

Duck stock is a marvelous bonus of a duck dinner. After your guests have enjoyed all the delicious meat, the remaining bare bones provide a glistening amber broth to enjoy as is or to use in a more complex soup or sauce. Don't be timid about snatching back the bones from the plates. Remember the bones will boil.

Good duck stock also results from my method of cooking Roast Duck (page 173). Use it to make a full-tasting gelatinous soup seasoned with kosher salt and a good bit of coarsely ground black pepper. You can put in precooked broad egg noodles or blanched, julienned leeks, carrots, celery, or string beans. If you're feeling ambitious, try adding the duck ravioli on page 100.

• • •

4 duck carcasses, broken into small pieces

Place the duck carcasses in a large stockpot and add enough water just to cover. Place over high heat, bring to a boil, and skim off the scum that rises to the surface.

Reduce the heat so the liquid just simmers. Skim the fat and impurities from the surface from time to time. The more often you skim, the clearer your stock will be. Cook for about 12 hours. Discard the solids. Cool the stock, then refrigerate or freeze. Remove any remaining fat.

MAKES ABOUT 7 CUPS

FISH STOCK

It's a myth of French cooking that bones for fish stock must not be cooked for more than twenty minutes. Ignorant, I for many years cooked my fish stocks for long hours just as I did my other stocks. Even as I learned more I persisted in my very satisfactory habit. It was not until years later, when I began to work with restaurants, that I understood the shibboleth. French restaurant chefs use the flat frames of flounder and sole for their stock. These bones do give a bitter stock if cooked longer than twenty minutes—forty at the outside. If you do not use flatfish bones you can follow my method and have wonderful rich broths. You would think that any country that produced bouillabaisse would have figured this out.

It is also important to avoid oily fish, such as mackerel, bluefish, and salmon, unless you are making an unusual soup like a fish solianka.

• • •

FISH STOCK, CONTINUED

> *3 pounds non-oily fish heads and bones such as cod*
> *and whiting (not flatfish)*
> *2 quarts water*

Wash the fish heads and bones very well to eliminate all traces of blood. Cut out the oil-rich gills with scissors. Put the fish heads and bones in a pot and cover with the water. Place the pot over high heat and bring to a boil. Skim off the scum that rises to the top. Lower the heat, and simmer the stock for 4 to 6 hours, or until approximately 4 cups of broth remain. Skim as necessary. Refrigerate, freeze, use, or reduce to make a glaze, as needed.

MAKES 1 QUART

...

COLD SOUPS

CUCUMBER SOUP

This classic egg-and-cream binding used to show up in lots of my soups, hot and cold. Now, with a growing taste for lighter foods, it does so less often. In this very fragrant soup (yes, cucumbers are fragrant; wait until you are cutting them all up—the world's best air freshener), the cream is a nice contrast and turns the soup the palest of greens.

...

> *5 cucumbers*
> *2 tablespoons unsalted butter*
> *2 tablespoons chopped shallots*
> *2 teaspoons kosher salt*
> *1 teaspoon sugar*

1 quart Chicken Stock (page 110)
6 egg yolks
1 cup heavy cream

GARNISH
½ cucumber, peeled, halved lengthwise, and
   seeded, blanched in salt water, cubed
Chopped mint

Peel and seed the 5 cucumbers. Cut them into chunks. Process in a food processor until smooth.

Melt the butter in a large skillet. Add the shallots and cook until soft but not brown. Add cucumbers. Continue to cook at low heat for 5 minutes. Add the salt and sugar. Cook over medium heat for about 30 minutes to thicken the mixture.

Add the chicken stock and cook 10 minutes longer. Pour the mixture through a dampened cloth in a sieve, squeezing to get out all the liquid. Reheat the soup. Discard the solids.

Beat the egg yolks and cream together. Stir in some of the hot soup to raise the temperature of the yolks. Stir the yolk mixture into the soup, and cook, stirring constantly, until the mixture thickens. Do not let the soup boil or you will have scrambled eggs. Strain it and cool to room temperature, then chill. Garnish with the cubed cucumbers and chopped mint.

SERVES 6

DILLED CHICKEN MADRILÈNE

Chicken with lemon and dill is one of my favorite combinations of flavors. When making this soup, remember that the lemon taste will grow stronger when cold, while the other tastes will dim. Don't cook the ground pepper in the broth any longer than specified or it will cause the soup to become bitter. Wait until the soup is cool before mixing in the dill or it will turn color. Besides, the dill won't stay properly suspended.

DILLED CHICKEN MADRILÈNE, CONTINUED

1 quart clear, rich Chicken Stock (page 110)
1 small onion, quartered
½ carrot, peeled and roughly chopped
Freshly ground black pepper
4 teaspoons unflavored gelatin, unless your stock
    sets really firm
2 tablespoons fresh lemon juice
¾ teaspoon kosher salt
2 tablespoons chopped fresh dill
Dill sprigs
Lemon wedges
Sour cream

Put 3½ cups of chicken stock, the onion, carrot, and pepper into a saucepan. Place over moderate heat and simmer 20 minutes.

Put the remaining ½ cup of chicken stock into a small dish, and sprinkle the gelatin over it; stir to blend. Add to the broth and cook over moderate heat until the gelatin is dissolved, stirring constantly. Strain through dampened cheesecloth into a serving bowl. Season with lemon juice and salt.

Chill until cooled and slightly thickened, then stir in the chopped dill. Chill until set, either in a glass serving bowl or in individual consommé bowls. Top each portion with a dill sprig. Put lemon wedge on each saucer or rim of the bowl. Pass sour cream.

SERVES 4

BORSCHT

Cold borscht is the most beautiful of the summer soups and is elegant enough to serve in winter. Its rich ruby red is turned into a valentine pink with lashings of sweet and sour cream.

Beets contain sugar, and the amount varies from beet to beet. Therefore, it is difficult to give exact measurements for the flavoring of borscht. From season to season beets can vary in cooking time from twenty minutes to four hours; give yourself plenty of time. Always season the borscht when it is warm or the sugar and citric acid will not properly dissolve. It is the acid that turns the beet liquid from purple to red. I use three different kinds of acid because each has its own acidity and taste. Together they give balance. Also, some acids, like lemon, intensify with the cold while others diminish. Add a little of the sweet and then balance with sour. Keep tasting and adding. This is the only way to know what you are doing as you are seasoning. The basic beet preparation freezes well for winter use.

• • •

1 pound beets
5 cups water
2 teaspoons vinegar, approximately
4 teaspoons lemon juice, approximately
3 citric acid (sour salt) crystals (each about ¼ teaspoon), available at grocery or pharmacy
9 tablespoons sugar
1½ teaspoons kosher salt
½ cup sour cream
⅔ cup heavy cream

GARNISHES

Chopped onion
Chopped cucumber
Chopped dill
Lemon wedges
Sour cream
Heavy cream
Reserved grated beets
Cold boiled potato
Chopped hard-boiled eggs

Scrub the beets well and cut off all but 1 inch of the stems. Place the beets in a 2½-quart saucepan with the water. Bring the water to a boil, then lower to a simmer. Let cook until the beets are tender when pierced with a skewer.

Drain the beets through a cloth-lined sieve. Reserve the cooking liquid. Run the beets under cold water; when cool enough to handle, peel them. Grate the beets in a food processor fitted with a grating disk. Return half the grated beets to the cooking liquid. Reserve the rest for garnish or another use.

Season the liquid to taste with vinegar, lemon juice, citric acid, sugar, and salt. Chill. Add the sour cream and heavy cream.

Serve cold to your lucky friends with any or all of the garnishes listed above in separate little bowls. Which garnishes are considered essential and which irrelevant will depend on previous experience and family background. I usually serve the first 6.

SERVES 6

VARIATION

Another trick to play with this soup is to put gelatin in the seasoned beet liquid and then chill without adding the creams. Serve jellied, topped with whipped cream that has an equal quantity of sour cream folded into it. Top the cream with caviar: soup for a tsar.

CREAM OF SORREL SOUP

———————•———————

For this recipe, you can use French sorrel, wild sorrel, or sour grass. French sorrel, which has a large shield-shaped leaf, can be grown in your garden. Keep cutting the plant back and it will grow more.

Wild sorrel has smaller leaves, also shield-shaped. It is a pestiferous weed that, once you can identify it, may cause you to look at weeding your garden with a different eye. If you use the wild variety, pull it up with the roots but be sure to break off the roots and dirt before saving for the kitchen.

Sour grass is a common sorrel that looks like clover. All have a sour lemony taste.

The leaves are fibrous, which is why they must be carefully cut into narrow strips across the main vein, so the soup is not stringy. A sieve will not do the job. When working with sorrel, it is absolutely essential that no aluminum come near it. It will not only become nasty-tasting but will also turn a revolting color.

• • •

2 handfuls (2 cups loosely packed, 1 cup tightly
packed) sorrel leaves, washed, stems and brown
spots removed
3 tablespoons unsalted butter

*5 cups Chicken Stock (preferably homemade, page
    110, without fat, but a good commercial brand
    may be used)*
5 egg yolks
1½ cups heavy cream
Salt, if needed

Either roll the leaves up and cut them by hand into a thin chiffonade or bundle them into a compact ball and place in the feed tube of a food processor fitted with the thin slicing blade. With the plunger in place, process quickly.

Melt the butter in a 1-quart non-aluminum pot. Add the sorrel leaves and stir with a wooden spoon until they are limp and concentrated. Pour in the chicken stock. Bring to a boil and lower the heat to a simmer. Let cook over low heat for 20 minutes. (The soup can be made up to this point a day or two ahead and refrigerated if you are serving it hot. Do this next step just before you are ready to serve. If serving cold, continue without stopping.)

Beat the egg yolks and cream together in a bowl. Slowly spoon in some of the hot soup, whisking constantly, until you have added about one-third of the soup and raised the temperature of the egg yolks. Now, while whisking the soup, slowly pour in the egg-yolk mixture. Cook just until the soup thickens slightly. Salt if you wish. Serve immediately or . . .

If you wish to serve the soup cold, pour it into a bowl and keep stirring until it is fairly cool so that it doesn't separate. Then refrigerate.

I find that if I keep this in quart jars in the refrigerator it disappears behind my back.

MAKES ABOUT 6 CUPS TO SERVE 4 TO 6

GAZPACHO

———————•———————

It is a humbling thought that, with all the recipes I have developed and written, the one that people mention most is this gazpacho recipe. So here it is.

• • •

½ medium Bermuda or other sweet white onion,
* peeled and quartered*
1½ firm medium cucumbers, peeled and cut into
* eighths*
1 big green pepper, stemmed, seeded and cut into
* eighths*
1 big red pepper, stemmed, seeded and cut into
* eighths*
6 medium to large ripe tomatoes, peeled and cut
* into eighths*
5 large garlic cloves, peeled
1 cup or more tomato juice
½ cup light olive oil
¾ teaspoon chili powder or 1 small piece fresh chili
* pepper*
Kosher salt
Beef bouillon (optional)

Place the onion in the work bowl of a food processor fitted with the metal blade. Process, turning on and off rapidly, until the onion is finely chopped, about 4 or 5 seconds. Transfer onion to large bowl.

Repeat with the cucumbers, then with the green and red peppers, adding each to the onion in the bowl. Process five of the tomatoes until evenly chopped into small pieces. Transfer to the bowl with the other chopped ingredients.

Process the remaining tomato with the garlic, tomato juice, olive oil, and chili until a smooth liquid is formed. Combine with the chopped vegetables and chill in a covered container.

Before serving, taste for salt and season to taste. If the texture is too thick, add more tomato juice or a combination of half tomato juice and half beef bouillon.

Serve in colorful bowls to 6 guests if you can hold them to one serving, which I never can. I just triple the recipe.

MAKES ABOUT 1½ QUARTS TO SERVE 6

GREEN GAZPACHO WITH CITRUS FRUIT AND YELLOW SQUASH

There are so many gazpachos in Spain I thought there could be no objection if I added a slightly freaky one of my own. I love the colors, the rich aromas of citrus fruits, garlic, and coriander. The taste has a rich balance too. I think you might find this a nice addition to the repertoire.

• • •

1 medium onion, peeled and quartered
2 medium green bell peppers, stemmed, seeded, cut into 1-inch pieces
2 medium cucumbers, peeled, coarsely sliced
½ cup packed parsley leaves
½ cup packed coriander leaves
1 cup Spanish olive oil
3 medium to large garlic cloves, peeled
2 small, fresh, hot green peppers, cut into ¼-inch lengths
Kosher salt
3 slices soft bread, crusts removed, torn in pieces
1 medium yellow summer squash, trimmed, coarsely sliced
2 lemons
1 navel orange

In a food processor fitted with the metal blade, process—one at a time—the onion, green peppers, cucumbers, parsley, and coriander, using on/off motion until finely chopped. Stop the machine frequently to scrape the sides of the bowl. Transfer each ingredient once chopped from the processor bowl to a bowl large enough to hold them all. Put the olive oil, garlic, hot peppers, 1½ tablespoons salt, and bread into the processor bowl and process until finely puréed. Add to chopped ingredients. Process the squash until coarsely chopped; add to bowl.

Cut 1 lemon and the orange into quarters. Reserve one quarter of the orange for another use. Remove the seeds from the remaining citrus quarters. Place lemon and orange, peel and all, in the work bowl of the food processor and process until minced, frequently scraping the sides of the bowl. Stir into the bowl with the rest of the soup. Squeeze the remaining lemon and add the juice to the soup.

Add enough water to thin the soup to the desired consistency. Add additional salt to taste. Refrigerate until ready to serve. After refrigerating, the soup may need to be thinned with more water, since oil thickens as it gets cold.

SERVES 4

HOT SOUPS

PARSLEY SOUP

I developed this recipe for a class that I was giving with James Beard at the Stanford Court in San Francisco. I wanted students to realize that parsley is not a tasteless garnish but a taste-rich ingredient. It worked; they loved the soup.

...

3 bunches Italian flat-leaf parsley
3 bunches curly parsley
6 tablespoons unsalted butter
¾ teaspoon ground coriander
3 cloves garlic, crushed
3 cups Chicken Stock (page 110)
¾ cup cottage cheese
Fresh lemon juice
Freshly ground black pepper
Salt if you need it

Pick over the bunches of both kinds of parsley and remove and discard the stems. Rinse the leaves well under cold running water. Drain well and squeeze dry.

Melt the butter in a saucepan over medium heat. Add the drained leaves and toss to coat well. Lower the heat and cook the parsley for 5 minutes, stirring occasionally.

Add the coriander and garlic, and cook until the garlic becomes fragrant, 1 to 2 minutes. Add the chicken stock and bring the soup to a boil. Lower the heat and simmer for 7 minutes. Remove from the heat and stir in the cottage cheese.

Let the soup cool slightly and then purée it in a food processor until it is smooth and the parsley is chopped fine. Season to taste with lemon juice and pepper. Return to the heat and heat through before serving.

SERVES 6

SCALLION AND RADISH SOUP

This is a perfect early-spring soup made from the first promising notes out of the garden. It is pretty too.

• • •

1 quart Chicken Stock (page 110)
1½ packed cups chopped scallions, white part only
  (about 3 bunches)
¼ cup heavy cream
1½ teaspoons fresh lemon juice
¼ teaspoon kosher salt
1 cup sliced scallions, green part only (about 3
  bunches)
3 radishes, very thinly sliced, blanched 15 to 20
  seconds in boiling water
Sprigs of dill, optional
Cucumber slices, optional

Heat the stock in a saucepan. Stir in the scallion whites and cook at a slow boil for 15 minutes. Purée 1 cup of the stock and the cooked scallions in a food processor. Return the purée to the saucepan and place over medium heat. Stir in the cream, lemon juice, and salt.

Just before serving, stir in the scallion greens. Place 3 radish slices in each of 6 small bowls and pour in the soup. Garnish with sprigs of dill and cucumber slices.

SERVES 6

JULIENNE OF FIVE-LETTUCE SOUP

·

Just before my lettuce bolts in the hot August sun, I have more lettuce of different kinds than I can use. The Haitians recommend lettuce soup to calm the stomach and the nerves. This soup does that and uses up the extra lettuce as well. If you don't grow lettuce, you can certainly find excellent varieties in the stores. Different lettuces can be substituted but try to preserve the ratio of bitter to sweet and soft to firm.

...

1 cup packed romaine lettuce leaves, ribs removed
1 cup packed Boston lettuce leaves
1 cup packed leaf lettuce
1 cup packed escarole leaves
½ cup packed chicory leaves
2 tablespoons unsalted butter
5 cups boiling Chicken Stock (page 110)
½ cup heavy cream
6 egg yolks
1½ teaspoons kosher salt
¼ teaspoon freshly ground black pepper

Wash the romaine, Boston, and leaf lettuce, the escarole and chicory. Dry well, then cut into an ⅛-inch chiffonade. This is easiest to do if you stack several leaves, roll them into a tight wad and slice them crosswise into ⅛-inch slices. You can also use the medium slicing disk of a food processor.

Heat the butter in a medium saucepan. Add the lettuces and toss with the butter. When the lettuces are wilted, add the chicken stock. Cook over medium heat for about 10 minutes, or until the toughest leaves are tender.

In a small bowl, mix the cream with the egg yolks. Stir a small amount of hot soup into the cream mixture to slowly raise the temperature of the egg yolks. Keep adding soup until the mixture is warm. Whisk the egg-yolk mixture into the soup, and cook, stirring constantly, but not letting the soup boil, over medium heat until the soup thickens enough to coat the back of the spoon. Season with salt and pepper.

SERVES 6 TO 8

CHICKEN SOUP WITH PASTINA AND GREENS

If the soup before this was summer and the one before that spring, then this chicken-broth-based soup is late fall and winter. I find the lightly bitter taste of the greens sensational.

• • •

1 bunch broccoli rabe or head of escarole, washed
2 tablespoons olive oil
½ cup minced onions
2 quarts Chicken Stock (page 110)
4 cloves garlic, whole, unpeeled, tied in a
  cheesecloth bag
Kosher salt
Freshly ground black pepper
½ cup pastina
4 teaspoons fresh lemon juice

• • •

Freshly ground Parmesan cheese

Remove and discard the tough stems from the broccoli rabe. Cut the remainder into 2-inch pieces. (If using escarole, wash very well in several changes of water to remove the grit; then cut into 2-inch pieces.)

Heat the olive oil in a soup pot. Add the onions and sauté until translucent. Add the broccoli rabe and sauté for 2 minutes longer. Add the chicken stock and the bag with the garlic cloves. Season to taste with salt and pepper. Bring to a simmer, and simmer for 30 minutes. Remove and discard the bag with the garlic cloves.

Add the pastina and simmer just until done, not raw in the middle but not mushy either. Watch it; this goes quickly—a minute or two. Stir in the lemon juice.

Let your guests add the Parmesan at the table.

SERVES 8

THAI CHICKEN SOUP

If all the world loves chicken soup, this sinus-clearing version is the one I love best. Aromatic balances hot: lemon grass, salaam, and coriander pivoting against red chili. Lemon and lime juice acid balance the salty nuoc nam—divine. It is worth looking for the special ingredients. They can do a lot for other dishes in your kitchen. If you live in a mild climate, consider planting lemon grass. If you can't find it whole, you may be able to find it as a dried powder—sereh powder—in Dutch or Indonesian stores or from the mail-order source listed at the end of the recipe.

• • •

2 quarts Chicken Stock (page 110)
1 whole dried red chili
¼ cup nuoc nam (see note)
10 two-inch pieces fragrant lemon grass, bruised
*   with a hammer*
4 leaves salaam (biblical basil)
3 tablespoons fresh lemon juice
3 tablespoons fresh lime juice
¼ cup scallions, green and white parts, cut in ¼-
*   inch pieces*
¾ cup washed and loosely packed fresh coriander
*   leaves*

In a non-aluminum soup pot, combine all ingredients except the citrus juices, scallions, and coriander. Simmer for an hour. Taste to correct seasonings. Strain the soup. Add the remaining ingredients and cook for 5 minutes more.

SERVES 8

NOTE: Nuoc nam is a clear fermented fish sauce used in Thailand, Indonesia, Vietnam and throughout the Malay Straits area. It is bought by the bottle and used, as was the Roman garum, instead of salt or soy.

Thai ingredients can be mail-ordered from Gourmets' Bazaar, 3 Purdy Avenue, Rye, New York 10580. Telephone number: (914) 967-0898.

BASIL CONSOMMÉ WITH BASIL QUENELLES

To me, this soup is an essence of late summer, the only time when I can have basil not only to spare but in mind-boggling overabundance.

...

BASIL CONSOMMÉ
3 quarts packed basil stems
1½ tablespoons kosher salt

BASIL QUENELLES
½ of a whole chicken breast, skinned and boned (about 3 ounces)
1½ cups packed basil leaves
1 egg white
½ cup heavy cream
½ teaspoon kosher salt
Freshly ground black pepper to taste
12 cups Basil Consommé

...

12 basil leaves (for garnish)

BASIL CONSOMMÉ

Place the stems in a large pot and add enough water just to cover them. Bring to a boil, cover the pot, and lower the heat to a simmer. Cook for 1 hour.

Strain the stock and discard the stems. Season the stock with salt. If not using the stock immediately, refrigerate or freeze it.

BASIL QUENELLES

Place the chicken breast and basil leaves in the work bowl of a food processor. Process until you have a smooth purée. With the machine running, pour the egg white through the feed tube. With the machine still running, pour in the cream, salt, and pepper.

Bring the basil consommé to a full boil, then reduce the heat so the liquid gently simmers. Shape the chicken mixture into quenelles by mounding on one demitasse spoon and smoothing with a second. Drop each quenelle gently into the hot liquid. Do not crowd the quenelles. Depending on the size of your pot, you can cook 6 to 10 at a time. Cook for about 2½ minutes, bobbing the quenelles in the liquid after a minute to ensure even cooking. When they are firm to the touch, remove them with a slotted spoon. Keep warm.

With each new batch of quenelles, add enough water to the pot to bring the liquid back to its original level. You should have about 65 quenelles.

When all the quenelles are cooked, strain the basil consommé and heat. Season to taste with salt.

Place one basil leaf and 5 or 6 quenelles in each of 12 bouillon or small soup cups. Ladle the hot, strained basil consommé into the cups.

ABOUT 3 QUARTS CONSOMMÉ TO SERVE 12

NOTE: If making the quenelles ahead, store them at room temperature in warm water rather than in the basil consommé.

GREEN SOUP

·

This soup started out with a recipe of Lila Jaeger's, one of the owners of Rutherford Hill Winery in California's Napa Valley. I played with her recipe a bit and came up with this version. It takes as inspiration the mustard greens that grow along the rows of grapevines in the early spring and late fall when the vines are bare.

• • •

1 tablespoon unsalted butter
1 cup shredded tender young mustard greens or
*   kale*
2 cups hot Chicken Stock (page 110)

1 cup shredded sorrel leaves (see discussion of
  sorrel, page 118)
4 egg yolks
½ cup heavy cream
1 cup finely julienned zucchini
3 tablespoons Basil Sauce (page 224)
¼ cup shredded fresh basil leaves
½ teaspoon kosher salt
Freshly ground black pepper

Heat the butter in a saucepan. Stir in the mustard greens and toss to coat, cooking over medium heat for about 1 minute. Add the chicken stock and bring to a boil. Reduce the heat and simmer 15 to 20 minutes or until the mustard greens become tender. Stir in the sorrel and continue to simmer 5 minutes longer.

In a small bowl, beat the egg yolks with the cream. Add a small amount of the hot soup, stirring constantly. Stir this egg-yolk mixture back into the soup. Add the zucchini, basil sauce, basil leaves, salt, and pepper. Do not let the soup boil or the eggs will curdle. Stir the soup over moderate heat until it is slightly thickened and coats the back of a wooden spoon.

SERVES 6

OYSTER SOUP WITH BROTH

In New England and beyond, oysters used to be a poor man's food. In the nineteenth century, the peddlers' carts that went from town to town had a pail containing shucked oysters hooked over the long back handles. Oysters were stuck in everything—including beefsteak pie—to fill everyone up with cheap protein. Turkey stuffings had oysters in them, and steaks were cooked with them. A lot of the dishes taste very good, once prejudices are discarded. Unfortunately, oysters are no longer cheap.

Some stores still sell shucked oysters in their liquor. If you find one that does, try this soup as it makes a sumptuous first course. It is not a dish for anybody watching his or her cholesterol, but it is a lot lighter than the usual oyster stew. It makes a better introduction to a meal also. I often serve it as a festive start for Thanksgiving.

Any white wine will taste bigger and fuller with this dish; but once I've gone all out on oysters, I often go all out on the wine.

• • •

1 quart Chicken Stock (page 110)
5 pints shucked oysters, drained, liquor reserved
½ cup chopped shallots
½ teaspoon hot red-pepper sauce
2½ tablespoons kosher salt (exact amount depends
  on the saltiness of the oysters)
Freshly ground black pepper
1 cup coarsely chopped flat-leaf parsley
1 cup thinly sliced scallion greens
3 tablespoons fresh lemon juice

Bring the stock and oyster liquor to a boil with the shallots. Lower the heat and simmer for 20 minutes. Then add the hot pepper sauce, salt, and pepper. Cook another 5 minutes.

Add the parsley and scallion greens, immediately followed by the oysters. Bring back to a boil and cook for another minute. Do not cook longer or you will toughen the oysters. Add lemon juice. You can prepare the soup ahead right up to the point when the oysters are added.

SERVES 6 TO 8

CANNELLINI SOUP

This is an instant hearty bean soup that can easily disguise canned stock.

• • •

2 cups canned cannellini, drained and rinsed
1 quart Chicken Stock (page 110) or canned stock
4 cloves garlic, thinly sliced
2 teaspoons freshly ground black pepper
2 tablespoons fresh lemon juice
½ teaspoon kosher salt
6 tablespoons ¼-inch unpeeled tomato cubes

Put the beans, stock, garlic, and pepper in a pot. Bring to a boil, then lower the heat, and let simmer for 15 minutes, or until the garlic is transparent. Stir in the lemon juice and salt.

Place the tomatoes in a serving bowl or individual bowls and pour the soup over them.

SERVES 6

ASPARAGUS SOUP

Here's the answer to what to do with the spears when you've used the tips in another dish.

· · ·

6 cups Chicken Stock (page 110)
8 cups 1-inch pieces of asparagus spears without
* tips, ends trimmed (see note)*
8 egg yolks
1 tablespoon plus 1 teaspoon fresh lemon juice
2 teaspoons kosher salt
Freshly ground black pepper to taste

In a large saucepan, bring the chicken broth to a boil over high heat. Add the asparagus. Reduce the heat and cook until it is tender enough to be pierced with a sharp knife point. Turn off the heat. Using a slotted spoon, remove half the pieces of asparagus from the broth and place them in the work bowl of a food processor. Using the steel blade, purée the asparagus pieces for 3 minutes.

Pour the purée through a medium-fine strainer set over a bowl. Use a spatula or your fingers to force the purée through the strainer until all that is left is the tough outer fibers of the asparagus. Discard the fibers. Repeat with the second batch of asparagus. Alternately you can put them through a food mill fitted with a fine disk.

Once the purée has been strained, pour it back into the chicken broth. Heat to just below boiling, then reduce the heat to low. Put the egg yolks into a small bowl. Whisk a ladleful of the purée into the egg yolks. Then whisk the yolk mixture into the hot soup. Stir constantly about 4 or 5 minutes, until the soup thickens. Do not boil the soup once the egg yolks have been added or it will scramble the eggs and ruin the soup. Stir in the lemon juice, salt, and pepper.

SERVES 6

NOTE: If you only have the woody ends left, don't expect them to get really soft; just cook them for 30 minutes. Don't process them; just put through a food mill.

SPRING-VEGETABLE GUMBO

I proudly think this recipe is a triumph. Please try it.

• • •

2 tablespoons unsalted butter
1½ cups diced onion
¼ teaspoon minced garlic
2 cups drained canned whole tomatoes, crushed
1 quart Meat Stock (page 109)
1 quart Chicken Stock (page 110)
2 to 2½ tablespoons kosher salt
Freshly ground black pepper to taste
Cayenne pepper to taste
Hot red-pepper sauce to taste
2 cups thinly sliced fresh (preferably) or frozen okra
⅓ cup diagonally sliced scallions (green and white parts)
¼ cup julienned carrots (2½- to 3-inch-long strips)
⅓ cup blanched asparagus spears, cut into 1-inch pieces
¼ cup cooked fresh peas
Extra diagonally sliced scallions for topping

Melt the butter, add the onions and garlic, and cook until translucent; do not brown. Add tomatoes, stocks, salt and pepper, cayenne and hot pepper sauce. Simmer the mixture about 30 minutes. Add the okra and cook until tender—roughly 3 minutes. In a bowl, mix together ⅓ cup scallions, the carrots, asparagus and peas. As you serve, stir into each portion a small amount of the spring-vegetable mixture. Sprinkle with scallions and serve immediately.

MAKES ABOUT 2½ TO 3 QUARTS; SERVES 10 TO 12 AS A FIRST COURSE

FULL-FLAVORED TOMATO SOUP

—————————— • ——————————

While summer brings out my most ardent soup-making frenzy, there are times in winter when I crave a light, full-tasting vegetable soup. There are also times when I have used a can of plum tomatoes, carefully draining the tomatoes. I hate waste, so when the times coincide, I make this soup, using the remaining tomato liquid as a base.

If you don't have fresh basil (I nurse mine along through the chilly winter on the windowsill of my kitchen), do not substitute dried. Create. Add chopped celery leaves or fresh coriander or minced chives—whatever you can find that is fresh and green. If you are using a very aromatic herb, such as thyme, reduce the quantity.

• • •

Drained liquid from one 35-ounce can plum
*   tomatoes (tomatoes reserved for another use)*
3 cups Chicken Stock (page 110)
½ cup fresh basil
½ cup fresh dill
½ cup parsley leaves
3 cloves garlic, smashed, peeled, and minced
Kosher salt
Freshly ground black pepper
½ teaspoon hot red-pepper sauce
Pinch cayenne pepper
Juice of 1 lemon

Heat the tomato liquid and stock to boiling in a non-aluminum pot.

Chop the basil, dill, and parsley in a food processor until medium fine. Add to the liquid with the garlic and salt and pepper to taste. Simmer for 15 minutes. Adjust the seasoning with the hot pepper sauce, cayenne, lemon juice, and more salt and pepper if needed.

SERVES 6

NOTE: If you have made Duck Burgers (page 210) and have some left over, break them into ½-inch pieces, and add them with their sauce to the soup for a more filling variation. This is not a pallid soup, especially if you use leftover Duck Burgers. It can easily take a red wine.

ACORN SQUASH SOUP

This soup is the spirit of fall, a perfect introduction to Thanksgiving dinner. Despites its radiant golden color, almost no one can guess the main ingredient. Baking the squash has the effect of intensifying its flavor. Sometimes, after the soup sits, it thickens until it needs to be thinned again with some extra chicken stock. In this case, check for additional salt and pepper. Reserve the seeds for toasting if you like.

• • •

4 medium-size acorn squash
⅓ pound (1⅓ sticks) unsalted butter
1 large onion, sliced
1 quart Chicken Stock (page 110)
Salt
Freshly ground black pepper
¼ teaspoon ground nutmeg

Heat oven to 300°F. Split the squash crosswise; scoop out the seeds. Place the squash, cut side down, on a baking sheet. Bake until very tender when pierced with a knife, about 1 hour. Remove and cool.

While the squash cools, melt the butter in a large saucepan over low heat. Sweat the onions in butter about 20 minutes, until softened. Add the chicken stock, 1 tablespoon salt, ⅓ teaspoon pepper, and the nutmeg. Simmer, covered, until the onions are tender, about 30 minutes.

Cut the squash into large cubes. Stir into the chicken stock until heated through. Pass stock, onion, and squash through the fine blade of a food mill. Taste for seasonings and thin with additional chicken broth if necessary. Check seasoning and thickness each time soup is reheated.

SERVES 6

QUICK BOURRIDE

A bourride or bourrida is a fish soup-stew from southern France or the Mediterranean coast of Italy—in France it's "e" and in Italy it's "a." The characteristic of these soups is that they are unified, or bound, by an aïoli, a garlicky mayonnaise, which miraculously doesn't separate when added to the hot soup. In this recipe for aïoli, I add a few drops of hot red-pepper sauce, which is definitely not classic. If you need an aïoli for vegetables, just omit the hot sauce.

There are other kinds of aïolis. Some are bound not with egg yolks but with the flesh from a baked potato or with a purée—called panade—made from white bread. The hardest to make is done only with garlic, which is placed in a mortar and continuously pounded and turned as the olive oil is dripped into it.

Aïoli is also the name of a regal meal in Provence. Boiled vegetables, meats, cod, and sausages are combined on a large platter in any grouping that appeals. The eaters keep on going, liberally slathering everything with aïoli to the point of exhaustion, which is aided by the consumption of vast quantities of the local highly alcoholic red wines.

This bourride is richly satisfying, creamy in texture and quick to prepare. If you have time to make a fish stock or have a bit of fish stock on hand to work with, the soup will be even better. If you wish to make this more elegant or more of a main-course meal, you can add shellfish. All of which is a warning to stay tuned for the next section, which is full of soups that make a meal.

• • •

QUICK BOURRIDE, CONTINUED

AÏOLI

2 large eggs
4 teaspoons lemon juice
12 drops hot red-pepper sauce
2 teaspoons kosher salt
¼ teaspoon freshly ground black pepper
½ cup light olive oil
6 to 8 cloves garlic, peeled

FISH SOUP

Stems from 2 bunches broccoli
3 cups Chicken Stock (page 110) or canned broth
2 cups bottled clam juice or Fish Stock (page 113)
1½ pounds cod or flounder fillets, cut into ½-inch
*   cubes, or 1 pound fish fillets and ½ pound small*
*   clams or mussels, cleaned, or shrimp*
Salt
Pepper

AÏOLI

Put the eggs, lemon juice, hot pepper sauce, salt, and pepper into a food processor. Process until blended. With the machine running, pour in the oil in a steady stream until it is incorporated and the mayonnaise is smooth. Add garlic. Process until smooth. The mayonnaise is now an aïoli. Set aside.

FISH SOUP

Peel the broccoli stems. Cut them crosswise into ¼-inch "coins." Measure 1½ cups of the coins and set aside.

In a 4-quart saucepan, bring the chicken and fish stocks to a boil over high heat (see note). Add broccoli stems. Bring back to the boil and cook 1 minute longer. Stir in the fish and cook 3 minutes. Place the aïoli in a small bowl. Slowly whisk in 2 cups of the soup liquid. Pour the liaison into remaining soup. Stir over medium heat until slightly thickened. Adjust seasonings. Serve immediately out of old-fashioned, large rim soups with lots of bread or, even better, thin slices of French bread sautéed in garlic-imbued olive oil until golden brown. Use oval not round soup spoons, oyster forks if you've used mussels or clams, large napkins, and possibly even finger bowls.

SERVES 8 AS A FIRST COURSE, 4 AS A MAIN COURSE.

NOTE: If using shellfish in addition to fillets, proceed as follows: Add clams to broth first, and boil for 3 minutes; add broccoli stems. If using mussels, add mussels with broccoli, and boil 4 minutes. Add fillets and continue as described above. If using shrimp, add peeled or not (depending on the informality of your guests) 1 minute before the end of the boiling.

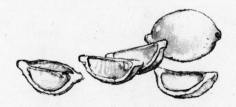

WHOLE-MEAL SOUPS

—————————•—————————

Fake Pelmenyi

Red-Cabbage Borscht

Shrimp and Chicken Gumbo

Bouillabaisse

Larder Fish Stew

On cold winter days or raw ones in March or October, my favorite meal to eat and serve is a large soup full of wonderful things. I begin with only a light nibble, perhaps Roasted Red Pepper Spread (page 19), then serve lots of wine along with the soup, peasanty bread, a salad, cheese, and nothing but fruit for dessert. The more elegant the friends, the happier they seem to be with these simple good foods.

. . .

FAKE PELMENYI

Among the many peoples who have discovered the succulence of ground and seasoned meat cooked inside a noodle wrapper the Siberians have not been the least inventive. (They also invented deep freezing.) In the fall, when the meat was butchered, they would grind up the little end pieces and form it into their own wontons, pelmenyi. Then they would put them outside to freeze. As needed during the winter, the individual pelmenyi would be broken from the block and put to simmer in stock rich with winter root vegetables and a precious hoarding of ukrop—dill.

I call this soup Fake Pelmenyi because I use frozen tortellini instead of making pelmenyi from scratch. It may not be authentic but it tastes delicious.

At restaurants like the Russian Tea Room in New York the pelmenyi are served with less broth than I use here and pieces of gizzard, heart, and neck (which you too could add if you have saved them from making the broth). They serve it only at lunch on

Wednesdays, when many of the Russians in town make an event out of being there.

• • •

> *6 cups Chicken Stock (page 110)*
> *2 whole chicken breasts, bone in, skinned*
> *1 cup white turnips in ¼-inch dice*
> *1 cup peeled, halved, and thinly sliced carrots*
> *1 cup thinly sliced scallions, white parts only*
> *2 cups frozen meat-filled tortellini, preferably beef*
> *⅓ cup coarsely chopped fresh dill and 1 tablespoon*
> *   for garnish*
> *⅓ cup sliced scallion greens*
> *1 teaspoon lemon juice*
> *Salt and freshly ground black pepper*
> *1 cup sour cream, plus approximately 2*
> *   tablespoons per person for garnish*
> *Chopped scallion greens for garnish*

In a medium-size saucepan, heat the chicken stock to simmering over low heat. Put the chicken breasts in the simmering stock and remove the pan from the heat. Let the breasts cool in the stock for 12 minutes. They will be barely pink in the center. Remove from the liquid.

When the chicken breasts are cool enough to handle, take the meat off the bones. Cut or tear into ½-inch-wide strips and set aside.

Over low heat, simmer the turnips, carrots, and scallion whites in the stock for 5 minutes. Add the frozen tortellini, ⅓ cup chopped dill, ⅓ cup sliced scallion greens, and lemon juice. Salt and pepper to taste. Simmer until the tortellini and vegetables are tender, about 4 minutes. Add the strips of chicken breast to the soup.

Place 1 cup of sour cream in a small bowl. Slowly whisk in about 1 cup of the hot stock. Whisk the sour cream and stock into the soup, stirring constantly. Taste and adjust the seasonings. Garnish each portion with chopped dill and scallion greens. Pass additional sour cream separately.

SERVES 6

NOTE: Blanched vegetables such as snow peas, small fresh peas, broccoli, and green beans can be added to the soup along with the tortellini.

RED-CABBAGE BORSCHT

———————————•———————————

With soup like this in the world, nothing can be that bad. Serve it out of a tureen or the pot into large rim soups. Top with dollops of sour cream and sprinklings of fresh dill. Accompany with Russian pumpernickel. Remember that, as with so many Russian dishes, you are balancing sweet with sour, dense and winy flavors with the freshness of dill, the acid of sour cream.

The only thing wrong with this soup is that you must start it the day before you wish to serve or eat it.

• • •

*1 pound beets (about 3 medium-size beets),
    trimmed of greens and scrubbed
3 pounds ham hocks or end pieces of ham with
    bone, split
1¼ cups red wine vinegar
½ cup red wine
1½ pounds red onions (4 medium-size onions),
    peeled and quartered
4 pounds red cabbage, trimmed and cut into
    eighths
½ cup packed dark brown sugar
6 juniper berries, crushed
4 whole cloves garlic, peeled
10 grinds black pepper from peppermill
Scant 2 tablespoons kosher salt
1 tablespoon fresh lemon juice
2 citric acid (sour salt) crystals (each about ¼
    teaspoon), available at grocery or pharmacy
½ cup packed coarsely chopped fresh dill, stems
    removed
Sour cream for garnish
Coarsely chopped fresh dill for garnish*

In a high, narrow soup pot, bring 3 quarts of water to a boil over high heat. Add the beets and simmer 40 to 50 minutes, until tender. Remove the beets form the water and set aside to cool. When you can handle them comfortably, slip the skins from the beets and discard. Set aside the whole beets until needed.

Add 3 more cups of water and the ham hocks to the soup pot. Bring to a boil. Skim off any scum that rises to the surface. Add vinegar, red wine, onions, and cabbage. Return to the boil. Then reduce heat to low and simmer for 5 hours.

Take the pot off the heat and allow the soup to cool to room temperature. Cover and store overnight in the refrigerator.

The next day, remove the meat, bones, and pieces of fat from the soup. Break the ham hocks into 1-inch pieces and set aside. Discard the bones and fat. Slice the beets into ⅓-inch-thick slices. Then cut each slice into strips. Stir the beet strips, meat, and 3 additional cups of water into the soup. Add all the remaining ingredients, except sour cream and extra chopped dill for garnish. Bring the soup to a boil over medium-high heat. Reduce the heat to low and simmer for 1 hour, stirring occasionally.

Serve topped with dollops of sour cream and coarsely chopped fresh dill.

MAKES 4 QUARTS; SERVES FROM 6 GREEDIES TO 16 FIRST-COURSE TASTERS

SHRIMP AND CHICKEN GUMBO

·

I particularly like to serve this kind of one-dish meal on formal occasions on a beautifully set table gleaming with crystal and silver. It loosens things up. Tapenade (see page 24) could introduce the meal, and gewürztraminer, Champagne, or beer goes well with it.

• • •

4 pounds large shrimp (one size smaller than jumbo), peeled; use the shells for the Shrimp Butter, the shrimp for the gumbo
5 chickens (3- to 3½-pounds each), cut into serving pieces
10 to 12 cups Chicken Stock (page 110), made without salt
2 pints pearl onions
¾ cup Shrimp Butter (page 146)
¼ cup unsalted butter
¾ cup all-purpose flour
1 large head garlic, peeled and finely minced to make ⅓ cup

14 to 16 small, fresh jalapeño peppers, thinly sliced
3 thirty-five-ounce cans Italian plum tomatoes,
    drained and crushed to make 4 cups
Kosher salt
Fresh lemon juice
3 twelve-ounce packages whole baby carrots,
    peeled and trimmed
2½ yellow bell peppers (red, if yellow are
    unavailable), stemmed, seeded, and thinly sliced
3 large stalks celery, peeled with a carrot peeler
    and sliced diagonally ¼ inch thick
Tips from 4 pounds asparagus (see Asparagus Soup,
    page 131)
2 ten-ounce packages frozen tiny peas, thawed
2½ pounds okra, trimmed and thinly sliced
3 bunches scallions, both green and white parts,
    diagonally sliced ¼ inch thick
Freshly ground black pepper
Hot red-pepper sauce, cayenne pepper, or ground
    hot red chilies to taste (optional)

• • •

Cooked rice

Prepare the shrimp and refrigerate. Skin the chicken breasts, thighs, and drumsticks. Discard the skin. Save the backs, tails, necks, and wings for future use in stock.

In a 4-quart pot, bring the chicken stock to a boil over high heat. Poach the drumsticks and thighs in the stock for 10 minutes. Remove the meat from the stock and set it aside to cool. Bring the stock to a boil once again and add half the chicken breasts. Poach for 7 minutes. Remove the breasts from the stock and set aside to cool. Repeat with the remaining chicken breasts. Reserve the stock.

When the chicken is cool enough to handle, remove the meat from the bones. Save the bones for future use in stock and discard any fat and cartilage. Tear any large pieces of meat into pieces about 1½ inches in size. You should have about 8 cups of chicken meat. Set aside.

Trim the root ends of the pearl onions. In a small saucepan, bring 3 cups of water to a boil. Plunge the onions into the boiling water. Remove from the heat and let stand for 30 seconds. Drain the onions in a colander. You can now slip off the skins quite easily. Trim the tops, if necessary, and set aside.

In a very large, heavy soup pot melt ½ cup Shrimp Butter with the unsalted butter over low heat. When the butter is bubbling, stir in the flour and cook, *stirring constantly,* until you have a very dark, chestnut-brown roux. This will take about 40 to 50 minutes. Do not let it burn.

Slowly pour in 6 cups of chicken stock, stirring constantly, until the mixture is smooth and well-blended. Stir in the garlic, jalapeño peppers, tomatoes, 5 tablespoons salt, and 3 tablespoons lemon juice. Simmer for 10 minutes. Add the pearl onions and baby carrots. Reduce the heat to low and cook for 30 minutes. Add 4 more cups of chicken broth, the yellow peppers, celery, asparagus tips, peas, okra, and scallions. Cook for 2 minutes, until the asparagus can be easily pierced with a sharp knife point.

Add the shrimp and reserved chicken meat. Cook about 3 minutes, stirring constantly, just until the shrimp become opaque. Taste and add more salt and lemon juice to taste. Add pepper to taste. If you wish, add either hot red-pepper sauce, cayenne pepper, or ground hot red chilies to taste.

In the center of each dinner plate, place a large spoonful of rice flavored with the remaining ¼ cup Shrimp Butter. Ladle Shrimp and Chicken Gumbo around the rice in a wreath. Top with another spoonful of rice in the center of the plate.

SERVES 12 TO 14

• SHRIMP BUTTER •

This is the recipe for which I have been exhorting you to save your shrimp shells. Store them tightly sealed in the freezer, keeping a running tally of the amount on an outside label. In addition to the gumbo (page 144) the shrimp butter can be used for seafood sauces which will be sieved, for sautéeing fish and for enriching seafood soups. The butter itself can be frozen in 1- or 2-tablespoon quantities, making it easy to use. This also works well with lobster shells.

• • •

4 tablespoons (½ stick) unsalted butter
Shells from 4 pounds shrimp (about 2 packed cups)
14 tablespoons (1¾ stick) unsalted butter, chilled

In a large skillet, melt 4 tablespoons of butter over medium-high heat. Sauté the shrimp shells, stirring frequently for 10 to 15 minutes. When the shells are golden, take them off the heat and place in the work bowl of a food processor. Using the steel blade, process the shells about 5 minutes, until they are very finely chopped. Remove the lid of the food processor and let the shells cool for 5 minutes. Cut the chilled butter into tablespoon-size pieces. Place the butter in the food processor and use on/off pulses to blend it with the crushed shells.

Scrape the mixture from the work bowl into a very fine sieve set over a bowl. Force the shells and butter through the sieve with either your fingers or a plastic spatula. Discard the crushed shells. This process will take a bit of time and effort, but the results are well worth it. When you have finished, the resulting butter will have a wonderful strong shrimp flavor. You should have enough shrimp butter for the Shrimp and Chicken Gumbo and to season the accompanying rice.

MAKES ¾ CUP

BOUILLABAISSE

Bouillabaisse is one of the world's most famous dishes. There is no such thing as an authentic one. Each person has his or her own ideas. This version is very non-French, being made in America with American fish that are filleted and with fish stock. I have many friends who are not happy wrestling with fish bones in the soupy, murky depths, so I created this panic-free version and satisfied the gelatinous requirement with rich fish stock, though it must be made ahead. This is one case in which a gelatin-rich base is boiled to bind in the loose ingredients.

In Paris, they add lobster, which cannot be filleted but which can be cut up in small easy-to-cope-with pieces.

The rouille should be placed on the table in a bowl, and guests can stir it into their soup as they go, adding more as their taste buds numb. The rouille is first cousin of Aïoli (page 136). The reddish difference is created by hot peppers and a last-minute thinning with the tomato-red soup. This rouille is strongly flavored with Pernod or pastis.

BOUILLABAISSE, CONTINUED

ROUILLE WITH PASTIS

4 egg yolks
½ teaspoon kosher salt
¼ teaspoon dry mustard
2 cups olive oil
6 cloves garlic, cut into pieces
3 dried red peppers, crumbled
1 teaspoon white wine vinegar
1 gram (small test-tube container) stem saffron,
*   dissolved in 2 tablespoons white wine*
½ teaspoon pastis or Pernod

BOUILLABAISSE

1 cup green virgin olive oil
4 large yellow onions, finely chopped
½ cup freshly chopped parsley
2 eels (preferably sea), about 1½ pounds each,
*   skinned, cut into 1½-inch lengths, heads and*
*   tails reserved for later use in stock*
2 pounds cod fillets cut into 2-by-4-inch pieces
2 pounds mackerel, hake, or whiting fillets, or a
*   mixture, cut into 2-by-4-inch pieces*
¾ cup pastis or Pernod
8 good-size ripe red tomatoes, peeled and chopped
2 quarts Fish Stock (see page 113)
3 grams stem saffron, dissolved in ½ cup dry white
*   wine*
8 large cloves garlic, peeled and chopped
3 tablespoons kosher salt
¼ cup fennel greens, finely chopped
1½ tablespoons chili powder
Cayenne pepper
4 pounds red-snapper or striped-bass fillets, cut in
*   large pieces*
30 medium hard-shell clams, scrubbed
30 mussels, well cleaned (see page 61)
30 raw medium shrimp in their shells

• • •

French bread, cut into ½-inch-thick slices, lightly
*   toasted*

ROUILLE

Process the egg yolks, salt, and mustard in a food processor for a full 2 minutes. Slowly add the 2 cups of oil until the mixture thickens; then add the oil faster. Add the garlic and peppers. Then add the vinegar, saffron wine, and Pernod. Set aside until ready to use.

BOUILLABAISSE

Place ½ cup of the olive oil in a large soup pot. Over low heat, add the onions; cook and stir until they are soft but not brown. Add the parsley and the eel. Cook and stir until the eel is lightly browned.

Add the cod and 2 pounds of assorted fish to the pot. Place the Pernod in a small pot to heat gently. Set a match to it to ignite. Pour the flaming liquid over the fish. When the flames die down, add the tomatoes, fish stock, saffron wine, garlic, salt, fennel greens, chili powder, cayenne, and the remaining ½ cup olive oil. Raise the temperature to high and bring the liquid to a violent boil. Cook for 7 minutes. Add the red snapper or striped bass and continue to boil for 3 minutes.

Add the clams and cover the pot; cook 3 minutes. Add the mussels and shrimp; cover the pot again and cook until the mussels open. Remove the fish and shellfish to a serving platter. Let the soup continue boiling until amalgamated. Then stir 3 tablespoons of it into the rouille.

Spread 2 slices of bread per person with a little rouille. Place in the bottom of each huge soup bowl. Strain the broth and spoon over. Serve the fish and extra bowls of rouille on the side.

SERVES AT LEAST 12

LARDER FISH STEW

A simple but surprising combination of vegetables and fish. All the ingredients can be kept on hand and easily turned into this warming stew. The flavorful broth is lightly thickened with rouille, the fiery mayonnaise of Provence. Serve with garlic croutons.

...

ROUILLE WITH ROASTED RED PEPPERS

3 egg yolks
3 tablespoons coarsely chopped jarred roasted red
 peppers
2 tablespoons lemon juice
4 whole dried red chilies
3 cloves garlic
1 teaspoon kosher salt
½ teaspoon cayenne pepper (optional)
1 cup light olive oil or blend of olive and vegetable
 oils

STEW

2 small sweet potatoes, peeled, cut lengthwise into
 thin wedges
1 ten-ounce package frozen baby lima beans,
 defrosted
1⅓ cup Chicken Stock (page 110)
⅔ cup bottled clam juice
¾ pound frozen cod fillets, separated
Lemon juice to taste

ROUILLE

Place the egg yolks, roasted red peppers, lemon juice, chilies, garlic, salt, and cayenne, if used, in a food processor. Process until the peppers are finely minced. With the motor running, pour the oil into the egg mixture in a thin, steady stream until the oil is incorporated and the mayonnaise is very thick. Transfer ¾ cup of the rouille to a small bowl and reserve the remainder.

STEW

In a large saucepan of boiling salted water, blanch the sweet potatoes until tender, about 14 minutes. Drain them and rinse under cold running water. Blanch the lima beans in a large saucepan of boiling salted water until crisp-tender, about 2 minutes. Drain and reserve.

In a heavy 2-quart saucepan heat the chicken stock and clam juice over medium heat to simmering. Add the fish fillets, potatoes, and lima beans. Simmer until the fish is cooked and the vegetables are heated through, about 5 minutes. Slowly beat about 1 cup of the hot broth into the measured rouille, scraping the sides of the bowl as you beat. Then stir the rouille-and-broth mixture into the soup in the saucepan. Reduce the heat to low. Cook, stirring constantly, until the soup is slightly thickened, about 4 minutes. If desired, stir in additional lemon juice to taste. Serve immediately, passing the remaining rouille separately.

SERVES 4 TO 6

OF FISH AND SEAFOOD

Broiled Frozen Salmon

Striped Bass with Shellfish

Salmon in Nage of Spring Vegetables

Sole in Pink Wine Sauce

Baked Whole Bass with Tomatoes and Cucumbers

White Fish Stew

The reason this is a short chapter is not that I don't like fish and seafood. In fact, I love them; but, with my taste for red wine, I seldom make them the main course at dinner. They and their recipes turn up in the early parts of the meal: Hot First Courses, Cold First Courses, Pasta, and Soups. When I do serve a fish main course, it tends to be simple. The best lobster for me is the freshest one-and-a-quarter-pound lobster boiled for eleven minutes and served with melted butter and halved lemons. The best fish is poached and served with a sauce on the side. Often these same simple preparations for lobster or fish will turn up in smaller portions as first courses.

The basic rule for cooking fish, whether poaching or broiling or baking, is to measure it at the thickest part and allow ten minutes per inch or a fraction of the time for a fraction of an inch. If you are in a hurry, fish can be satisfactorily poached in plain water. A little more time and ambition allow a court bouillon. In your fish poacher place enough liquid to just cover your fish. The liquid should be two-thirds water and one-third dry white wine. Peel and slice one or two onions into the liquid. Add two or three cloves of garlic, five peppercorns, one clove, a thinly sliced lemon, a scraped and sliced carrot, a few branches of parsley and some dill if appropriate. Bring to the boil; reduce heat; simmer one-half hour. Then poach your fish, covered.

• • •

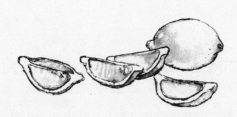

BROILED FROZEN SALMON

This recipe is like the letter the Madwoman of Chaillot received each morning telling her what to do with her day—carefully self-prepared in anticipation of impending disaster. With this salmon laid away in the freezer, I am prepared for the most unexpected or forgotten guest.

• • •

1 tablespoon peanut oil
1 three-and-a-half-pound side of salmon, frozen
  (see note)
1 recipe Gravlax Sauce (page 14)

Heat the broiler. Using 1 teaspoon of the oil, grease a metal baking sheet large enough to hold the salmon.

Place the frozen salmon, skin side up, on the baking sheet, and brush with the remaining 2 teaspoons oil. Place the fish 3 inches away from the broiler heat. Broil for 5 minutes. Using two long spatulas, carefully turn the fish over and broil 10 minutes longer. (Begin testing the fish for doneness after 7 minutes on the second side.) The outside should be lightly browned and the inside slightly undercooked. It will continue cooking after it is removed from the oven.

Transfer the salmon to a warm serving platter, and serve with Gravlax Sauce and steamed new potatoes.

SERVES 6

NOTE: Before freezing the fish, remove all the small bones in the thicker foresection with tweezers or needle-nosed pliers. Freeze flat.

STRIPED BASS WITH SHELLFISH

This recipe can be prepared in a fish poacher rather than in a skillet, and with a whole fish rather than fillets. Red snapper is a good alternative if striped bass is unavailable. In that case, do not precook the clams. Put them in the simmering court bouillon at the same time as the fish. Plan the cooking time by the ten-minute-per-inch rule (page 155) and insert mussels and shrimp at the appropriate times. You can serve an Aïoli (page 136) or a Rouille (page 148 or 150) with this. I serve it plain.

• • •

18 cherrystone or littleneck clams, well washed
5 cups (approximately) court bouillon (page 155)
6 six-ounce pieces striped bass, filleted (these
    should have the skin on and be weighed after
    filleting)
24 mussels, beards removed, well-washed
24 large shrimp in the shell
Freshly ground black pepper
Sea salt

Place the clams in a saucepan over low heat. Cover and steam just until they open. Set aside.

Meanwhile, in a large, deep skillet, bring the court bouillon to a simmer. It should be deep enough to cover the bass. If not, add more liquid. Add the bass and adjust the heat to keep the liquid at a simmer. After 3 minutes, add the mussels and cover the pan tightly. Cook 2 minutes longer, then add the shrimp and opened clams. Cook another 1 to 1½ minutes.

Serve portions of fish surrounded by shellfish. Moisten the top with a little of the broth. Grind over a little fresh pepper and sprinkle on some sea salt.

SERVES 6

SALMON IN NAGE OF
SPRING VEGETABLES

This recipe is written for individual servings since I like to serve the salmon right in the bowl in which it cooks. If you choose to do the same thing, just multiply by the number of guests or bowls with which you want to finish. This dish has a pretty contrast of colors.

SALMON IN NAGE OF SPRING VEGETABLES, CONTINUED

When serving it, be careful not to spill hot broth on yourself or on your guests.

• • •

½ cup julienned peeled carrots
½ cup julienned white part of leek
½ cup julienned peeled celery
Salt
Freshly ground black pepper
1 eight-ounce salmon fillet
¼ cup julienned zucchini with skin on
Chopped parsley
¾ cup Fish Stock (page 113)
¼ cup dry white wine

Scatter half of the carrots, leeks, and celery in a buttered 6-inch pan or ovenproof soup bowl. Sprinkle with a pinch of salt and pepper. Snuggle the salmon fillet into the vegetables. Scatter the remaining julienned vegetables, including zucchini, on top of the fish. Sprinkle with chopped parsley and a speck of salt and pepper. Carefully pour in the fish stock and dry white wine so as not to disarrange the vegetables.

Cover (aluminum foil will do), and cook gently on top of the stove or, if the fish is in soup bowls, on a baking sheet in a preheated 350° F. oven. Remove from the heat approximately 5 minutes after the stock has come to a simmer, or just before the fish is done. It will continue cooking on the way to the table.

Serve with small steamed potatoes.

SERVES 1

SOLE IN PINK WINE SAUCE

This is a variant on a classic dish. Here, the rosé wine turns the sole and sauce a delicate pink. I serve the fish on pale pink plates or directly from the baking dish since the arrangement of the rolls of the sole is extremely pretty. I always give people a spoon for the sauce.

The baking dish should be just large enough to hold the twelve pieces of fillet rolled up and standing on end. It should be approximately a two-quart, seven-inch round dish, three inches deep.

I tend to serve this as a first course, allowing two rolls per person. If you want to make it a main course, serve four rolls per person with some rice and possibly sautéed spinach. You could add some thinly sliced mushrooms to the fish while it cooks.

Serve the same wine to drink as you use in the dish. Pink or rosé wines have myriad designations in California. I particularly like blanc de pinot noir, which turns out to be a lovely rosy-apricot.

• • •

6 fillets of sole or flounder, 8 to 10 inches long,
    skinned
Juice of 1 lemon, or to taste
2 tablespoons thinly sliced shallots
2 cups good rosé wine
2 cups heavy cream
1 tablespoon chopped fresh tarragon or ¼ teaspoon
    dried tarragon
2 egg yolks

Preheat the oven to 350° F.

Cut each fillet lengthwise down the center and remove any bones or large tendons that may remain. Put the fillets in a bowl and add the lemon juice and enough cold water just to cover. Let sit 10 to 15 minutes. Drain them and pat dry. Generously butter a baking dish that will hold the fillets snugly when rolled.

Roll up each fillet, skinned side out. Stand the rolled fillets on end side by side in the dish. Sprinkle the shallots over the top. Pour the wine over the fish, and cover with buttered waxed paper, buttered side down.

Bake the fish in the preheated oven for 10 to 12 minutes, or until the outside of the fish is opaque.

While the fish is cooking, pour the cream into a wide pan and begin reducing over moderate heat.

When the fish is done, turn off the oven. Carefully, pour the fish juices into a second pan. Return the fish, covered again with waxed paper, to the turned-off oven.

Add the tarragon to the fish juices and begin to reduce over high heat. From time to time, pour into the saucepan any additional juices that the fish releases.

When the cream and fish juices have each reduced to about 1 cup, combine them in one pan.

Place the egg yolks in a small bowl and beat lightly. Slowly pour about ½ cup of the hot cream mixture into the eggs, whisking constantly. Continue adding cream until the egg yolks are warm. Then, while whisking the sauce, pour the yolk mixture into the cream. Cook, stirring constantly, over low heat about 1 to 2 minutes, or until the sauce is slightly thickened. Taste the sauce and adjust the taste with lemon juice. If desired, strain the sauce. Pour over the fish and serve.

SERVES 6 AS A FIRST COURSE, 3 AS A MAIN COURSE

BAKED WHOLE BASS
WITH TOMATOES AND CUCUMBERS

I would serve smaller portions of this as a first course; but it makes a spectacular and light main course for those who like it. Do find a pretty platter and serve the fish whole. If you can get the fishmonger to do the butterflying, congratulations. However, if you have to do it yourself and have never done it before, allow enough time to get all the bones out. Butterflied fish are completely boned, but fillets are left joined along the backbone. The purpose is to create a boneless pocket for stuffing while still retaining the shape of a whole fish. The stuffed fish can then be easily sliced.

This can also be served cold. A light white wine is the choice, whether the fish is served hot or cold.

• • •

1 striped bass (3½ to 4 pounds), butterflied
3 tablespoons olive oil
2 tablespoons lemon juice
Kosher salt
Freshly ground black pepper
1 medium tomato, cored, thinly sliced
4 medium-size kirby (pickling) cucumbers, thinly
    sliced
½ cup (loosely packed) coarsely chopped fresh dill

Make sure all traces of viscera are removed from the cavity of the fish, including the dark red air sac located just behind the head. Pat the fish dry inside and out with paper towels. Heat the oven to 350° F.

Whisk the olive oil and lemon juice in a small bowl. Open the fish. With the skin side down, lightly sprinkle the flesh with about 2 tablespoons of the oil and lemon juice. Add salt and pepper to taste. Arrange overlapping slices of tomato and cucumber along one fillet. Use 3 slices of cucumber to every 1 of tomato. Sprinkle with dill. Reserve any remaining vegetable slices for garnish. Fold the plain fillet over the topped fillet. Tie the fish gently but securely with butchers' twine at 2-inch intervals.

Place the fish in a baking dish large enough to hold it comfortably. An oval dish is ideal. Bake about 20 minutes or until the flesh along the thickest part of the backbone is opaque. Baste occasionally with the remaining oil and lemon juice and pan juices.

With two large spatulas, carefully transfer the fish to a serving plate. Remove the strings. Gently lift up the top fillet and spoon the juices from the baking dish over the tomato and cucumber slices. Replace the top fillet. Garnish with the reserved tomato and cucumber slices. To serve, slice the fish crosswise with a serrated knife. Serve warm or at room temperature.

SERVES 6 AS A FIRST COURSE, 3 TO 4 AS A MAIN COURSE

BUTTERFLYING A WHOLE FISH

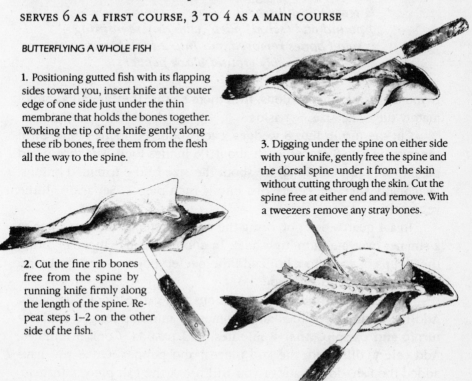

1. Positioning gutted fish with its flapping sides toward you, insert knife at the outer edge of one side just under the thin membrane that holds the bones together. Working the tip of the knife gently along these rib bones, free them from the flesh all the way to the spine.

3. Digging under the spine on either side with your knife, gently free the spine and the dorsal spine under it from the skin without cutting through the skin. Cut the spine free at either end and remove. With a tweezers remove any stray bones.

2. Cut the fine rib bones free from the spine by running knife firmly along the length of the spine. Repeat steps 1–2 on the other side of the fish.

WHITE FISH STEW

— • —

This is clearly the fraternal twin of the Quick Bourride (page 135), but it has a nice group of wintery vegetables to make it into a substantial meal.

• • •

*6 whole small yellow onions, peeled and trimmed,
   or 2 medium-size onions, peeled and cut in
   quarters
1 medium-size turnip, peeled and trimmed
1 medium-size parsnip, peeled and trimmed
2 small ribs celery, scraped with a carrot peeler
4 cups Chicken Stock (page 110)
2 cups bottled clam juice
2 cups water
¾ pound small Maine potatoes or medium-size cut
   in halves, peeled
6 large cloves garlic, peeled
1½ tablespoons egg pastina
½ teaspoon dill seed
1 pound cod (scrod) fillets, with any remaining
   small bones removed, cut into 2-inch pieces
⅛ teaspoon freshly ground black pepper*

If you are using small onions, trim them so that they are all approximately the same size. Set aside.

Cut the turnip into 8 wedges, each about 1½ inches long. Slice the parsnip into 8 pieces, each about 1½ inches long. The turnip and parsnip wedges should all be about the size of the trimmed onions. Diagonally slice the celery ribs into ¼-inch pieces. Set aside all the vegetables.

In a 4-quart stock pot, bring the chicken stock and clam juice to a simmer over medium-high heat. In another small saucepan, bring the 2 cups of water to a boil; add the peeled potatoes and boil for 5 minutes. Drain and set aside.

To the simmering broth add onions and garlic. Cook 7 minutes. Add the drained potatoes and simmer 10 minutes longer. Add the turnip and parsnip. After 8 minutes, add pastina. Cook 3 minutes. Add celery, dill seed, the cod pieces, and pepper. Once you have added the fish, do not stir or you will break the fish pieces. Instead, gently shake the pot to distribute the vegetables more evenly. Cook for an additional 1½ minutes. Serve immediately. If you do not plan to serve the stew immediately, cook fish for 1 minute only and re-move the pot from the heat.

SERVES 6 AS A FIRST COURSE

NOTE: To prepare as a main course use 2 pounds of cod and increase the liquid to 4⅔ cups chicken stock and 2½ cups bottled clam juice. Serves 6.

ROAST MEATS

———————•———————

Roast Chicken

To Herb-Roast a Chicken

Roast Turkey with Sauerkraut Stuffing

Grits Stuffing (for Turkey)

Crisp Roast Duck

Duck Hash

Roast Leg of Lamb

Roast Beef

Beef Salad with Horseradish Dressing

Roast Fresh Ham with Olives and Almonds

Roast Loin of Pork

Pork, Apple, and Celery Salad

I am a strange creature, thrifty in some ways—saving bones to make my soups and chicken livers to make my terrines—but profligate in others. I always roast my meats at high temperatures and shrinkage be damned. I do it because I am a naturally hurried person and because I like my meats juicy and rare. The high heat quickly caramelizes the surface of the meat or the skin of the bird, sealing in the rich juices and flavors. If you turn down the heat after your meat has caramelized, the steam will soften the crust. Continuous low-heat cooking is more like steaming or pot roasting than real roasting, the exemplar of which is open-flame cooking. The high heat also creates a rich pan glaze that can be degreased and then deglazed with wine or stock to make the best of natural gravies.

The strong flavors brought out by roasting are a perfect foil for red wine and virtually any kind of vegetable. For me, these are the perfect centerpieces of a meal. The oohing and aahing have gone with the first course and now we can settle down to serious conversation and serious eating.

One of the advantages of this form of cooking is that it is quick. I can turn on the oven as I walk in the door, and by the time we are ready for a main course it is ready for us. Variety can be achieved by rotating the guests and changing sauces and side dishes, so do look in those chapters for ideas. Since almost all of the first-course dishes in this book could go before a roast, the only thing you have to be careful of when planning a meal around a roast is not to repeat in the vegetables ingredients and flavors in the first course.

They used to say one had to be born a roast cook; but I think the principles are simple enough to be learned. Do buy a good meat thermometer. Professional cooks can tell the doneness of the meat by pushing with a finger on the outside of a roast. The roast becomes firmer to the touch—hardens—as it cooks; but it takes practice and sometimes burned fingers. A thermometer is safer. Don't get a thermometer that tells what well done or rare is, as the markings are invariably wrong. The reason I can't give you absolute so-many-minutes-at-such-a-temperature indications is that the shape of a piece of meat, the weight and shape of the bone, and the percentage of fat will change the cooking time extraordinarily. However, I can give you pretty good outside indications. If the roast is done early, take it out of the oven. Mercifully, roasts tend to be largish and therefore retain heat well. The only time when it is not a good idea to take the roast out early is when you want a crisp skin on a bird. By now most commercially grown birds are so standardized that, for them, I can give you fairly good timing.

...

ROAST CHICKEN

A well-roasted chicken is still worthy of Sunday dinner, even if the festivities fall on a midweek night. If I have leftovers, I don't refrigerate them (the flesh toughens); I eat them at midnight or the next day at room temperature, keeping the carcass for soup. If you feel you should refrigerate the chicken, remove meat from bones and mix the leftover meat with mayonnaise or other good dressing before refrigerating; the protective covering will prevent toughening. I think the citrus fruit stuffed in the chicken perfumes without overwhelming it.

The reason I don't truss birds when I roast them is that it seems to me illogical to force the thickest, longest-to-cook part of the bird up against the body of the bird. This insulates the thighs and makes them take yet longer to cook. That is the sure way to have dry white meat and red blood at the thigh joint. Do it my way and the bird may look vaguely drunk and obscene but it will be properly roasted. I also don't cook my chicken on a rack as my friend James Beard does, nor do I turn it from side to side. Occasionally, at the beginning of the roasting, I give the pan a good hard shake so that the chicken doesn't stick to the bottom of the pan.

Sometimes, when I am more interested in richness of flavor than in crisp skin, I stick four tablespoons of butter inside the chicken along with the flavoring ingredients and baste the chicken from time to time with the juices. The butter can easily be omitted in the interests of sane diet, though chicken is very lean meat. If you want a crisp skin omit the basting as I do in this recipe. Be careful when removing the bird to the platter; first tilt it so that the hot butter and juices in the bird fall back into the roasting pan and not onto your arm or the floor.

In most houses, this serves 4. I don't count on more than 2 or at most 3 people being served by one chicken, since I can never tell how many people will want white and how many dark.

Among the white wines, a sauvignon blanc with some acid and some fruit, and among the reds a round, soft merlot would do the trick.

* * *

1 five-pound chicken
1 lemon, halved
5 cloves garlic
½ orange
1 medium onion
4 tablespoons unsalted butter
Salt
Freshly ground black pepper
½ cup water or Chicken Stock (page 110)

Preheat the oven to 500° F.

Remove the fat from the crop and cavity of the chicken. Freeze the neck and gizzards for stock. Put the liver with your other chicken livers (page 22). Stuff the cavity of the chicken with the lemon, garlic, orange, onion, butter, salt, and pepper. Season the skin with salt and pepper.

Place the chicken in a roasting pan, breast side up, and roast for 45 minutes to an hour, or until the juices run clear. During the first few minutes, either shake the chicken or move it frequently with a wooden spoon to keep it from sticking. When chicken is done, tilt the bird over the roasting pan to allow cavity juices to fall into it. Remove the chicken to a platter.

Put the roasting pan on top of the stove. Add the water or chicken stock and bring the contents of the pan to a boil, while scraping the bottom vigorously with a wooden spoon. Serve the pan juices over the chicken or, for crisper skin, in a sauceboat.

SERVES 2 TO 4

TO HERB-ROAST A CHICKEN

•

The simplest method is to set your oven to 450° F. Then go to your window box or garden and pick as large a bunch of one herb or an assortment of herbs as you think you can cram into the interior of the chicken. Wash the herbs under cold running water in a sieve. Dry well.

Depending on the size of the chicken, peel a quantity of garlic cloves. Put the garlic, freshly ground pepper, a knob of butter, kosher salt, and herbs in the cavity of the chicken. Do not truss. Roast until browned and crisp.

•••

1 four-and-a-half-pound roasting chicken
½ cup thyme
½ cup winter savory
¼ cup rosemary
6 chives
4 large cloves garlic
1 teaspoon freshly ground black pepper
1 tablespoon kosher salt
4 tablespoons unsalted butter

Follow the procedure as explained above. Roast for 45 minutes.

ROAST TURKEY WITH SAUERKRAUT STUFFING

•

Think of a turkey as a large chicken without much fat of its own. I cook turkeys in a rather unorthodox way: quickly at high heat. Not only is this the way I do most roasting; but I also find that it gives a much juicier turkey. As with chickens, I do not truss and I do not rack—same reasons (see page 168). I do baste: the skin is thin; the bird is large. It still stays crisp.

Make the extra effort of finding a fresh turkey. It usually only requires ordering ahead. Make sure it has not been injected with anything. Turkey is one of those fortunate ingredients with a low enough price so that we can afford the best. Injected turkeys are tougher and you are paying for water.

When I invented this stuffing I felt very original; then Jim Beard told me that in Maryland they serve turkey with sauerkraut. Well, a good idea for them seems a great idea to me—but as a stuffing.

For those who want more stuffing, simply double the amounts given below. Bake extra stuffing in a buttered heatproof casserole, moistening with additional chicken stock and bacon fat as required.

• • •

*1 fifteen-pound turkey, preferably fresh, giblets
    reserved*
1 quart Chicken Stock (page 110)
Freshly ground black pepper
1 pound sliced bacon
4 medium onions, peeled, thinly sliced
*1 to 1¼ pounds sour rye bread, with seeds and
    crusts, cut into ½-inch cubes*
1 tablespoon caraway seeds
Freshly ground black pepper
*2 sixteen-ounce cans sauerkraut, placed in a sieve
    and pressed to drain well*
Salt as necessary

Remove giblets; set aside liver for another use. In a small saucepan, place the giblets, neck, and enough stock to cover. Simmer 4 to 5 hours over low heat. Replace stock as necessary.

Rinse the turkey body cavity. Pat dry with paper towels. Sprinkle the outside with pepper.

Separate the bacon slices. In a heavy frying pan, sauté them about 6 minutes over medium heat. The bacon should be just crisp, but not dry. Drain it on paper towels. Crumble coarsely.

Pour off all but 3 tablespoons of the fat from the bacon pan. Reserve the extra fat. Add the onions to the pan. Sauté over medium heat, stirring frequently, about 10 minutes, until wilted and golden brown.

In a large bowl, toss the bread, bacon, onions, caraway, and ¼ teaspoon of pepper until mixed. Add the sauerkraut, a handful at a time, mixing well after each addition. Add salt to taste carefully; the bacon and sauerkraut may give you plenty of salt. Moisten with about ½ cup of chicken stock.

Stuff the body cavity and crop of the turkey. Secure the crop with a long metal skewer if desired. Roast the turkey in a 500° F. oven until the leg joint near the backbone wiggles easily, about 2 hours. Baste the turkey with bacon grease every 20 minutes during roasting. Let it rest at least 10 minutes before removing the stuffing and carving.

While the turkey is resting, remove the giblets from the stock. Slice the heart and gizzard. Pick off the meat from the neck bone. Return the heart, gizzard, and neck meat to the stock. Season with salt and pepper. Keep hot over low heat until ready to serve. This is your gravy and wonderful it is. I have been known to skip the turkey and just have stuffing and gravy, grits and gravy, or mashed potatoes and gravy.

MAKES 12 SERVINGS PLUS LEFTOVERS

GRITS STUFFING

This is another wonderful stuffing. This recipe makes enough for a fifteen-pound turkey to roast as above, but you will need to sprinkle the turkey with salt as well as pepper, since this stuffing is less salty. Make your gravy as in the preceding recipe.

• • •

3½ cups Chicken Stock (page 110)
4 cloves garlic, peeled and left whole
12 tablespoons (1½ sticks) unsalted butter
1½ cups grits
½ pound chicken livers, cleaned
¼ pound turkey liver, cleaned
1 medium onion, sliced lengthwise, then cut in half
½ pound mushrooms, cut into ¼-inch-thick slices
⅔ pound green apples, peeled, cored, and sliced
   lengthwise (kept fresh in acidulated water)
½ cup shelled pecans
1 tablespoon kosher salt or to taste

Heat the oven to 450° F. Butter a 2½-quart soufflé dish, if desired.

In a pan, bring the stock to a boil with the garlic cloves and 8 tablespoons of butter. When the stock is boiling, slowly add the grits, stirring so it does not stick. Stir and cook for 8 minutes over medium heat.

Meanwhile, in a skillet melt the remaining 4 tablespoons of butter. Add the livers and cook, stirring, for 2 minutes, just to seize. Remove them from the pan with a slotted spoon. To the skillet add the sliced onion and cook for 1 minute. Add the mushrooms and apples, and cook 5 minutes longer.

While the apple mixture is cooking, cut the chicken and turkey livers into ¼-inch slices, removing the veins. Add them to the skillet. Stir to mix, then add the contents of the skillet to the grits. Mix well. Cook for 5 minutes over low heat. Stir in the pecans. Season to taste with salt.

Now either stuff your turkey and roast as in the preceding recipe or bake the stuffing as a side dish to eat with the turkey. In the latter case, put the mixture in the buttered dish, making sure to eliminate all the air bubbles (press down firmly with a spoon as you add the mixture). Cover with a sheet of buttered aluminum foil, buttered side down. Bake for 1 hour and 10 minutes, or until firm. Turn off the heat and let rest in the oven 10 minutes longer.

MAKES ENOUGH STUFFING FOR A 15-POUND TURKEY

NOTE: This mixture can also be used in a casserole made with leftover turkey. In that case, replace the turkey liver with ¼ pound of chicken livers. When you stir in the pecans, add 2 cups skinned and boned cooked turkey, cut into ½-inch pieces. If you do not want to eat the stuffing mixture right away, it can be frozen and then reheated.

CRISP ROAST DUCK

Despite all the fancy and cut-up versions of duck, there are days when a simple crisp roast duck is really what we crave. I developed the following recipe to deal with the fact that, by the time the duck skin is crisp enough to please most Americans and the fat under the skin has melted away, the meat has become dry, microscopic, and

CRISP ROAST DUCK, CONTINUED

stringy. Poaching the duck helps to eliminate the fat under the skin. It also keeps the meat juicy and plump. The resulting broth is a delicious duck stock. It's particularly rich if you use duck stock as your poaching liquid. You may have to start with canned chicken stock the first time, but from then on you are in business.

Duck is really inexpensive and you can treat this dish as festively as you care to, or as informally. Any red wine from a jug to your finest vintage cabernet will improve in taste when served with this deep-tasting duck.

If you are making the bird in the spring, you might try browning lightly blanched tiny carrots and turnips in the duck fat until they are golden. In the fall or winter, a purée of half potatoes and half turnips with lots of butter would be good.

As I can never tell exactly how much duck each person can eat, I inevitably make so much I have leftovers. For that reason and by reason of its wonderful taste, I developed the duck ravioli on page 100. Don't throw out the bones on people's plates. Remember boiling will sanitize them. Throw into the remaining broth and boil away. If you are not going to serve the broth soon, freeze as stock or reduce to a glaze (page 309) for sauces.

• • •

1 duck (4½ to 5½ pounds)
8 to 10 quarts Chicken, Meat, or Duck Stock (pages
110, 109, 112)
½ teaspoon kosher salt
¼ teaspoon freshly ground black pepper

Thoroughly prick the duck skin with the tines of a fork. Pour stock into a 10- to 12-quart stockpot, leaving enough room in the pot for the duck. There should be enough stock to cover the duck generously. If you use a narrow stockpot, you need less stock than with a wider pot. Bring the stock to a boil over high heat. Carefully lower the duck into the stock, neck end first, allowing the cavity to fill with stock so the duck sinks to the bottom of the pot. Place a plate or other weight on the duck to keep it submerged.

When the stock returns to the boil, reduce the heat and simmer, with pot uncovered, for 45 minutes. Since the duck will tend to float to the surface, check weight about every 10 minutes to ensure that the duck remains submerged. Keep the stock at a gentle simmer; if it boils the duck will rise to the surface.

After 30 minutes, preheat the oven to 375° F.

When the duck has finished simmering, spoon 2 to 3 table-spoons of the duck fat off the top of the stock and spread it in the bottom of a shallow roasting pan. Remove the plate and carefully lift out the duck, holding it over the pot to drain any liquid from the cavity. Reserve the stock.

Pat the duck thoroughly dry and sprinkle the skin with the salt and pepper, gently pressing them against the skin. The duck is hot and the skin is tender, so work carefully. Transfer the seasoned bird to the greased roasting pan, breast side up. Do not tuck the neck flap under the duck.

Roast for 45 minutes. Every 10 minutes, pour off the fat that accumulates in the roasting pan, and slide the duck around to pre-vent the skin from sticking to the bottom of the pan.

Remove the duck from the pan. Pour off the fat and deglaze as described on page 179 with ½ cup of the cooking liquid.

SERVES 2 TO 4

NOTE: If you are in a hurry, you can, with very little loss of quality although a loss in drama, cut the duck into quarters and then pro-ceed to poach the legs for 20 minutes and the breasts for 14 minutes. Then place, skin side up, under a preheated broiler for 6 minutes. A nice way to serve these cut sections is on a bed of coriander. The juices drip into and warm the coriander, which should be portioned out with the duck.

DUCK HASH

As I said above, I always end up with leftover duck—often those delectable oysters of meat along the backbone that are too messy to get out when you are carving the hot bird. Duck hash is an unex-pected dish and one that's festive enough for company. If you get addicted, you can always just poach the duck whole and go on from there. It has been known to happen.

• • •

3 tablespoons rendered duck fat (page 209)
2 cups chopped white cabbage (¾-inch pieces)
1 cup chopped onions (½-inch pieces)
1¾ cups cubed cooked skinned and boned duck
  meat (1-inch pieces)
3 tablespoons unsalted butter
2 tablespoons all-purpose flour
1 cup Duck Stock (page 112)
2 tablespoons celery leaves
1 tablespoon celery seed
2 teaspoons kosher salt
Freshly ground black pepper
1 cup bread crumbs

In a skillet, heat 2 tablespoons rendered duck fat. Add the cabbage and cook slowly until transparent, about 5 to 7 minutes. Do not brown. Lift the wilted cabbage to a large mixing bowl. Leave the fat in the pan.

In the same skillet, put the remaining tablespoon duck fat, and cook the onions until soft and transparent. Add to the cabbage. Add the duck meat to the bowl.

In a small pan, melt 2 tablespoons of the butter. Add the flour and cook, stirring constantly, for 5 to 7 minutes to make a light roux. Slowly stir in the stock. Mix well. Bring to a boil and lower the heat. Allow the sauce to simmer for 5 minutes. Stir in the celery leaves and set aside to cool. When cool, add to the duck mixture. Stir in the celery seed, salt, and pepper.

In a small pan, melt the remaining tablespoon of butter and remove from the heat. Stir in the bread crumbs. Set aside.

Heat the broiler until hot. In a baking pan, form a round loaf with the hash. Cover with a layer of buttered bread crumbs. Put under the broiler for 3 to 5 minutes, or until nicely brown.

SERVES 4

ROAST LEG OF LAMB

———————•———————

I make roast leg of lamb so often that I sometimes think its garlicky perfume has taken over the entire house. Variations in the deglazing liquid will provide variations in sauce. Consider bourbon and orange juice or Calvados and cream. This roast makes my life easy because I can pop it in a hot oven when my guests walk in the door. That way I know it will be done when I need it and not cold or overdone. Bordeaux is the traditional wine to serve with lamb. It does well with a good Médoc or a similar style of cabernet.

Good and trusted side dishes are the Garlic-Roasted Potatoes (page 256), Zucchini Custard (page 273), Melting Tomatoes Provençale (page 272), and Marinated, Roasted Baby Eggplants (page 269). The Navy Bean Purée (page 259) is very traditional; strong-tasting purées do very well. The possibilities are virtually endless; all you have to do is choose some with an assertive enough flavor to stand up to the lamb and something that will make an attractive contrast in color and texture.

For me, lamb must always be served rare or medium rare. Sometimes, in classes, I will find someone with a prejudice against lamb. Usually what they don't like is the smell, and they have never eaten rare lamb. Lamb fat can have a strong smell when it melts into the meat. With short, high-temperature cooking, this problem doesn't arise.

• • •

> 3 cloves garlic
> 1 short leg of lamb (see note)
> 1 teaspoon dried rosemary
> Kosher salt
> Freshly ground black pepper
> ¾ cup decent dry red wine

Preheat the oven to 500°F. Peel the garlic and cut it into slivers.

Place the lamb on a work surface. With a small sharp knife, make 1-inch-deep slits toward the center of the leg. Place a sliver of garlic and a needle of rosemary in each of the slits. Rub generous amounts of salt and pepper into the roast on all sides. Put any remaining garlic and rosemary in the bottom of a shallow roasting pan. Place the leg on them, skin side up.

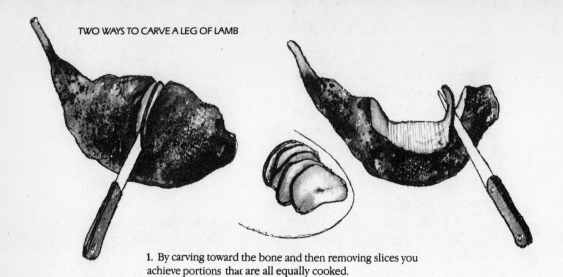

1. By carving toward the bone and then removing slices you achieve portions that are all equally cooked.

2. By carving parallel to the bone you will have better-done slices from the first cuts and rarer slices the closer you get to the bone.

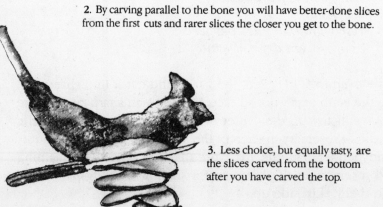

3. Less choice, but equally tasty, are the slices carved from the bottom after you have carved the top.

Place the lamb in the preheated oven and roast for 10 minutes. Lower the heat to 425°F. and roast it 35 minutes longer. Remove it to a platter. Let rest for 10 minutes, if possible, before carving.

Pour off any fat from the roasting pan. Place the pan over high heat. Pour on the wine. Holding the pan firmly with one hand, scrape it hard with a wooden spoon. Scrape and boil until all the glaze has joined the wine in a lovely, slightly reduced pan gravy. Pour over the meat or place in a sauceboat.

There are basically two ways to carve a leg of lamb. For both of them it is best to grab the shank bone with the hand that doesn't hold the knife. There used to be wonderful silver bone holders. I don't have one and tend to use a clean kitchen cloth to grab with.

Leg of lamb will vary in weight; most should serve 8 people. If I have more people to serve, I prefer to find two very small legs rather than one large one.

NOTE: A short leg of lamb is one with the "steaks" beyond the joint cut off. If your butcher insists on selling the leg as a whole, still ask him to cut the "steaks" off. An untrimmed leg weighs approximately 8 pounds; whole but trimmed, approximately 6½ pounds; and short, approximately 5¾ pounds. The steaks can be broiled for family meals, ground for patties, or cut into chunks and made into spiffy stews (see Lamb Stew with Cucumbers, page 242, and Fall Ragout of Lamb, page 241). Any time you are roasting lamb, the fell should of course be removed.

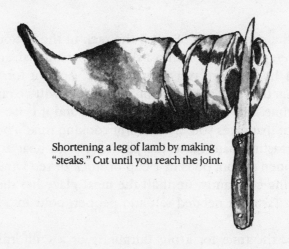

Shortening a leg of lamb by making "steaks." Cut until you reach the joint.

ROAST BEEF

———————————•———————————

Roast beef is a matter of philosophy and a good butcher rather than brilliant cooking. Start earlier than your estimate of weight or size indicates, since the amount of bone and varied configurations can change cooking time radically. Because of its mass your roast will not get cold if it waits out of the oven.

It used to be that the only cut of beef to roast was a standing rib roast, which is very difficult to roast evenly and even harder to carve properly. Then there was the steamship round, an imposing cut to be carved by a knife-wielding chef at an imposing buffet. I was relieved to find that the great Connaught Hotel cooks, as I do, a whole shell of beef, boneless and relatively even in shape for perfect, even cooking. It is expensive but there are times when it is a perfect solution to festive entertaining.

I always serve one of these at Thanksgiving along with the turkey. Many in my family find the turkey a necessary reassurance; but they really prefer to eat the beef. This is a good buffet dish if there are tables, china plates, and knives and forks. Otherwise it is too difficult to eat.

This meat is so good it doesn't require anything but a little salt and pepper or a few cloves of garlic in the bottom of the pan. The butcher will already have done all the trimming and tying.

• • •

Heat the oven to 500° F. with the rack in the bottom third. Put the room-temperature shell into a shallow roasting pan and stick it in the oven 1 hour before you want to serve. Cook it for 45 minutes, remove from the oven and place on a platter. It will be rare; anything else is a crime. The meat cooks like a steak, and it is its shape rather than weight that gives you the uniform cooking time. Pour off the fat from the roasting pan. Place the pan over high heat and, scraping with a wooden spoon, pour in 1 cup of stock or red wine. Cook like crazy, stirring constantly, until all the meat glaze has dissolved into the liquid. Taste for needed salt and pepper; pour into a sauceboat and serve.

This is the time for a big Burgundy or a California cabernet. Mashed Potatoes (page 258) or Garlic-Roasted Potatoes (page 256) and one simple green vegetable are all that are needed at dinner. At a buffet, Shrimp and Chicken Gumbo (page 144), a green salad with

Soy-Sesame Vinaigrette (page 266), a platter of cheese, a basket of individual rye rolls, and a fruit salad do it.

BEEF SALAD WITH HORSERADISH DRESSING

———————————•———————————

This is a way of using leftover roast beef if it doesn't all disappear in snatches and sandwiches. It can also be made with the leftover meat from making Meat Stock.

• • •

6 cups ¾-inch cubes roast beef (or boiled beef
  reserved from making Meat Stock, page 109)
⅓ cup finely cut chives
¾ cup drained prepared horseradish
2¼ cups Mayonnaise (page 312)
Kosher salt
Freshly ground black pepper

Place the beef and the chives in a mixing bowl.

In a separate bowl, mix the horseradish with the mayonnaise. Pour the dressing over the beef and chives, stirring to combine. Add salt and pepper to taste. Serve at room temperature.

MAKES ABOUT 6 CUPS

ROAST FRESH HAM WITH
OLIVES AND ALMONDS

———————————•———————————

Fresh ham is great food, gives delicious gravy, is inexpensive, and can be homey with Fresh Applesauce with Horseradish (recipe follows) or elegant with olives and almonds as I prepare it here. Cook it the same way but just serve the pork plain if you are going to make the applesauce.

½ fresh ham (shank end), about 9 pounds
12 cloves garlic, unpeeled

OLIVE AND ALMOND SAUCE

1¼ cups Chicken Stock (page 110)
1½ cups pitted green French olives (about 6
ounces unpitted); reserve ¼ cup of the brine
1 cup slivered blanched almonds
6 cardamom pods, bruised (see note)
2 teaspoons ground dried lemon grass or 2
tablespoons fresh (see page 126)
1 teaspoon ground cumin
3 tablespoons lemon juice
Freshly ground black pepper
Salt to taste

Heat the oven to 400° F.

With a very sharp knife or an artist's mat knife, diagonally score the skin of the ham at one-inch intervals. Cut only halfway through the fat; do not penetrate the meat. Place the garlic cloves in the center of a roasting pan. Set the ham on top of the garlic cloves.

Roast, basting with pan juices occasionally, about 3½ hours, or until the center of the thickest part of the roast reaches 165° F. Remove the roast to a carving board. Let it stand while you prepare the sauce.

OLIVE AND ALMOND SAUCE

Tilt the roasting pan so that the juices run to one corner. With a large spoon, skim off and discard the fat. Place the pan with the juices over medium heat and add the chicken stock. Bring to a boil, scraping the sides and bottom of the pan with a wooden spoon. Cook until the liquid reduces by half. Add the olives, almonds, reserved olive brine, cardamom seeds (see note) and pods, lemon grass, and cumin. Simmer 1 to 2 minutes. Add the lemon juice and a generous amount of freshly ground pepper and salt to taste.

Slice the ham thin against the grain. Arrange overlapping slices on a serving plate. Spoon a small amount of the sauce over the sliced ham. Pass the remaining sauce separately.

SERVES 8, PLUS LEFTOVERS

NOTE: Smack the cardamom pods with a large, heavy pot so that the shells crack open, releasing the seeds. Bruise the seeds by smacking them with the pot. Use both the seeds and the cracked pods.

• FRESH APPLESAUCE WITH HORSERADISH •

This is quick and good applesauce. Greenings or early acid Macs are best for this.

8 apples, peeled, cored, and cut into eighths
4 tablespoons unsalted butter
2 tablespoons water
1 scant teaspoon kosher salt
½ cup squeezed-dry white prepared horseradish

Cook the apples in a saucepan with the butter and water for about 15 to 20 minutes, or until the apples are tender. Place the mixture in a food processor and purée.

When smooth, add the salt and horseradish and stir to mix.

MAKES ABOUT 5 CUPS

ROAST LOIN OF PORK

This is my favorite economy roast. You buy it boned and rolled by the butcher. It is the kind of meat you can buy by the inch. If I have a substantial first course, I buy an inch per person—eight inches for eight people. If the first course is light, I buy an inch and a half per person—twelve inches for eight people. Ask the butcher to include the bones.

• • •

Heat the oven to 500° F. Peel 1 clove of garlic for each 2 inches of meat. Sliver lengthwise. With the point of a small knife make small incisions toward the center all around the roast. Insert the slivers of garlic. Pat lots of kosher salt, freshly ground pepper, and some

ROAST LOIN OF PORK, CONTINUED

needles of rosemary onto the roast. Put the bones in the center of a roasting pan and use as a rack for the roast. No matter what the length of the roast, leave it in the oven for 50 minutes. As long as the meat reaches an internal temperature of 140° F. at the center, don't worry if it is slightly pink. The traditional worst crime against pork is cooking it to a dry and dusty death.

You can place the bones back in the oven for 15 minutes longer to crisp them. Cut them apart and serve them with the roast, if you have the kind of guests that don't mind using their fingers, or save the bones to crisp up the following day for a private orgy.

Pour any fat from pan. Deglaze with red wine. Serve with sautéed spinach or the full-tasting Couscous Risotto (page 261).

This simple roast can be varied in any number of ways. Instead of the salt, pepper, and rosemary on the outside, the roast can be marinated in soy sauce and fresh ginger for a couple of hours, if you have the time. Then use some of the marinade to deglaze the pan. Try rubbing cracked coriander seeds, ground cumin, and salt on the outside of the roast. Deglaze the pan with a little Meat Stock (page 109).

The roast can be seasoned with Hungarian paprika and caraway. When it is removed from the pan, sauté some sliced onions and extra garlic in the roasting pan. Then deglaze with a small amount of Meat Stock. Heat some drained sauerkraut in the gravy. Off the heat, so it doesn't separate, stir in some sour cream. Check if salt and pepper are needed. Serve the sliced roast on the flavored sauerkraut.

The variations are endless and the rich flavor of the meat goes with countless vegetables, from celery root and potato purée to braised leeks.

PORK, APPLE, AND CELERY SALAD

Here is a way of serving some of the best leftover roast pork you're ever likely to have. The easiest way to destring the celery is with a potato peeler.

• • •

*4 cups sliced roast boneless loin of pork or fresh
  ham, cut into 2-by-½-by-⅛-inch strips, at room
  temperature*
*1 cup sliced celery, strings removed (cut on the
  diagonal into ¼-inch slices)*
*1 cup diced, cored, red McIntosh apples, skin on
  (½-inch dice)*
½ cup coarsely chopped walnuts
2 tablespoons lemon juice
1 to 1½ cups Mayonnaise (page 312)
2 teaspoons dried tarragon
Kosher salt
Freshly ground black pepper

In a mixing bowl, combine the pork, celery, apples, and walnuts. Sprinkle the lemon juice over the mixture and toss.

In a separate bowl, mix together the mayonnaise and tarragon. If the mayonnaise is too thick, add a little water. Pour the dressing over the salad ingredients. Mix well. Season to taste with salt and pepper. Serve at room temperature.

MAKES ABOUT 6 CUPS, ENOUGH FOR LUNCH FOR 6

VARIOUS BIRDS

Poached Chicken Breasts

Chicken Breasts with Cèpes

Chicken Breasts with Strawberries

Chicken Breasts with Pepper

Chicken Breasts with Sauce Supreme and Kumquats

Poached Chicken

Curried Chicken Salad

Chicken, Avocado, and Bacon Salad
with Blue-Cheese Dressing

Chicken Provençale

A Winter Chicken

Chicken Legs, Bell Peppers and Sausage

Cornish Hens Stuffed with Purple Grapes

Spicy Grilled Pigeon (Squab)

Duck Burgers

Duck Breasts with Transparent Noodles

Duck Breasts with Pears

------------•------------

Herewith a spate of recipes for nonroasted birds. When you are not sure of the company, birds are almost always safe. They can be light and simple or sumptuous. In the European manner, I serve red wine with my birds, but a rich white or chilled rosé works equally well—whatever's on hand. Most birds cook quickly, which is helpful. As emergency rations, I always keep some individually frozen skinned and boned chicken breasts on hand. They can be poached while still frozen in about thirteen minutes or cut up frozen and sautéed. Though they are rather bland, they can be varied, are easy to eat, and look attractive on the plate.

...

POACHED CHICKEN BREASTS

------------•------------

3 cups Chicken Stock (page 110)
1 rib celery, coarsely chopped
1 small onion, quartered
4 sprigs parsley
1 clove garlic, unpeeled
½ teaspoon kosher salt
Freshly ground black pepper
2 tablespoons dry white vermouth
4 whole chicken breasts, split, skinned, and boned,
*   fresh or frozen*
6 egg yolks
1 teaspoon fresh lemon juice
Fresh chives, snipped into 1-inch lengths

In a saucepan that will hold the chicken breasts snugly in a single layer put the chicken stock, celery, onion, parsley, garlic, salt, pepper, and vermouth. Place over moderate heat, bring to a simmer, and add the chicken breasts. Make sure they are covered by stock. Adjust the heat to maintain a bare simmer, and poach the chicken for about 7 minutes if fresh, 13 minutes if frozen.

Remove the breasts from the liquid and keep them warm. Strain the poaching liquid into a clean saucepan and boil it over high heat until it is reduced to ½ cup. Meanwhile, place the egg yolks and lemon juice in the work bowl of a food processor. With the machine on, slowly pour the boiling reduced poaching liquid into the egg yolks. Return to the saucepan.

Stir the sauce over low heat until it thickens. Pour over the breasts and garnish with the chives.

SERVES 4 TO 8

CHICKEN BREASTS WITH CEPES

———————————•———————————

This is a simple and luxurious preparation, whose ingredients, except for the spinach, can be kept on hand. (See page 189 for frozen chicken breasts.) You can serve a half breast or a whole breast per person—or compromise, as I would, and serve half breasts to 6 guests, which leaves 4 portions for second helpings.

■ ■ ■

5 whole chicken breasts (see note)
1 ounce dry cèpes (boletus, black forest
*   mushrooms, or Italian porcini mushrooms*
Chicken Stock (page 110), at room temperature
1 tablespoon unsalted butter
1 tablespoon arrowroot
½ cup milk
½ cup heavy cream
1 tablespoon kosher salt, or to taste
Freshly ground black pepper
2 dashes hot red-pepper sauce
2 pounds fresh spinach

Split the chicken breasts and remove the skin and bones. Discard the skin; freeze the bones for stock. Soak the dried mushrooms in enough chicken stock just to cover for 30 minutes, or until the mush-rooms are soft. Remove mushrooms from stock and reserve. Strain stock through moistened cloth; reserve.

Heat the butter in a 10-inch skillet. Add all the chicken, and cook, tossing it, until the breasts have seized (lost their raw look but are not brown).

Place the arrowroot in a bowl and add 2 tablespoons milk to dissolve it. When the mixture is smooth, stir in the remaining milk and the cream. (If you prefer, use 1 cup half-and-half in place of the milk and cream.) Set aside.

When the chicken has all seized, add the mushrooms and their liquid. Let simmer for 3 to 4 minutes. If your stock is unsalted, add 1 tablespoon salt. If it is salted, taste it, and add more if necessary. Also add some pepper and the hot pepper sauce.

Whisk some of the skillet liquid into the cream-milk mixture. Keep adding the liquid until the mixture is warm. Then pour the liquid over the chicken and bring to a slow boil. Let cook for about 7 minutes, or until the chicken is done.

Meanwhile, remove the stems from the spinach. Remove any dry or wilted portions. Wash in several changes of cold water until all sand is removed. Shake out and put on a towel to dry.

Place the spinach in a heavy skillet and cook, turning and toss-ing, just until it begins to wilt. It should be neither raw nor mushy. Remove it with a slotted spoon (leaving any liquid in the pan) and arrange it in a circle on the serving platter. Place the chicken in the center and pour the sauce on top. I prefer to serve the chicken just on its green bed with sauce on top, but either noodles or rice cooked in a little chicken broth, drained and turned with salt and butter, would go well.

SERVES 6

NOTE: You can use individually frozen skinned, boned and split chicken breasts for this recipe without having to thaw them. I find it's a good idea always to have frozen chicken breasts on hand.

CHICKEN BREASTS WITH STRAWBERRIES

———————— • ————————

This recipe came about when I was asked to make a dish on television that was both colorful and quick. It came out very well.

• • •

20 strawberries
2 tablespoons unsalted butter
4 whole chicken breasts, split, skinned, and boned
½ cup framboise (white raspberry brandy, not sweet)
¼ cup raspberry vinegar
3 tablespoons peeled, seeded, and chopped tomatoes
⅛ teaspoon finely chopped garlic
2 tablespoons Meat Glaze (page 309)
1 teaspoon tomato paste
¾ cup heavy cream
4 teaspoons kosher salt
Freshly ground black pepper to taste
¼ cup very thinly sliced scallion greens
8 basil leaves, washed and dried

Wash and hull the strawberries. Cut 12 into quarters and leave 8 whole for the beauty spots.

Heat the butter in a 10½-inch skillet. Add the chicken in a single layer, and cook about 2 minutes, or until the chicken is white. Turn and cook the chicken for 2 minutes longer. The chicken should have just lost its raw look.

In a small pot, heat the framboise until warm. Ignite and pour the flaming brandy over the chicken. Shake the pan gently until the flames die down. Remove the chicken to a platter and keep warm.

Deglaze the pan with the raspberry vinegar, scraping the bottom with a spoon to loosen any stuck bits. Then stir in the tomatoes, garlic, meat glaze, tomato paste, and ½ cup of the cream. Stir to blend everything together. Bring the mixture to a boil, and cook for 1 minute, or until the sauce is fairly thick. Season with salt and pepper.

Return the chicken and any liquid that has accumulated on the platter to the pan, add the cut-up strawberries and the remaining ¼ cup cream. Cook for another 2 minutes, or until the strawberries are soft and the chicken is almost cooked through. Stir in 2 tablespoons of the scallions and cook 1 minute longer.

To serve, divide the sauce among 4 heated dinner plates. Place 2 matching chicken pieces on each plate facing each other with space between. Place 2 basil leaves so they join in the center of each plate and flank by two whole strawberries. Sprinkle some scallion greens on top of each chicken piece. Serve bread but don't add anything else to the plate; it will muck up the taste and the look.

SERVES 4

CHICKEN BREASTS WITH PEPPER

This is one of those dishes for which our readily-available and inexpensive chicken breasts come into their own. It is a lighter version of a pepper steak. Even with about one tablespoon of heavy cream for each person, it is a rather unfattening dish. If you have the ingredients ready, it is a question of minutes from starting to cook to being ready to eat.

Ask the butcher to skin and bone the chicken breasts for you and give you the bones to freeze for stock. Do not buy already cracked peppercorns (they tend to be acrid). Instead, place a small handful of peppercorns on a dish towel on top of a sturdy table. Cover them with the towel so they do not fly all over the room when you proceed to whack them with the bottom of a heavy pot. Fabulous for aggressions. If you do not keep chicken glaze, or, alternatively, meat glaze, on hand, you can find frozen varieties in the stores. If you omit the glaze altogether, you might consider a teaspoon of tomato paste in its place to round the sauce.

This simple dish can take an elegant wine—a good chardonnay or, if it were I, a cabernet with some age. Unless you want to double the portions, you will need a first course like the Smoked Whitefish Mousse (page 43) and an unexpected non-creamy dessert, like the Maple-Syrup–Baked Rome Beauties (page 284).

• • •

CHICKEN BREASTS WITH PEPPER, CONTINUED

2 whole chicken breasts, split, skinned, and boned
½ to ¾ teaspoon cracked black peppercorns
1 tablespoon vegetable oil
Kosher salt
1 tablespoon brandy
⅓ cup Chicken Stock (page 110)
1 tablespoon Chicken Glaze (page 309)
3 to 4 tablespoons heavy cream
¼ to ½ teaspoon fresh lemon juice

Sprinkle both sides of the chicken breasts with the pepper, pressing it gently into the meat.

Heat the oil in a medium-size skillet. Sprinkle ⅛ teaspoon of salt over the oil. When the salt begins to brown, add the chicken and cook 2 minutes. Turn and cook another 2 minutes, or until the meat gives only slightly under the pressure of your finger.

Briefly warm the brandy over low heat. Ignite and pour it, still flaming, over the chicken. Shake the pan until the flames die down. Remove the chicken to a plate. Deglaze the pan with the stock, glaze, and cream, cooking just until the sauce is slightly thickened. Add lemon juice and more salt to taste. Return the chicken to the pan, turning it in the sauce to warm.

Slice the breasts on the bias and serve them with the sauce.

SERVES 4

CHICKEN BREASTS WITH SAUCE SUPREME AND KUMQUATS

It is slightly ironic that two of my recipes that I consider most inventive combine flesh and fruit, a combination that I ordinarily loathe. It only goes to show . . . Not only is this sauce the most beautiful pale tangerine in color, but the aromatic slight bitterness of kumquats and tangerines is a surprising balance to the cream. There is a precedent for this recipe, unthought of at the time I concocted it. The Swiss scrape the very bitter white pith from the inside of the tangerine rind, cut the rind into strips, and dry it. At this point it keeps almost indefinitely without refrigeration. They drop one or more strips—it is a strong taste—into their stews for a regional flavor.

This is not a quick and easy recipe but it is very festive. I have used chicken breasts because they look very spiffy on the plate; but I originally made it with chicken on the bone and cut up into sections. If you try it that way, cook the chicken for forty minutes after you add it to the sauce instead of the fifteen minutes for the breasts.

• • •

> 9 whole chicken breasts, split, skinned, and boned,
>   bones reserved
> 6 cups Chicken Stock (page 110) or water
> 5 tangerines
> 1 pound unsalted butter
> ½ cup finely chopped onions
> ½ cup finely chopped Italian flat-leaf parsley
> 1 cup finely chopped carrots
> 1 cup finely chopped celery
> 2 large cloves garlic, peeled and finely chopped
> 2 large shallots, finely chopped
> ½ cup (¼ pound) finely chopped mushrooms
> ½ cup all-purpose flour
> 1 tablespoon tomato paste
> 2 teaspoons ground cayenne pepper
> Kosher salt
> ¾ pound kumquats, sliced ⅛ inch thick
> 1 cup heavy cream
> 1 tablespoon fresh lemon juice

In a stockpot, put the bones from the chicken breasts. Cover with the chicken stock or water. Bring to a boil and lower the heat to a simmer. Cook for 4 or 5 hours, skimming off the scum and fat. If you are using water, you can let it simmer overnight. Strain and discard the bones. You will need 3 cups for this recipe.

Peel the tangerines. With a sharp knife, scrape the bitter white part off the rind and discard. Cut the rind into long strips ⅛ inch wide. The rinds of 3 tangerines should be enough. Put the strips on a rack in a very low—180° F.—oven until they are completely dry. They should crumble between your fingers. Once they are dried, crumble the tangerine rinds; they can be kept in a closed jar for weeks. For this recipe you will need 1 tablespoon crumbled rind.

Squeeze the peeled tangerines with your hands over a sieve so the sieve catches the pits and membranes. You will need 1 cup juice.

In a skillet, melt ½ pound of the butter. Add the onions, parsley, carrots, celery, garlic, and shallots. Cook slowly for 15 to 20 minutes. Add the mushrooms and continue cooking slowly for another 10 minutes. When everything is soft, add the flour and stir well with a wooden spoon, scraping the bottom and sides of the pan. Cook, stirring, for at least 10 minutes so the flour is cooked through.

Add the tomato paste and mix well, then season with the cayenne pepper and 1 teaspoon salt. When well blended, add 3 cups chicken stock. Mix well and cook over low heat for another 30 minutes.

Meanwhile, in another pan, melt ¼ pound of the butter. Add the kumquats and cook over low heat until they start to form a glaze. Add ¾ cup tangerine juice, and let it simmer gently for 5 minutes. Set aside.

Put the vegetable mixture through a very fine sieve, pressing firmly against the vegetables with the back of a spoon to release all the liquid. Discard the solids. Put the sauce in a large flameproof casserole and bring to a gentle simmer. Add the cooked kumquats, heavy cream, lemon juice, and dried tangerine rind. Continue cooking gently for a few minutes.

Separate the thin fillet from the main part of the breast, remove the tendon, and cut the main part of the breast in half, lengthwise. Cut away any fat.

In a skillet, melt the remaining ¼ pound of butter over low heat. Add the chicken in batches and cook until white on all sides. Do not let it brown. As each batch is done, remove it to a plate. When all the chicken is white, add it to the sauce with any liquid that has exuded and any butter still in the pan. Cook very gently for another 15 minutes. You can prepare this a few hours before serving. Reheat over very low heat. Just before serving, stir in the remaining ¼ cup tangerine juice to enhance the flavor, and add salt to taste. I usually serve a little steamed rice in a ring around each serving—no vegetable, but a salad afterward.

SERVES 10 TO 12

POACHED CHICKEN

This is that basic chicken in the pot that Henri IV wanted to assure his subjects. It can be simple or elegant; but it is always good. It can be served with a little broth and individual dishes of kosher salt. You can add one or more sauces: Mayonnaise (page 312), Aïoli (page

136), Basil Sauce (page 224), a spicy tomato sauce, or Everyday Vinaigrette (page 316) enriched with chopped fresh parsley, a chopped hard-boiled egg, a few chopped capers and, possibly, chopped dill. Leftover chicken can be cubed and added with any leftover vegetables to the remaining sauce to eat cold the following day, or can simply be put, cut with the vegetables, into some of the broth with blanched broad egg noodles for tomorrow's soup. The real issue is not to refrigerate the chicken without a protective covering of sauce or liquid, or it will toughen irretrievably.

When choosing the vegetables, think of the balance of flavors as well as the balance of colors and shapes. I serve a light red wine, anything from a chilled Beaujolais to a Chianti.

The marvelous dividend is the doubly rich stock.

• • •

1 truffle (optional)
1 four- to five-pound chicken
Vegetable oil
14 cups Chicken Stock (page 110)

VEGETABLES
(USE 3 OR MORE, 1 SCANT CUP EACH)

Turnips, peeled and trimmed
Peas, shelled
Whole baby carrots, peeled and trimmed
Very tiny new potatoes (if red, remove a thin band
    of peel from around the middle)
Zucchini, trimmed and cut into ½-inch rounds
Broccoli, cut into flowerets (no stems)
Cauliflower, cut into flowerets (no stems)
Radishes, trimmed
Very young whole green beans, trimmed
Whole thin scallions, trimmed
Pearl or small white onions, peeled and trimmed
Mushroom caps
Thin asparagus, woody ends removed
Small Italian artichokes, halved, chokes removed

• • •

Lemon juice

Slice the truffle. Slide your hands under the chicken skin and slip in the truffle slices evenly between the skin and breast meat of the chicken.

Open up a 2-yard length of cheesecloth and fold it in half lengthwise. Oil it so the chicken will not stick to it. Place the chicken on the cheesecloth so its length goes along the length of the cheesecloth. Bring up the two long sides of the cheesecloth, pull them together, so they meet, then roll them down until the cheesecloth is taut around the chicken. Tie the cheesecloth at either end as close to the chicken as you can. This way, you won't have to truss it. Tie the cheesecloth again just before the ends so they don't unravel (drawing 1).

In a large stockpot with handles, bring the chicken stock to a boil. Lower the heat to a simmer and slowly, holding both ends of the cheesecloth, lower the chicken into the simmering stock (drawing 2). If possible, tie the ends of the cheesecloth to the pot handles for easy removal when cooked. Let the chicken simmer 30 to 40 minutes.

VEGETABLES

Cook the vegetables separately in plenty of boiling salted water until just tender. For mushrooms and artichokes, add some lemon juice to the water.

Gently lift the chicken from the stockpot. Peel off the cheesecloth and transfer the chicken to a platter. Serve the poached chicken hot, surrounded by cooked vegetables.

SERVES 4

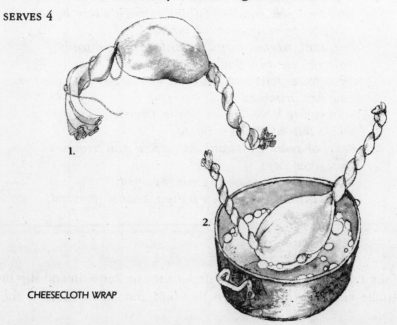

CHEESECLOTH WRAP

CURRIED CHICKEN SALAD

———————•———————

The curry has to be cooked before it is added to the mayonnaise or the flavor won't develop and it will taste raw. Chutney can be served on the side. Walnuts or grapes can be mixed in. A good summer meal. Try making a Cucumber Pachadi (page 267) to serve on the side instead of a salad to follow.

•••

2 tablespoons olive oil
1 tablespoon curry powder
¼ cup Chicken Stock (page 110)
3 drops hot red-pepper sauce
About 3 cups Mayonnaise (page 312)
6 cups cubed cooked chicken, ½-inch cubes
1½ cups celery, cut into ¼-inch-thick slices
6 tablespoons finely chopped onion
6 tablespoons chopped coriander leaves
3 cups iceberg lettuce, cut in chiffonade
3 cups sorrel leaves, cut in chiffonade (see Cream
    of Sorrel Soup, page 118)

Heat the olive oil in a small pan. Add the curry powder and cook for about 2 minutes, or until it is well browned. Add the chicken stock and cook 1 minute. Let the mixture cool.

Add the curry mixture and hot pepper sauce to the mayonnaise. Put the chicken, celery, onion, and coriander in a bowl. Add just enough mayonnaise to bind.

Mix the lettuce and sorrel together. Put the chicken salad in the center of a platter and surround with a wreath of lettuce and sorrel.

SERVES 6

CHICKEN, AVOCADO, AND BACON SALAD WITH BLUE-CHEESE DRESSING

———————•———————

It may be that this recipe doesn't even belong in this book, as I almost never entertain at lunch and this salad really is neither a first course nor a dinner main course. It is so good and uses any leftovers from the poached chicken so nicely that I couldn't resist. It is a knock-off of a fabulous salad that the Plaza Hotel in New York used to make for lunch. I tried to get it right for quite some time and now I think I have it. Serve with the pale inside leaves of romaine arranged like flower petals underneath. Iced tea with lots of lemon is the right drink.

• • •

1 cup Mayonnaise (page 312)—commercial is fine
    if it has no sweetener
½ cup sour cream
6 tablespoons chicken stock
2½ tablespoons blue cheese, in small chunks
Freshly ground black pepper
¼ cup fresh lemon juice
4 cups poached chicken meat, still warm, cut into
    approximately 1½-inch pieces
2 cups diced peeled avocado
½ teaspoon kosher salt
1 head romaine lettuce, torn into 2-inch pieces
8 strips bacon, cooked until crisp, broken into
    1-inch pieces

Put the mayonnaise, sour cream, stock, blue cheese, pepper, and half the lemon juice in a bowl. Mix well.

Toss the chicken and avocado lightly with the salt and the remaining lemon juice. Arrange the romaine in 4 salad bowls. Divide the chicken mixture evenly among the bowls. Sprinkle the bacon pieces on top. Serve with the blue-cheese dressing.

SERVES 4

CHICKEN PROVENÇALE

When I first started in the kitchen, it was the heyday of Dione Lucas, who was a remarkable cook. After reading her *Cordon Bleu Cook Book,* I gradually came to realize that almost all of her recipes for savory dishes contained tomato paste, meat glaze, and bay leaf—to me, at that time, exotic ingredients. Then I read *The Joy of Cooking* and James Beard's *Fireside Cookbook*. In that brilliant book, he treats cooking as a series of base recipes with the potential for almost endless variation. I discovered that recipes for the same dish could incorporate different ingredients and different approaches; that cooks have personal styles as clearly marked as architects'.

My copy of Elizabeth David's *A Book of Mediterranean Food* is a yellowed Penguin that came out in 1955. It was she who introduced me to the regionality of food and the joys of olives and a plenitude of garlic.

This recipe—made as I cooked then, stealing, like a magpie, a bit here and a bit there to build my nest—is my awkward tribute. Use and serve a rather strong, coarse red wine such as a Cahors.

• • •

1 tablespoon unsalted butter
1 tablespoon vegetable oil
1 two-and-a-half-pound chicken, cut into serving
    pieces
1 tablespoon all-purpose flour
⅓ to ½ cup dry red wine
½ to 1 cup Chicken Stock (page 110)
2 cloves garlic, unpeeled
1 sprig fresh thyme or oregano, or ¼ teaspoon dried
    thyme or oregano soaked in chicken stock
2 medium tomatoes, peeled, seeded, and cut into
    ½-inch cubes
1 teaspoon tomato paste
1 bay leaf
1 strip lemon zest
1 strip orange zest
Kosher salt
Freshly ground black pepper
1 teaspoon fresh lemon juice
⅓ cup Nice olives
A large handful of finely chopped parsley

In a large sauté pan, heat the butter and oil until hot. Add the chicken pieces, skin side down. Cook until golden brown on the bottom. Turn the pieces over and cook until golden brown on the other side. Remove the chicken from the pan and set it aside.

Discard all but 1 tablespoon of the fat. Stir in the flour and cook over moderate heat for 1 to 2 minutes. Add ⅓ cup wine and ½ cup stock to the pan and deglaze, scraping the bottom with a wooden spoon. Add the garlic, thyme or oregano, cubed tomatoes, tomato paste, bay leaf, and zests. Stir until roughly blended.

Return the chicken to the pan and partially cover it. Cook for 15 to 20 minutes, or until the chicken juices run clear when chicken is pricked with a knife. If the sauce seems too thick, add the remaining wine and stock. Taste the sauce and add salt and pepper to taste. Add the lemon juice and olives, and cook for 5 more minutes with the pan partially covered. Remove the bay leaf. Sprinkle with parsley. Serve from the hot cooking pot (copper, if possible) with a generous ladle. A few steamed potatoes would not come amiss.

SERVES 4

A WINTER CHICKEN

This is really a fricassee (creamed chicken with the bone in) with some available-in-winter vegetables concealed in ivory splendor in the ivory sauce. Unusual and very good. If you prefer to serve white wine with your chicken, then this is the recipe. A dry Alsatian riesling would be perfection. The Alsations love cream with their chicken too. Taking another hint from them, if you insist on a starch, use buttered broad noodles. The dish is not quite as rich as it sounds. I omitted egg yolks and/or flour to give a lighter sauce.

• • •

4 tablespoons unsalted butter
1 three-and-a-half-pound chicken, cut into quarters
1½ cups cut fennel (¼-inch matchsticks)
1½ cups cut celery root (¼-inch matchsticks)
1½ cups cut endive (¼-inch crosswise strips)
1 medium onion, halved, sliced crosswise into ¼-inch slices
2 teaspoons kosher salt
1½ cups Chicken Stock (page 110)
1 cup heavy cream

Heat the butter in a 10-inch skillet. Add the chicken, bone side down, and cook just until the meat turns white; do not brown. Turn and cook on other side until flesh is white.

Add the vegetables, pushing them into the spaces between the chicken pieces. Add the salt, stock, and cream. Bring the liquid to a boil, then lower the heat so it simmers. Cover and cook for 40 minutes, or until the chicken is done. Turn the chicken pieces over every 10 minutes as they cook.

Serve with rice or noodles.

SERVES 4

CHICKEN LEGS, BELL PEPPERS AND SAUSAGE

This book has many recipes for chicken breasts. Sometimes, I just buy breasts. Often, I buy whole chickens and use the breasts for one purpose and the various other parts for soup, chicken livers, whatever. When I need a recipe for the second joints and legs, this Italian classic is simple and good.

▪ ▪ ▪

8 whole legs and thighs (from 4 chickens)
Flour seasoned with salt and pepper
¼ cup vegetable oil
16 sweet Italian sausages, halved crosswise
8 cloves garlic, smashed and peeled
2 onions, peeled and thinly sliced
4 red bell peppers, stems removed, cut into 2-inch strips
4 green bell peppers, stems removed, cut into 2-inch strips
Scant ¼ teaspoon red pepper flakes
2 cups dry white wine
4 cups chicken stock
2 teaspoons crushed dried rosemary
¼ cup fresh lemon juice
Kosher salt
¼ cup chopped parsley

Separate legs from thighs. Cut each thigh into two equal pieces. In a bag, shake chicken pieces with flour until lightly coated. Heat oil in

CHICKEN LEGS, BELL PEPPERS, AND SAUSAGE, CONTINUED

a large skillet. Brown the chicken pieces in two batches. Remove to a plate.

Add the sausage pieces to the skillet and cook until well browned. Reserve sausage with chicken.

Reduce heat in skillet. Add garlic, onions, bell peppers, and pepper flakes. Cover the skillet and cook ingredients without browning until soft—about 5 minutes. Add wine, stock and rosemary to skillet. Skim off surface fat.

Add reserved chicken and sausage to pan. Simmer uncovered for 25 minutes.

Remove vegetables, chicken and sausage and reserve. Degrease the liquids in the skillet. Boil them to reduce by half. The dish can be made ahead to this point. Before serving, reheat the sauce to a simmer. Add lemon juice and reserved meats and vegetables. Simmer until chicken is warm, about 3 minutes. Taste the sauce and add salt if necessary. Stir in parsley and serve.

SERVES 8

CORNISH HENS STUFFED WITH
PURPLE GRAPES

Cornish hens are a particularly American development, giving individual portions and plump breasty birds. Here, stuffed with purple grapes, they have a delicate flavor and an astonishing, gently lavender sauce.

The sauce is bound by the blood-rich puréed livers which coagulate when heated and thicken the sauce. The thing you have to be careful about is the temperature—hot enough to coagulate the blood but not so hot that it separates into nasty, gritty bits as egg yolk also can. The existence of the food processor makes it all easy by puréeing the livers and amalgamating the boiling liquid into them rapidly and safely. If you have some sauce left over, put it in little crocks and it will set up into creamy terrines. You can do the same thing on purpose by using livers, butter, and some stock in the same ratio.

• • •

4 Cornish hens, each weighing about 1 pound
¾ pound unsalted butter, melted
4 to 5 cups purple grapes, halved, seeds removed
Seeds from 2 cardamom pods, crushed
1 tablespoon fresh lemon juice
1 teaspoon kosher salt
Freshly ground black pepper

Heat the oven to 375°F.

Remove the bags of innards from the hens. Trim the livers and set them aside. If desired, reserve the gizzards for another use.

Place the hens, breast up, in a baking pan just large enough to hold them tightly side by side. Pour the melted butter over the birds and place them in the oven. Spoon the butter over the birds to baste every 5 to 10 minutes.

After 30 minutes, remove the pan from the oven. Pack the grapes tightly into the hens' cavities. Sprinkle the remaining grapes (about 2½ cups) over the birds. Return the pan to the oven and cook another 15 minutes, basting again with the butter every 5 to 10 minutes. The hens should be nicely browned. Remove them from the oven and put them on a serving platter. Cover and keep warm.

Place the livers in the work bowl of a food processor. Turn the machine on and let it run for a full minute. Add the cardamom seeds. With the machine running, pour the hot pan liquids, including the extra cooked grapes, through the feed tube. Keep the machine running for 2 minutes after everything is added. Season to taste with lemon juice, salt and pepper. The livers will cook and the sauce thicken.

Serve the birds with the liver sauce and an elegant wine such as a petit sirah or a zinfandel.

SERVES 4 TO 8

SPICY GRILLED PIGEON (SQUAB)

———————— • ————————

Some ideas are so good it is even worth stealing from oneself. This dish is intimately related to the Cayenne Quail on a Coriander Nest (page 76). It is also related to chicken tabaka from Georgia in the USSR and chicken mattone from Italy. In the Italian version, there is a special weight, traditionally terracotta, that is placed on the flattened bird as it cooks so that it comes to table like a thick, crisp pancake. As weights, lacking enough mattones, I have used aluminum-foil-covered weights from a bar bell or saucepans with two cans inside. If you want to make this dish, inspiration will come to you. The flatness is not simply a visual element; it also insures even cooking and crisp skin while the meat remains juicy.

Again it is not a dish for friends who are picky eaters. Grits (page 262) or Gorgonzola Polenta (page 263) would do well with this. You may serve green salad or asparagus someplace in the meal.

• • •

4 half-pound pigeons (weighed with innards)
1 cup olive oil
4 teaspoons fresh lemon juice
2 tablespoons cayenne pepper

Heat a grill or broiler until hot.

Cut out the pigeons' backbones. Cut off the wing tips and leg tips. Wing tips, backbones, leg tips, and giblets can be added to chicken stock garnerings. They can also be turned into a small soup of their own with some dried wild mushrooms and barley. Open the birds out on a steady table. Take the palm of your hand or the bottom of a heavy pot and bring it down sharply on the breastbone to break it so that the birds lie flat.

Combine the oil, lemon juice, and pepper. Spread the mixture over the birds to coat evenly. Leave on a plate to marinate for at least 30 minutes.

Place the birds on the hot grill, skin side up, for 5 minutes. Turn them over with tongs and cook 1 minute. Weight the birds and cook another 4 minutes (for a total of 5 minutes on that side). This can be done in a very heavy well-seasoned skillet.

If using a broiler—a third best since you can't weight the birds—begin cooking with the skin side down, then turn after 5 minutes and cook 5 minutes on the other side.

SERVES 4

...

DUCK

Duck is one of those strange foods that people are delighted to eat in restaurants and afraid to make at home, which is really silly. Look at the procedure for roasting on pages 173–175. It relieves you of the problem of dealing with lots of hot fat in the oven. If you work with cut-up birds, you can roast only the legs and save the breasts for another use. One of the benefits of the nouvelle cuisine and of an awakened interest in the cooking of Southwest France (of which Paula Wolfert is the doyenne) has been the cooking of duck breasts on their boned own. They come to the table pink inside, browned outside, and with just a hint of pearly fat under the skin. Sliced on the diagonal, they are ravishing with a variety of sauces.

Ducks divided yield more dividends than ducks entire. From four ducks, you can get six full portions of breast, even eight if your guests are modest eaters. You can have four dinners of grilled thighs. You can make Duck Burgers (page 210) for a few from the leg meat. You have enough carcasses for lots of rich, delicious stock. With the giblets, you can make for four a dinner of Dirty Rice (page 246), and you still have the livers to sauté with garlic, salt, and pepper, deglazing with a touch of Madeira, and to serve on croutons as a first course for four.

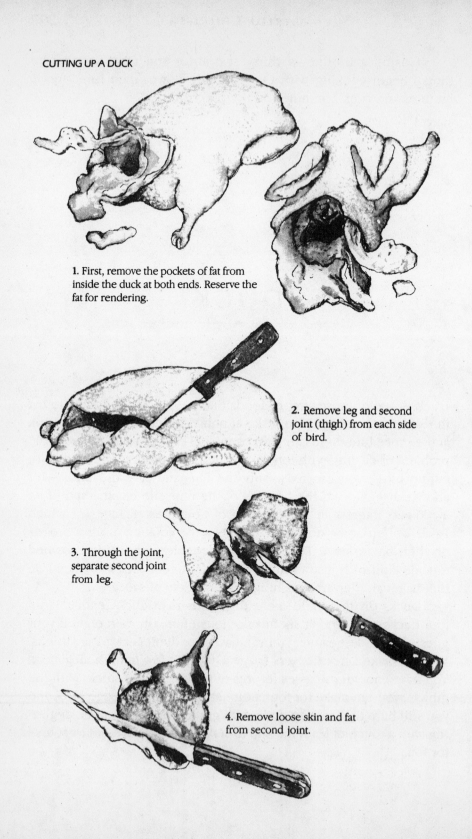

1. First, remove the pockets of fat from inside the duck at both ends. Reserve the fat for rendering.

2. Remove leg and second joint (thigh) from each side of bird.

3. Through the joint, separate second joint from leg.

4. Remove loose skin and fat from second joint.

I haven't even mentioned the guilty, fattening delight of cracklings that can be made with the duck skin if you are cooking skinned birds. Cut the skin in long quarter-inch-wide strips. Put them in a heavy pot with the fat from the ducks, cut in chunks, and a little bit of water. As the fat renders, the skin will turn crisp and golden. Remove it with a skimmer to paper toweling. Sprinkle with kosher salt and eat as hot as you can tolerate. If the cracklings don't disappear immediately, you can store them in a closed jar in the refrigerator and then reheat as the better olive to serve with drinks. Place the cracklings on paper toweling on a baking sheet. Place in a 350° F. oven. Take them out as soon as they are hot; salt and eat.

That leaves only the fat; but what a golden treasure. It is only second to goose fat as a prize. Fry potatoes in it. Sauté eggs in it. Read Paula Wolfert's *The Cooking of South-West France* and feel prepared.

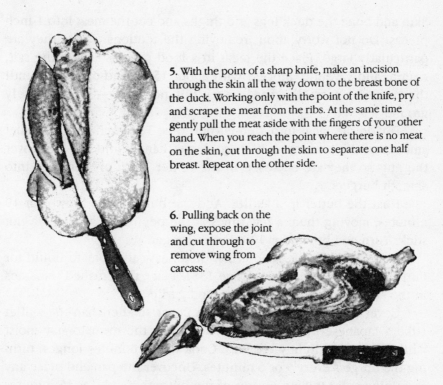

5. With the point of a sharp knife, make an incision through the skin all the way down to the breast bone of the duck. Working only with the point of the knife, pry and scrape the meat from the ribs. At the same time gently pull the meat aside with the fingers of your other hand. When you reach the point where there is no meat on the skin, cut through the skin to separate one half breast. Repeat on the other side.

6. Pulling back on the wing, expose the joint and cut through to remove wing from carcass.

7. Any extra skin should be removed from the carcass. It, along with the skin from the breasts if you are removing it, can be fried for crackling. The stripped carcass can now be cut up for stock (see page 112). Duck is carved in the same way that it is cut up.

DUCK BURGERS

Of all the parts of the duck, the legs are the hardest to use on their own. Here is an excellent and informal recipe. Sometimes I vary it by stirring a little sour cream into the sauce at the last minute.

• • •

Legs and thighs of 4 ducks
1 teaspoon kosher salt
¼ teaspoon ground cumin
Pinch cayenne pepper
1 tablespoon pine nuts
1 teaspoon unsalted butter
1 thirty-five-ounce can plum tomatoes
12 large basil leaves
4 cloves garlic, peeled and smashed

Skin and bone the duck legs and thighs and cut the meat into 1-inch pieces. Do not worry about removing the tendons unless they are particularly large. Place the meat in a food processor with the salt, cumin, and cayenne. Process with about 15 on-and-off pulses until the meat is in small, even pieces but not pasty—as if coarsely ground.

Divide the meat into 4 equal portions. Top each with an equal amount of the pine nuts. With cool, wet hands, fold the meat over the nuts so they are enclosed in the center. Turn over and pat into smooth burgers.

Heat the butter in a skillet. Add the burgers and brown for 10 minutes, moving them a few times at the beginning so they do not stick. Turn and brown for 10 minutes longer.

Drain the tomatoes and crush them. Save the tomato liquid for Full-Flavored Tomato Soup (page 133). Place the crushed tomatoes in the skillet with the basil leaves and garlic.

Cover the pan, preferably with a cover smaller than the skillet (like a Japanese otoshi-buta). This permits the meat to stay moist while the sauce slightly reduces. Cook for 30 minutes longer, turning the burgers every 5 or 6 minutes. Uncover the pan and place any remaining solid tomato on top of the burgers. Cook for 15 minutes more so the liquid reduces and thickens.

Serve with the hot sauce and Mashed Potatoes (page 258). If

there are any leftovers, they can go in the Full-Flavored Tomato Soup
with the juice from the tomatoes.

SERVES 2 TO 4

DUCK BREASTS WITH
TRANSPARENT NOODLES

———————————•———————————

Previously, I said that the breasts from four ducks would make dinner for six, but here is a perfectly enchanting recipe that gets a light,
cool main course for six or a first course for ten out of only one
whole duck breast. As with most such economies a little more work
is needed; but not too much.

• • •

*1 quart Duck Stock (page 112; use chicken stock if
  duck is not available)*
1 whole breast of duck, skinned and boned
1 head Chinese cabbage
¼ cup vegetable oil
2 tablespoons chopped garlic
*2 tablespoons shredded ginger (½-inch-long, ⅛-
  inch-thick pieces)*
*12 snow peas, cut into long shreds about $\frac{1}{16}$ inch
  wide*
*2⅔ cups soaked transparent noodles (soaked in
  water to cover for 20 to 30 minutes and drained
  thoroughly)*
2 tablespoons soy sauce
10 to 12 drops hot red-pepper sauce
⅔ cup slivered scallions (white and green parts)
1 cup whole coriander leaves, well washed
1 teaspoon kosher salt

In a saucepan, bring the duck stock to a boil. Add the duck breast
and reduce the heat to a low simmer. Cook for 3 minutes, then remove the duck. Reserve ½ cup stock for later. Reserve the remaining
stock for another recipe.

Cut each half duck breast lengthwise into slices ⅛ inch wide. Turn each slice on its side and cut it lengthwise into 2 or 3 pieces, each ⅛ inch wide. Cut the cabbage crosswise into slices ⅛ inch thick—you will need 6 cups for this recipe—and set aside.

Divide all your ingredients, except the cabbage and salt, in half so you can work in batches.

Coat the inside of a wok with 2 tablespoons oil. Set the pan over medium heat. When the oil is hot, add 1½ cups sliced cabbage. Toss with chopsticks and cook for 90 seconds, until the cabbage begins to wilt. Add half the garlic and ginger. Toss for another minute, then add half the snow peas. Cook, tossing, 30 to 45 seconds longer.

Add half the noodles and mix well. Then add half the soy and hot-pepper sauces and stir to spread them evenly throughout. Add half the scallions and coriander leaves, then half the duck. Stir in ¼ cup reserved duck stock and toss for another minute.

Dump the mixture into a bowl and repeat for remaining ingredients, reserving 3 cups cabbage. Mix both batches together and add the salt. Mix well. Let everything sit for 10 minutes or more so the flavor develops.

Arrange the reserved raw cabbage in a ring on each of 6 salad plates. Put an equal portion of the duck-noodle mixture in the center of each.

SERVES 6

DUCK BREASTS WITH PEARS

·

This is the other side of the coin—the marvelous, festive dish that uses the duck breasts of the birds that you've so carefully separated into pieces (see Duck Hash, page 175, and Duck Burgers, page 210). Duck is traditionally served with a fruit sauce, but it should have some sharpness to it. Duckling à l'Orange is meant to be made with bitter oranges (Seville oranges). Duckling Montmorency is made properly with Montmorency cherries which are sour cherries. In this recipe the sharpness is provided by vinegar. Serve on a colorful plate to set off the paleness of the pears.

• • •

3 large unripe pears
1 cup scallions, diagonally sliced
1 tablespoon kosher salt
½ teaspoon freshly ground black pepper
Juice of ½ lemon
2 whole duck breasts, split, boned, wings removed,
*   skin left on*
3 tablespoons pear brandy, clear and not sweet

PEAR SAUCE

1 cup Duck Stock (page 112)
2 tablespoons Duck Glaze (page 309)
5 of the reserved pear halves
2 tablespoons red wine vinegar
2 teaspoons kosher salt
Generous amount freshly ground black pepper
¼ pound unsalted butter, cut into bits
½ cup scallions, diagonally sliced

Peel, halve, and core the pears. Place the peelings and cores in the bottom of an 8-inch-square pan. Toss together with the scallions, salt, and pepper. Rub the pears with the lemon juice. Place 5 halves in a bowl, cover with plastic, and refrigerate for the sauce. Eat the remaining half. Toss the duck breasts with the peelings. Place skin side down in the pan. Cover and refrigerate overnight.

Remove the duck breasts from the refrigerator. Add the brandy to the marinade. Let the ducks reach room temperature before continuing.

PEAR SAUCE

While you are waiting for the duck breasts to come to room temperature, make the sauce. In a medium saucepan, bring the duck stock and glaze to a boil. Slice the pears and add to the stock. Cover, and cook the pears 1 to 2 minutes, or until cooked through. With a slotted spoon, remove the pears to a bowl.

Boil down the uncovered stock-glaze mixture until ½ cup remains. From time to time, pour any liquid that exudes from the pears back into the pan of reducing liquid. Add the vinegar, salt, and pepper. Gradually beat in the butter, bit by bit, until the sauce is smooth. Return the pear slices to the pan and add the scallions. Let the sauce sit off the heat while you are grilling the duck breasts.

Heat a grill or a broiler. Remove the breasts from the marinade and pat dry. Score the skin side of each piece several times. Grill or broil 5 to 6 minutes on the skin side and 1½ to 2 minutes on the flesh side, grilling about 5 inches from the heat source. Slice at an exaggerated angle.

Serve with the sauce.

SERVES 4

MORE
MAIN COURSES

·—————•—————·

· LIGHT MAIN COURSES ·

Lobster and Chicken Liver Salad

Niçoise Salad

Pot Cheese and Vegetable Salad

Corn and Feta Cheese Omelet

· OTHER MAIN COURSES ·

Beef and Asparagus Sauté

Poached Filet of Beef with Basil Sauce

Black Pepper Steak

Beef Thulier

All-Day Beef Stew

Beef Bourguignon

Short Ribs of Beef

Grilled Mustard Rabbit

Ossobucco

Braised Breast of Veal with Spinach-Mushroom Stuffing

Veal and Artichoke-Heart Stew

Barbecued Leg of Lamb

Lamb Navarin

Fall Ragout of Lamb

Lamb Stew with Cucumbers

Lamb Kidneys with Applejack and Horseradish

Veal Kidneys with Mustard Sauce

Dirty Rice

Sauté of Chicken Livers with Okra

Venison Stew

Here are some more main-course recipes. There are other main courses in the sections on Roast Meats, Of Fish and Seafood, Pasta, and Soups. You'll even find recipes in the two chapters on first courses that happily make a meal.

Some of the recipes in this chapter are made rapidly, but many require time and attention. Lots are stews because I enjoy their full flavors and their informality, and cooking them is not a persnickety business—a bit less of this or a bit more of that will not be a hysterical differential.

...

LIGHT MAIN COURSES

Every once in a while—an elegant lunch, a hot summer's day—I need a main course light as dandelion silk and still evidencing culinary care. The light main courses that follow suit the occasion.

LOBSTER AND CHICKEN LIVER SALAD

The sauce for this salad is truly wonderful. As the recipe is written, you use the roe and scrapings from only one lobster and have enough sauce to serve six generously. However, with the same effort, you can double the ingredients and make extra sauce, delicious with grilled birds. I have served it with great success with pigeon and quail. It is also good with poached fish or mixed with leftover fish in a rice salad. The lobster sauce will keep for a week in the refrigerator. The combination of lobster and liver may sound nutty but is very good.

...

2 one-and-a-half-pound female lobsters
3 large egg yolks
⅔ cup plus ¼ cup olive oil
4 teaspoons fresh lemon juice
¼ teaspoon hot red-pepper sauce
¼ teaspoon ground cumin
½ pound chicken livers
30 spinach leaves, trimmed, washed, and dried

Begin your preparations several hours ahead so the taste of the sauce has time to develop.

Bring a large pot of water to a boil. Add the lobsters and boil for 10 minutes. Turn off the heat and let the lobsters cool in the water. Be sure to reserve the water.

Take one lobster out and, holding it over a bowl, break it in two where the tail meets the body. Let all the liquid from the lobster go into the bowl. With scissors, cut the soft part of the tail shell down its middle and pull out the tail meat in one piece. Set aside. Scrape into the bowl all the bits of lobster remaining on the shell.

Break off the claws and carefully crack the shells and remove the meat. Reserve the two main claw pieces (one large, one small) with the tail meat. Add the meat in the small joints to the bowl. Scrape the inside of the body-shell and the roe into the bowl as well. Set aside.

Of the second lobster you need only the tail and claw meat (unless you wish to double the amount of sauce). The carcasses can be used for lobster butter (page 146).

Place in a pot 2 cups of the water in which the lobsters were cooked. Bring to a boil and cook until reduced to ⅓ cup.

Put the egg yolks in the work bowl of a food processor, and process for 90 seconds. With the machine still running, slowly pour in the ⅔ cup oil, drop by drop, as if making a mayonnaise. After you have added 2 to 3 tablespoons oil, add 1 teaspoon lemon juice, then go back to the oil and continue alternating oil and lemon juice until you've added the ⅔ cup oil and 4 teaspoons lemon juice. Add the hot pepper sauce and cumin.

With the machine running, pour in the reduced lobster liquid and add the roe and any trimmings from the lobster meat to the bowl. Let run for 2 minutes to totally process. Refrigerate the sauce until ready to use.

Just before you are ready to serve, cut each lobster tail crosswise into 9 even pieces. Separate the claws into the large and small pieces. Hold them at room temperature.

Place a wok over high heat. Add the remaining ¼ cup oil and heat until hot. Add the livers and cook and toss, using cooking chopsticks or a wooden spoon, until the livers are nicely brown on all sides, about 3 minutes. Remove them from the wok with a strainer or slotted spoon. With the knife parallel to the cutting surface, slice each liver in half to form what looks like 2 livers. If a nerve is exposed, remove it.

Reheat the oil and add the spinach leaves. Toss to coat and just wilt, about 45 seconds. Remove, leaving the oil in the pan.

Arrange 5 spinach leaves on each of 6 dinner plates so they follow the inner rims in a half circle. Arrange alternate slices of chicken liver and lobster tail so they overlap over the spinach. Place either 1 large piece of claw or 2 small ones in the center of each plate.

Dribble 1 tablespoon sauce over the lobster and liver on each plate and put 2 tablespoons at the bottom of each claw. Serve the remaining sauce on the side.

SERVES 6

NIÇOISE SALAD

———————— • ————————

This is a classic from Nice, though more strange combinations have been perpetrated in its name than I can eat. It is a summer dish because of the need for small, fresh string beans. Serve as a main course preceded by a light soup or as a first course followed by a lovely runny omelet or a simple poached fish.

• • •

8 large eggs
2 pounds new potatoes
½ pound small (French) string beans, if possible
2 large tomatoes
2 seven-ounce cans solid white tuna, drained, in
*   large flakes*
½ cup Nice olives
1 cup olive oil
¼ cup red wine vinegar
1 teaspoon tarragon mustard
1 tablespoon kosher salt
Freshly ground black pepper
3 tablespoons freshly grated Parmesan cheese
4 slices Bermuda onion, halved
Lettuce leaves to decorate the plates

Put the eggs in a non-aluminum pot with cold water. Bring the water to a boil, cover the pot, and turn off the heat. Leave the eggs in the covered pot for 12 minutes. Rinse thoroughly and continuously under cold running water. The yolks will keep cooking until totally cool. Rap the egg shells sharply on a hard surface. Then, gently pressing, roll the eggs on the hard surface until they look like Chinese eggshell porcelains. At this point, pinch the shell and you should be able to pull it off in just a few pieces on its supporting membrane. It takes longer to describe than do. Cut 4 of the eggs into 8 wedges each. Put in a serving bowl.

Bring 2 pots of salted water to a boil.

Peel the potatoes and cut them into ¼-inch-thick rounds. Put into one of the pots of boiling water and cook until done, 7 to 9 minutes. Drain; add to the bowl with the egg wedges.

Break off and discard the ends from the string beans. If the string beans are not very small, cut them lengthwise into 4 pieces each. Drop the beans into the other pot of boiling water and cook for 1 to 2 minutes, or until barely done. Drain and rinse under cold running water. Pat dry and add to the serving bowl.

Cut the tomatoes into thin wedges, about 20 per tomato. Add to the bowl. Put the tuna and olives in the bowl as well.

In another bowl, mix together the olive oil, vinegar, mustard, salt, pepper, and Parmesan cheese. When the dressing is mixed, add it to the ingredients in the bowl. Mix well.

Cut the remaining 4 eggs into quarters and arrange on top of the salad. Separate the onion slices into separate half rings and scatter on top.

SERVES 6 AS A MAIN COURSE, 12 AS A FIRST COURSE

POT CHEESE AND VEGETABLE SALAD

When summer comes, I crave this salad that my grandmother used to make. The flavors, colors, and textures are all perfectly varied. For me this salad is lunch with a good rye bread. If real pot cheese is unavailable, use the driest uncreamed, large-curd cottage cheese you can find.

• • •

2 cucumbers, peeled, seeded, and diced
2 tomatoes, diced
1 green pepper, seeded, deribbed, and diced
1 red pepper, seeded, deribbed, and diced
2 bunches dill, chopped roughly
1 bunch scallions (white parts only), chopped
Salt
Pepper
2 cups pot cheese
2 cups sour cream

Mix the vegetables and dill together; season with salt and pepper to taste. Place them in the center of a platter. Arrange the pot cheese and sour cream on either side.

Guests can mix the salad to their own taste, using either pot cheese or sour cream or both.

SERVES 4 NORMAL PEOPLE OR 2 PEOPLE LIKE ME

NOTE: Instead of vegetables, you might serve fresh cut-up fruits.

CORN AND FETA CHEESE OMELET

Another all-vegetarian main course. Incidentally, if you have sophisticated friends you might try this as a first course. I find that many of my friends don't understand eggs as a first course unless they are in a cheese soufflé.

If you like, a little jalapeño pepper and coriander would jazz this up.

• • •

4 tablespoons unsalted butter
2 cups peeled, seeded, chopped tomatoes
2 cups corn kernels (fresh or canned)
1 cup sliced scallions
1 teaspoon kosher salt
Freshly ground black pepper
6 ounces (approximately 1½ cups) Feta cheese, crumbled
12 large eggs

Heat the butter in a skillet and add the tomato. Cook over moderately high heat for about 3 minutes, or until the tomatoes begin to give off liquid. Add the corn, scallions, salt, and pepper, and cook 1 more minute over low heat. Remove the pan from the heat and stir in the cheese.

Make four 3-egg omelets in a 9-inch skillet, one at a time. Before folding them over, spoon in some of the filling. Slide the folded, filled omelets onto plates. Spoon a little remaining filling over the tops.

MAKES 4 INDIVIDUAL OMELETS

OTHER MAIN COURSES

BEEF AND ASPARAGUS SAUTÉ

However complicated some of these recipes may be, this one is quick, easy and festive. It is another recipe that provides asparagus stems for the soup on page 131. It also gives filet of beef more flavor than it ordinarily has. (Though it's a tender, quick-cooking cut, it is not madly flavorful.) The small pieces stay rare yet brown all over and take good flavor from the shallots, garlic and glaze.

• • •

4 tablespoons unsalted butter
2 pounds beef filet, cut into strips, each 2 inches
*   long and ¼ inch thick*
2 tablespoons chopped shallots
2 teaspoons chopped garlic
5 cups asparagus tips, 2½ inches long (save
*   asparagus stalks for soup)*
3 tablespoons Meat Glaze (page 309)
½ cup water
2 tablespoons fresh lemon juice
1 teaspoon kosher salt
¼ teaspoon freshly ground black pepper
4 teaspoons arrowroot dissolved in 4 teaspoons
*   water*
2 tablespoons chopped fresh parsley

Heat the butter over high heat in a large skillet (or use two medium skillets and divide all the ingredients between them). Add the beef and sear on all sides. Add the shallots and garlic and toss for about a minute. Add the asparagus tips. Toss for another minute, then stir in the glaze.

When the glaze is melted, stir in the water and lemon juice, salt, and pepper. Cook another minute, then add the arrowroot and parsley. Cook and stir just until blended. Serve with a little rice.

SERVES 6

POACHED FILET OF BEEF WITH BASIL SAUCE

This is a really spectacular dish. It is the best way I know to serve beef in the summer. The Basil Sauce is a superb variation on pesto and is endlessly useful. If you have the time, turn some carrots, turnips, and potatoes, and blanch them. Heat them in some of the broth and serve them with the meat and sauce. Otherwise, serve just plain steamed potatoes. In the winter, serve the meat hot with the broth and vegetables. (I don't like the Basil Sauce with hot beef. If you want a sauce for the winter version, serve Chili Mayonnaise, page 31, instead.)

• • •

BASIL SAUCE

2 cups packed basil leaves
1½ cups olive oil
1 cup heavy cream
½ cup red wine vinegar
8 ounces shelled walnut pieces
6 cloves garlic, peeled
⅓ cup Gorgonzola
4 teaspoons kosher salt

POACHED FILET

1 eight-inch piece of beef tenderloin, trimmed of
   excess fat and tied at 2-inch intervals with
   butcher's string
Meat Stock (page 109) to cover (about 4 quarts)
1 onion, peeled and quartered
1 carrot, peeled and coarsely chopped
2 ribs celery, coarsely chopped
Salt and freshly ground black pepper to taste

BASIL SAUCE

Place the ingredients for the sauce in the work bowl of a food processor. Process until smooth. Cover and refrigerate until ready to use. This will allow the flavors time to blend.

POACHED FILET

Cut a piece of cheesecloth large enough to overlap twice when wrapped around the filet. Be sure that the cloth extends about 2 inches beyond each end of the meat. Dampen the cheesecloth and wrap the meat. Using one end of each of 2 twelve-inch lengths of string, tie each end of the cheesecloth. Leave enough string so that you can use the loose ends to immerse and remove the tenderloin from the simmering stock. (See the procedure for Poached Chicken, page 198.)

In a 6-quart stockpot, bring the meat stock, onion, carrot, and celery to a simmer over high heat. Salt and pepper. Lower the wrapped, tied tenderloin into the stock. Adjust the heat to a low simmer. Poach about 20 minutes or until the center of the tenderloin registers 115° to 120° F. on a meat thermometer. Take the pot off the heat. Carefully remove the filet from the hot stock. Let it stand for 10 to 15 minutes to cool.

Unwrap the filet and slice it into ¼-inch-thick slices. Serve with the Basil Sauce on the side. If you have turned and poached vegetables, arrange them attractively on each dish.

Strain the poaching liquid and reserve for another use, such as a superb soup.

SERVES 6

BLACK PEPPER STEAK

At a dinner for four close, beef-loving friends, make these steaks and serve with Shoestring Potatoes Fried in Suet (page 254).

• • •

4 twelve-ounce club steaks
4 teaspoons kosher salt
4 teaspoons freshly cracked black pepper (page 193)
½ cup brandy
¼ cup Meat Glaze (page 309)
¾ cup heavy cream
1 teaspoon fresh lemon juice

Heat a well-seasoned skillet large enough to hold the 4 steaks in one layer (or use two skillets and divide all the ingredients between them). Add the salt and pepper. When they begin to smoke, add the steaks and cook until crusty on the bottoms. Turn and cook until crusty on the other sides. This will take about 8 minutes altogether.

When the steaks are almost done, heat the brandy in a small pan. Ignite and pour over the steaks. Shake the pan gently until the flames die down, then remove the steaks to a serving platter and keep warm.

Scrape the bottom of the pan with a wooden spoon to deglaze, then stir in the meat glaze, cream, and lemon juice. (If using two skillets, deglaze one and add the contents to the other. Make the sauce in one skillet.) Stir until well blended and slightly thick. Pour over the steaks and serve at once.

SERVES 4

BEEF THULIER

This is a recipe only for the most lavish of nights. It was given to me years ago as the prize in a guessing game. Chef Thulier, at his breathtaking restaurant L'Ostau de Beaumanière, in Les Baux-de-Provence, served this dish and somewhat mischievously asked me if I could guess the ingredients. I replied: if I could, would he give me the recipe? The answer was yes. I went along swimmingly through the beef, shallots, wines, and even the foie gras. Then I bogged down. Thulier looked triumphant. Finally, my sense of history came to my aid. In the center of Roman Provence what could be more appropriate than some version of the fermented fish sauce, garum, which the Romans used to salt their food. Anchovies, I exclaimed. I got the recipe. It may sound like a weird combination; but it works.

A good Burgundy is just as expensive as the rest of the ingredients. In for a penny, in for a pound. Enjoy this with the very best of your friends.

• • •

2 tablespoons vegetable oil
2 tablespoons unsalted butter
6 good-sized shallots, finely chopped
¼ cup finely chopped fresh parsley

*1 whole filet of beef, approximately 4-5 pounds
   trimmed weight*
¾ cup dry white wine
¾ cup dry tawny port
3 tablespoons Meat Glaze (page 309)
½ cup bloc foie gras, cold, not room temperature
2 teaspoons anchovy paste
Freshly ground black pepper

Heat the oven to 400°F.

Heat the oil and butter in a large sauté pan until hot. (If the meat doesn't fit in your sauté pan, work directly in a roasting pan.) Add the shallots, parsley, and meat. Cook quickly just until the meat is browned on all sides, turning and stirring to keep the shallots from burning. Remove the pan from the heat. Remove the beef to a roasting pan and roast it in the oven for 15 to 20 minutes.

Add the wine and port to the sauté pan, scraping the bottom of the pan with a wooden spoon to incorporate the bits into the sauce. Bring to a simmer and add the meat glaze. Let the sauce simmer slowly for 15 minutes.

When the meat is done, remove it to a board and let it rest. Put the roasting pan over high heat; pour in the wine mixture from the sauté pan and deglaze. Strain the juices through a sieve into a saucepan. Put it over heat and simmer another 5 minutes.

In a small bowl, mash together the foie gras and anchovy paste with a fork. Remove the saucepan from the heat and beat in the foie gras and anchovy paste. (If using a 7¼-ounce bloc of foie gras, you may add all of it; in that case add more anchovy paste to taste.) Generously grind in pepper. Taste the sauce; it should have a thin consistency and slightly curdled appearance.

Slice the filet on the bias. Barely coat the slices with some sauce and serve the rest on the side.

SERVES 8 TO 12

NOTE: If there are truffles in the foie gras, thinly slice them and add to the sauce.

ALL-DAY BEEF STEW

With this recipe I can be away all day and arrive home to a cooked meal, or I let it cook all night and let it cool in the morning. You may want to add other ingredients, but remember not to reduce the liquid level.

...

2 medium tomatoes
2 pounds beef chuck, cut into 1-inch cubes
1 cup finely sliced carrots
1 cup finely sliced peeled potatoes
¼ cup finely chopped parsley
2 tablespoons kosher salt
Freshly ground black pepper to taste
½ cup finely sliced fresh mushrooms
1½ cups dry red wine
1 cup beef stock
2 large cloves garlic, smashed and peeled
1 bay leaf
½ teaspoon dried marjoram

Heat the oven at its lowest setting, usually to warm—below 200° F.

Put all the ingredients in a 3-quart casserole. Stir to mix. Cover. Place in the oven and allow to cook for at least 8 hours. The meat should be fork tender.

SERVES 4 TO 6

NOTE: This recipe can also be made in a crockpot.

BEEF BOURGUIGNON

This is one of the great classics. I have made only the smallest personal adjustments in my version. Serve lots of bread and a big spoon for the sauce but nothing else on the plate.

...

1 pound slab bacon, cut in 2-by-½-inch pieces
½ cup all-purpose flour

1 tablespoon kosher salt
Freshly ground black pepper
4½ pounds beef chuck, cut into 2-inch cubes
¼ cup Cognac
1 bottle (3 cups) dry red wine
1 cup Meat Stock (page 109)
3 tablespoons tomato paste
1 bay leaf
Cloves from 1 head garlic, unpeeled, smashed
¼ cup Meat Glaze (page 309)
1½ pounds small white onions or pearl onions
4 tablespoons unsalted butter
1½ pounds mushrooms, caps only

Put the bacon in a large skillet and cook over moderate heat until all the fat is melted and the meat is crisp. Remove the crisp pieces with a slotted spoon and set aside. Pour out all but about 5 tablespoons of the fat and reserve.

Season the flour with the salt and a little pepper to taste. Pat the meat dry and toss it in the seasoned flour so each piece is lightly coated. Shake off any excess.

Heat the fat in the skillet. Add half the meat and brown it on all sides. When the meat is all browned, heat gently half the Cognac in a small pan. Ignite it and pour it, still flaming, over the meat. When the flames die down, remove the meat and its juices to a bowl. Brown the remaining meat in the same way and flavor it with the remaining Cognac, also flaming. Add it to the rest of the meat.

Pour the red wine and stock into the pan and scrape the bottom with a wooden spoon to deglaze, loosening all the browned bits. Stir in the tomato paste, bay leaf, garlic, and meat glaze. When the sauce is well mixed, return the meat and its juices to the pan.

Bring the liquid to a boil, then cover the pan and lower the heat so the liquid just simmers. Cook at a simmer for 4 hours, or until the meat is fork tender. Skim off any surface fat.

While the stew cooks, bring a pot of salted water to a boil. Add the onions, unpeeled. Cook until tender, 15 to 20 minutes. Remove them from the water and set aside until cool enough to handle. Then cut off the root ends and slip the onions out of their skins. They should pop out easily. Pat dry.

Melt the butter and ¼ cup bacon fat in a large skillet over high heat. When the fat is hot, add the mushroom caps. Cook, stirring from time to time, until they are lightly browned. Remove them from the skillet, leaving the fat, and set them aside. Add the onions to the same skillet and cook until nicely browned.

When the meat is cooked, stir in the mushrooms, onions, and cooked bacon. Cook about 10 minutes, just to heat through.

Serve with boiled potatoes or buttered noodles. Encourage your guests to suck out the sweet meat from the garlic skins.

SERVES 8 TO 12, DEPENDING ON APPETITES

NOTE: If you make this the day before serving, do not add the mushrooms, onions, and bacon until just before serving.

SHORT RIBS OF BEEF

Another of the rich stews with which I like to comfort myself and my guests. This needs thorough skimming to get rid of the fat while you keep the richness. Mashed Potatoes (page 258) or Creamy Polenta (page 263) would be my favorite here; but steamed potatoes would be less fattening.

• • •

3 tablespoons vegetable oil
¾ cup diced onions
½ teaspoon minced garlic
4 short ribs of beef (about 2½ pounds total), each
    4½ by 2½ inches
⅔ cup all-purpose flour, seasoned with 1 teaspoon
    kosher salt and ¼ teaspoon freshly ground pepper
¼ cup rye whiskey
⅔ cup dry red wine
1 cup Meat Stock (page 109)
¼ cup fresh orange juice
3 two-inch strips orange zest (orange part only)
½ cup pitted Graber olives (pitted with a pitter)

Heat the oil in a Dutch oven and gently sauté the onions for 3 to 5 minutes. Add the garlic and continue to sauté until the onions are translucent. Meanwhile, dust the ribs with the seasoned flour, shaking off any excess.

When the onions and garlic are cooked, remove them from the pan with a slotted spoon, leaving the hot fat in the pan. Set aside.

Sear the short ribs in the hot fat on all sides. Remove the meat and reserve with the onions.

Pour the fat out of the pan. Over high heat, deglaze the pan with the rye, scraping the bottom with a wooden spoon and cooking rapidly. Add the wine and stock. Let the mixture boil rapidly for 2 minutes. Return the short ribs and onions to the pan. Add the orange juice and zest. Lower the heat to a gentle simmer. Cover and cook for an hour, skimming occasionally. Add the olives; cover and cook until the meat is tender, about 1½ to 2 hours longer.

Remove the meat to a serving platter. Skim the fat from the sauce. If it seems weak, remove the olives and reduce by rapid boiling. Then return the olives to the sauce, and either pour it over the meat or serve on the side. If you prefer, this dish can be cooked a day ahead, skimmed when cold and then reheated.

SERVES 4

GRILLED MUSTARD RABBIT

———————————•———————————

Rabbit is not America's favorite meat although it can now be bought frozen. If you don't have an interest or the right friends for this recipe, exchange chicken for rabbit and proceed. Since the meat needs to marinate for a day or more, plan ahead. A good Côtes-du-Rhône or Piedmont wine would have the body to accompany this recipe. Get a really good mustard; the recipe needs that sharpness.

• • •

6 cups milk
2 cups Dijon mustard
½ cup vegetable oil
¼ cup fresh lemon juice
1 teaspoon kosher salt
2 teaspoons freshly ground black pepper
2 skinned rabbits, 2 to 2½ pounds each, cut into
   serving pieces (if frozen, defrost first)

Whisk together the milk, mustard, oil, and lemon juice. Stir in the salt and pepper.

Put the rabbit in a deep, wide pan and pour the mustard mixture over it. Turn the pieces so they are coated. Cover and leave in the refrigerator for 1 to 2 days, turning the pieces from time to time.

To cook, heat a grill or broiler until hot. Place the rabbit pieces, along with whatever marinade adheres, fleshy side down on the grill or fleshy side up under the broiler. Cook until browned, basting often with the marinade. Turn over and cook, basting the other side until browned—about 5 minutes per side.

Serve with potatoes, rice, or noodles and some of the marinade as a sauce.

SERVES 4 TO 6

OSSOBUCCO

———————•———————

This great Italian dish always satisfies. Classically, it is served with saffron risotto—the only dish in Italy to be served with rice or pasta as an accompaniment. The priest-robe-colored rice surrounds the browned meat, which in turn surrounds its marrow. On top is sprinkled the brilliantly colored Gremolata. Before this, serve smoked fish or Marinated, Roasted Baby Eggplants (page 269). Finish the meal with a crisp green salad and a perfect pear with Brie.

• • •

3 tablespoons olive oil
Flour seasoned with salt and freshly ground black
* pepper*
1 six- to seven-pound veal shank, sawed into 6
* pieces, each about 2½ to 3 inches long*
4 tablespoons unsalted butter
1½ cups chopped onions
1 cup chopped carrots
1 cup chopped peeled celery
1 tablespoon chopped garlic
1 three-inch strip orange zest
2 three-inch strips lemon zest
1½ cups dry white wine
1 cup Meat or Chicken Stock (pages 109 and 110)

1½ cups canned Italian tomatoes, drained and
   coarsely chopped
Kosher salt
¼ teaspoon dried thyme
¼ teaspoon dried basil
1 bay leaf
3 sprigs parsley
Freshly ground black pepper
Pinch cayenne pepper
2 tablespoons Meat Glaze (page 309)

GREMOLATA

1 bunch washed parsley
5 peeled garlic cloves
5 strips orange zest (3 inches by ¼ inch)
1 strip lemon zest (3 inches by ¼ inch)

Heat the oven to 350°F.

Heat the oil in a heavy flameproof casserole. Lightly flour the veal shanks on all sides, brushing off the excess. Add the meat to the casserole and brown on all sides. Remove the browned meat to a plate.

Stir in the butter. When melted, stir in the onions, carrots, celery, garlic, orange and lemon zests. Cook over medium heat until the vegetables are soft but not brown, stirring occasionally. Stir in 1 cup wine, the stock, tomatoes, 1½ teaspoons salt, thyme, basil, bay leaf, parsley, ⅛ teaspoon black pepper and the cayenne pepper. Scrape the bottom of the pan. Return the veal shanks to the casserole and place in the oven. Cook 1½ to 2 hours, or until the meat is very tender. Remove the meat and keep it warm.

Skim the excess fat from the sauce. Pour the sauce into a food processor and process until coarsely puréed. Return the sauce to the pot, add the remaining ½ cup wine and the meat glaze. Cook over medium-high heat until the sauce is thickened and measures about 3 cups. Season with additional salt and pepper to taste.

GREMOLATA

Chop together the parsley leaves, garlic, orange and lemon zests.

Spoon the sauce over the veal shanks, and sprinkle with Gremolata. Serve with saffron risotto.

SERVES 6

BRAISED BREAST OF VEAL WITH
SPINACH-MUSHROOM STUFFING
(INEXPENSIVE VEAL FOR A FESTIVE PARTY)

———————————•———————————

We all need in our repertoire an inexpensive and festive dish that
will feed a large number. This is it. There is a price to pay: a fair
amount of preparation time is required. It can be done the day before the party.

• • •

STUFFING

6 pounds fresh spinach
2 tablespoons unsalted butter
6 ounces (about 3 cups) medium-size fresh
　mushrooms, sliced
½ pound (about 2 cups) diced Italian Fontina
　cheese (¼-inch dice)
1½ cups cooked rice
½ cup small basil leaves or coarsely chopped basil
Salt and freshly ground black pepper
1 tablespoon olive oil

VEAL

1 breast of veal, about 9 pounds, boned, trimmed,
　bones reserved
4 tablespoons unsalted butter
2 large heads garlic, separated into cloves,
　unpeeled
3 cups Meat Stock (page 109)
Salt
Pepper

TO ROAST BONES

3 tablespoons Dijon mustard
1 tablespoon dry red wine
2 cups fine fresh white bread crumbs

Stem the spinach completely. Rinse in several changes of cool water
to remove all the sand and grit. Place 8 cups of the washed leaves,
with the water that clings to them, in a large saucepan and cover.
Steam over medium heat, stirring occasionally, just until the leaves

are wilted but still bright green, about 4 minutes. Drain in a colander. Run cold water over the spinach until it is cool enough to handle. Squeeze all the moisture from the spinach with your hands. Chop coarsely. Dry and reserve the remaining spinach leaves.

Melt 2 tablespoons of unsalted butter in a large skillet over medium heat. Add the mushrooms. Sauté, stirring occasionally, until they begin to exude liquid, about 5 minutes.

In a bowl, blend together the cooked spinach, mushrooms, cheese, rice, and basil. Salt and pepper to taste. Set aside.

Spread out the veal, fat side down. Trim any ragged edges and reserve, along with other trimmings, for another use. Turn the veal so that one of the long sides of the rectangle is closest to you. Spread the spinach-mushroom filling in a 4-inch strip down the long side of the veal. Leave an inch between the filling and the edge of the veal (drawing 1). Roll the breast lengthwise, rolling tightly and evenly. You may have to stop and adjust the veal as you roll in order to keep it even. Tie the veal securely at 1½-inch intervals, making sure the stuffing is completely enclosed (drawing 2).

Preheat the oven to 300°F.

In a roasting pan large enough to hold the veal, melt 4 tablespoons butter over low heat. Increase the heat to medium high and sauté the reserved veal bones for 10 minutes, until they are golden brown on all sides. Scatter the garlic cloves over the bones and stir to incorporate. Push the bones to the sides of the pan and add the rolled veal to the center. Brown lightly on all sides, about 15 minutes. Pour the meat stock into the pan, scraping the bottom and sides with a wooden spoon. Salt and pepper the stock to taste.

STUFFING BONED BREAST OF VEAL

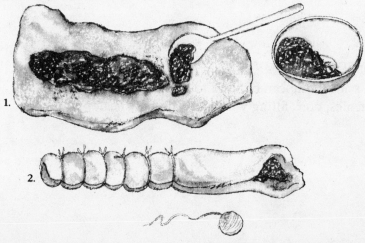

1.

2.

Set the pan in the preheated oven. Braise about an hour and 10 minutes, or until the veal reaches an internal temperature of 130° F. on a meat thermometer. Remove the pan from the oven and increase the oven temperature to 450° F.

Transfer the veal to a platter. Remove the bones to a plate. Strain the pan juices into a small saucepan, reserving the garlic cloves. Skim off and reserve 2 tablespoons of fat from the juices. Cover the saucepan with aluminum foil. Let it stand as you prepare the bones.

Beat the mustard, the 2 tablespoons of reserved fat and the wine in a small bowl. Brush the bones with the mustard mixture, then roll them in bread crumbs until they are completely coated. Place the coated bones in a clean roasting pan. Roast until the bread crumbs are crisp and golden, about 20 minutes. Brush the bones with additional drippings halfway through the roasting.

When ready to serve, skim the remaining fat from the juices in the saucepan. Heat. If necessary, boil the juices in order to concentrate the flavors. Season with salt and pepper to taste.

Heat the oil in a large wok or skillet over high heat until it is just beginning to smoke. Add the remaining spinach. Stir-fry until the leaves are wilted and bright green. Sprinkle with salt and continue to stir. Remove the spinach from the heat.

Cut the strings from the veal. Slice it into ½-inch slices. Overlap the slices along one side of a serving platter. Mound the garlic cloves at one end of the platter, and arrange the bones alongside the veal slices. Take the platter to the table to show it off.

At the table, place a small mound of spinach on each dinner plate. Add a slice of veal, a bone and some garlic to each plate. Moisten the veal with some of the skimmed pan juices, and pass the remaining juices separately.

SERVES 12 GENEROUSLY

STUFFED VEAL SCALOPPINE

The same filling can be used to stuff small scaloppine of veal. About 1½ tablespoons filling will be needed per scaloppine.

VEAL AND ARTICHOKE-HEART STEW

———————— • ————————

This can be made with an inexpensive cut of veal. I think it is better than a blanquette de veau and it is certainly a lot lighter. Since veal cooks quickly, it is rather rapidly done. The artichoke hearts lend a festive touch and an unusual flavor. Being frozen, they require no work, except shopping. You can cook the artichokes in the same fashion but without the veal and they make an almost instant and unexpected vegetable to go with a roasted chicken.

Incidentally, this stew is pale. Choose a colorful plate.

• • •

3½ tablespoons unsalted butter
2 pounds 1½-inch veal cubes, trimmed
2 medium-size onions, cut into 1-inch chunks
4 cups Chicken Stock (page 110) or as needed
Salt
Freshly ground black pepper
2 nine-ounce boxes frozen artichoke hearts,
    defrosted, drained
3 tablespoons lemon juice
½ cup coarsely chopped fresh dill
1½ tablespoons all-purpose flour

In a large skillet, melt 2 tablespoons of the butter over medium-low heat. Add the veal cubes and onions. Toss until they are coated with butter. Cook, stirring occasionally, about 10 minutes, until the veal is uniformly gray and the onions are wilted. Scrape the contents of the skillet into a small stockpot.

Pour into the stockpot enough chicken stock to just cover the veal and onions. Add 1 teaspoon of salt and ¼ teaspoon of pepper. Heat to simmering. Simmer, partially covered, for an hour, or until the veal is almost tender. Add the artichoke hearts. Cook about 10 minutes, until the artichokes are tender when pierced with a knife point. Stir in the lemon juice, dill, and additional salt and pepper to taste.

In a small bowl, beat the remaining 1½ tablespoons of butter and the flour until smooth to make beurre manié. Pour in ½ cup of hot liquid from the stockpot. Beat until incorporated. Stir the liaison back into the stew. Simmer 5 minutes, until the stew thickens. Taste and adjust the seasonings. Serve with rice.

SERVES 6

BARBECUED LEG OF LAMB

If the butcher will bone the leg for you, this is one of the quickest ways of cooking lamb I know. It is based on a recipe of James Beard's. I just happen to like more rosemary on my lamb than he does. While this is a super dish for making out of doors on a grill, it can be made under the broiler. If your oven is electric, leave the door a little ajar.

In the summer, you might lightly chill either some red table wine or some Napa Gamay. Leftover, this lamb makes a superb filling for sandwiches.

...

1 short leg of lamb (see note, page 179)
8 medium cloves garlic, minced
1 tablespoon rosemary, preferably fresh
1½ tablespoons kosher salt
2 teaspoons freshly ground black pepper

Remove the fell (the thin external membrane covering the leg) and most of the fat from the lamb. There will be one fairly thick bone in the leg. Make a lengthwise cut into the leg going to the bone and along the length of the bone. Then cut around the bone with a long, thin knife to separate the bone completely from the meat. Pat the meat dry and rub generously with the garlic, rosemary, salt, and pepper on all sides. Let sit for at least an hour at room temperature.

Heat the grill until hot. Rub the grate with a little fat to keep the meat from sticking. Place the meat on the hot grill and cook for 10 minutes. Turn and grill 10 minutes longer. The lamb should be juicy and rare to pink.

Remove the meat to a cutting board and slice on the bias into thin strips. Marinated, Roasted Baby Eggplants (page 269) and/or Roasted Yellow Bell Peppers and Tomatoes (page 35) make this an irresistible feast.

SERVES 6 TO 8

LAMB NAVARIN

It's clear by now that a good stew is dear to my heart; it seems to get my guests to relax. This one is for spring, with young lamb and young vegetables. The tastes should remain light and fresh. If fresh herbs are unavailable, tie the dried herbs in a double layer of cheesecloth before putting them in the stew. Remove before serving.

• • •

2 tablespoons unsalted butter

1 tablespoon vegetable oil

5 pounds lamb stew meat, preferably neck, or lamb steaks (see note, page 179) cut into 2-inch chunks with the bone

1¾ pounds small new potatoes, peeled (if large, cut into about 1½-inch chunks)

2 ten-ounce packages frozen peas (use fresh peas if young ones are available)

1 pound small white onions, peeled

1 cup Chicken Stock (page 110)

1 cup Meat Stock (page 109)

2½ tablespoons minced garlic

3 tablespoons finely chopped parsley

1¼ pounds mushrooms, stems removed (quartered unless button size)

1 tablespoon Meat Glaze (page 309)

3 small sprigs fresh rosemary

3 leaves fresh young sage

2 or 3 leaves fresh tarragon

2 fresh thyme sprigs

¼ cup loosely packed whole basil leaves

¾ pound baby carrots, peeled and trimmed

3 tablespoons kosher salt

½ pound string beans, julienned

3 tablespoons fresh lemon juice

2 tablespoons beurre manié (see page 240)

Freshly ground black pepper

Place the butter and oil in a large pot over medium heat. When the butter is melted, raise the heat to high and add as much meat as will comfortably fit in one layer. Brown each piece on all sides. When the meat is thoroughly brown, remove it to a bowl and add more lamb to the pot. Continue to brown the meat in batches, never crowding the pot, adding the browned meat to the meat in the bowl. The total browning should take about 15 minutes.

Meanwhile, drop the potatoes into boiling salted water. Bring the water back to the boil, and cook for 10 minutes. Drain and re-fresh under cold water. Set aside.

If using frozen peas, place them in a sieve under hot running water just until defrosted. Set aside.

When the meat is all brown, set it aside. Add the onions to the fat in the pot, and cook over medium heat until they are lightly browned. Leaving the onions in the pot, pour off the excess fat. Deglaze the pot with the stocks, scraping well. When the pot is thor-oughly deglazed, add to the pot the lamb and any meat juices that have accumulated in the bowl. Stir in 1½ tablespoons garlic, the parsley, mushrooms, and Meat Glaze. Cover and simmer over low heat for 1 hour.

If you are making the stew ahead, stop here and let it cool. Remove all the fat that rises to the surface. If serving immediately after cooking, skim as the stew simmers and continue skimming throughout the cooking time.

Add the rosemary, sage, tarragon, thyme, and basil, then the carrots, potatoes, and 1 tablespoon salt. Mix well. Continue to sim-mer, covered, until the carrots and potatoes are tender (pierce with a knife), approximately 15 to 20 minutes. Add the peas and string beans, and simmer until the beans are tender, about 7 to 8 minutes longer. Stir in the remaining tablespoon garlic with the lemon juice, beurre manié, 2 tablespoons salt, and a few grindings of black pep-per. Adjust the seasonings to taste. Cook for a few minutes to smooth the sauce and blend the flavors.

SERVES 6 TO 8

• BEURRE MANIÉ •

To make beurre manié, mix together equal amounts of flour and butter until smooth. In this case, 2 tablespoons flour and 2 table-spoons butter. Large quantities of beurre manié may be made in a food processor and stored in the refrigerator until needed.

FALL RAGOUT OF LAMB

This is a wonderful party dish, though basically a gussied-up version of Irish stew. One of the nice things about lamb stews is that you can make lamb stock so much more quickly than any other kind. Because of the softness and strong flavor of the bones, cooking them in water for only an hour or two will do the trick. If you don't need all the stock, save it for a soup that uses these fall vegetables, adding some garlic and some canned white beans rinsed in clear water. Serve the soup hot accompanied by a bowl of freshly grated cheese.

• • •

¾ cup vegetable oil
12 pounds boneless lamb shoulder (bones
   reserved), trimmed, or lamb from leg (page 179)
6 pounds onions, peeled, trimmed, and cut into 1-
   inch cubes
4 pounds very tiny new potatoes, scrubbed, thin
   strip of peel removed from the circumference of
   each
3 pounds carrots, peeled, trimmed, and cut on bias
   into ¾-inch ovals
3 pounds small white turnips, peeled and cut into
   1-inch cubes
6 ounces (1½ sticks) unsalted butter
¾ cup flour
¼ cup kosher salt
Freshly ground black pepper
3 tablespoons dry mustard
2 cups chopped Italian parsley

In a large braising pan over medium-high flame, heat ¼ cup of the oil until it is very hot. Add the reserved lamb bones. Brown on all sides. Pour off the fat from the pan. Add water to cover. Reduce the heat to simmering. Simmer 2 hours. Strain and reserve.

While the bones are simmering, heat the remaining oil in a second large pan over high heat. Brown the lamb cubes in a single layer, turning often. Don't add too many to the pan at one time or they will steam and not brown. As the meat browns, remove it from the pan with a slotted spoon and transfer to paper to drain. When all the meat is brown, add the vegetables to the pan. Sauté until softened and slightly browned, about 10 minutes. Remove the vegetables to a separate bowl.

Add the butter to the meat pan. Melt over medium heat. Whisk in the flour. Continue whisking over medium heat about 6 minutes, until the roux is cooked. Stir in the lamb stock, salt, pepper, and mustard. Heat to simmering. Add the lamb, and simmer 30 minutes. Add the vegetables. Simmer until the lamb and vegetables are tender, about 1 hour. Season with more salt and pepper, if needed. Stir in parsley.

Serve surrounded by a ring of buttered noodles or with lots of bread and big spoons for the sauce.

SERVES 12

LAMB STEW WITH CUCUMBERS

Once James Beard and I were going to teach a class all about lamb in San Francisco. We began to talk about lamb stew and somehow this idea emerged. I went on to develop it into a recipe. The class seemed to love it. So did Jim and I.

• • •

3½ pounds lamb neck with the bone or lamb from
    leg (page 179) cut into 1½- to 2-inch pieces
2 tablespoons vegetable oil
3 tablespoons unsalted butter
⅔ cup rice wine vinegar
3 cloves garlic, crushed
1⅓ cups Chicken Stock (page 110)
4 cucumbers
Kosher salt
Freshly ground black pepper
2 large egg yolks

Pat the meat dry. Heat the oil and butter in a heavy pot. Working in batches, brown the meat on all sides. As each batch is browned, use a slotted spoon to remove it to a bowl. When all the lamb is browned, pour out all but 3 tablespoons fat.

Pour the vinegar into the pan and scrape the bottom with a wooden spoon to deglaze. Bring the liquid to a simmer and cook for 3 minutes. Add the garlic, browned lamb, and Chicken Stock. Simmer for 45 minutes. Remove from the heat.

While the stew cooks, prepare the cucumbers by peeling them, cutting them in half lengthwise, and removing all the seeds. Cut the halves in half again lengthwise, then cut each strip into pieces 1½ inches long. Trim these by rounding the edges so they're "oval."

When the meat is cooked, add the cucumbers. Cook for 10 minutes. Remove from the heat. Season to taste with 1 teaspoon salt and ½ teaspoon pepper.

With a slotted spoon, remove the meat and cucumbers to a bowl. Put the egg yolks in a small bowl. Slowly whisk in some of the hot lamb liquid to raise the temperature of the yolks. When the yolks are quite warm, whisk them into the liquid. Cook over moderate heat, whisking constantly, until the liquid thickens slightly. Do not let it boil or the sauce will curdle. Add the lamb and cucumbers to the pot, and correct seasonings with salt and pepper to taste.

SERVES 6

LAMB KIDNEYS WITH APPLEJACK AND HORSERADISH

Even less than people eat lamb do they eat lamb kidneys. I persist. Kidneys are good, inexpensive, and nutritious. I suppose the aversion people have can only be overcome by tasting well-prepared kidneys made with a flavorful sauce that balances their slightly strong taste. Mustard does well in this connection, as does the horseradish in this recipe. In fact, I think this dish is so good that it will change almost anybody's mind about kidneys.

This full-flavored dish does not overwhelm wine but goes well with it. Almost any white that is not too sweet or any red will fit in and taste better than usual.

• • •

1 pound lamb kidneys
2 tablespoons unsalted butter
2 tablespoons applejack
½ cup hard cider
4 tablespoons freshly grated horseradish, or ⅓ cup
drained prepared white horseradish—not
creamed
½ cup heavy cream
1 tablespoon Meat Glaze (page 309)
Kosher salt
Freshly ground black pepper
2 to 3 teaspoons white wine vinegar
2 tablespoons chopped fresh parsley

With the kidneys flat on a cutting board and the knife parallel to the board, slice the kidneys in half lengthwise through the indentation. With a small knife, carefully remove the fat and membranes, particularly from the canal-like grooves.

Heat the butter in an 8-inch skillet. When very hot but not brown, add the kidneys and sear them on all sides, about 1½ to 2 minutes in all. Heat the applejack in a small pan. Ignite it and pour over the kidneys. Shake the pan until the flames die down. Using a slotted spoon, remove the kidneys to a bowl, leaving the liquid in the pan.

Add the cider and 2 tablespoons of the horseradish to the pan. Cook over medium heat until reduced by about half. Add the cream and glaze, and cook until about 1 cup of liquid remains. Season with ¾ teaspoon salt and ⅛ teaspoon pepper.

Return the kidneys to the skillet with any liquid they have exuded. Add the remaining horseradish. Adjust the seasoning with salt, pepper, and vinegar. Add the parsley, and cook until heated through.

SERVES 3 TO 4

VEAL KIDNEYS WITH MUSTARD SAUCE

Veal kidneys are a little lighter in taste than lamb kidneys, and the taste of this dish is a little lighter than that of the preceding one.

Incidentally, if you have a really good butcher, you may be able to get hold of veal kidneys surrounded by their pocket of fat. This is the cleanest fat available. Put the kidneys with the fat on a hot grill; turn once. Take them off when crusty and brown on all sides. Serve one per person with a selection of mustards, fresh sprigs of watercress, and Shoestring Potatoes Fried in Suet (page 254).

These kidneys with their mustard sauce take a robust wine: Côtes-du-Rhône, Cahors, Barbera, or zinfandel.

• • •

1 pair veal kidneys (about 1 pound)
4 tablespoons unsalted butter
2 tablespoons chopped shallots
6 to 8 ounces sliced mushrooms
1 teaspoon fresh lemon juice
1 cup Chicken Stock (page 110)
¼ cup Madeira wine
3 tablespoons Dijon mustard
2 tablespoons Meat Glaze (page 309)
Kosher salt
Freshly ground black pepper

Cut the kidneys in half lengthwise and remove the fat and canal-like membranes. Carefully pull the nodules apart, or use a knife if necessary. Set aside.

Heat 2 tablespoons of the butter in an 8-inch skillet. Add the shallots and cook over medium-high heat until soft, stirring occasionally. Raise the heat and add the mushrooms. Sauté about 1 minute, or until mushrooms are tender. Toss them with the lemon juice. Remove the mushrooms, shallots, and any liquid to a bowl.

Add the remaining 2 tablespoons of butter to the skillet. When hot, add the kidneys and sauté just to sear them on all sides, about 1½ to 2 minutes. With a slotted spoon, remove the kidneys to a bowl. Add the chicken stock, Madeira, and mustard. Cook, scraping the pan, until the liquid is reduced by about one-third, and add the glaze. Continue to cook until the sauce is slightly thickened.

Return the kidneys and their liquid and the mushrooms and their liquid to the sauce. Season to taste with salt and pepper. Stir from time to time, and cook until heated through. You can serve with rice or noodles or just lots of chunky bread.

SERVES 4

DIRTY RICE

———————————•———————————

I love Dirty Rice. It is perfect on a buffet or for an informal after-theater supper. It can be reheated, plus it uses up leftovers, plus it can be made with the giblets saved from birds used at other meals. Beer is fine with it. What more could you want except elegance?

...

*¾ pound coarsely chopped chicken giblets,
    excluding livers
5½ cups Chicken Stock (page 110)
2 cups long-grain rice
3 tablespoons unsalted butter
2 tablespoons all-purpose flour
1 cup finely chopped onions
¾ pound coarsely chopped chicken livers
1 cup chopped scallions, both green and white
    parts
½ cup chopped celery
½ cup chopped fresh parsley
½ cup chopped green bell pepper
1 teaspoon minced garlic
Kosher salt
Freshly ground black pepper
⅛ teaspoon cayenne pepper*

Place the giblets and 1 cup of the chicken stock in a small saucepan. Bring to a boil, cover, reduce the heat, and simmer 1 hour.

In a separate pot, bring 4 cups of the stock to a boil and stir in the rice. Cover and cook at a simmer until all the stock is absorbed and the rice is tender, about 18 minutes.

While the rice is cooking, heat the butter and flour in a large pot over medium heat, stirring constantly. Cook until the mixture is dark nutty brown. Add the onions and cook, stirring from time to time, until tender, about 3 to 5 minutes. Stir in the chicken livers, scallions, celery, parsley, green pepper, garlic, 1¼ teaspoons salt, ½ teaspoon black pepper, the cayenne, and the remaining ½ cup of stock. Cover and cook over high heat, stirring frequently, about 3 to 5 minutes.

Stir the chicken-liver mixture and giblet mixture into the cooked rice. Season with additional salt and pepper if necessary.

SERVES 6 TO 8

SAUTÉ OF CHICKEN LIVERS WITH OKRA

This is a quick and dirty gumbo. Served over about three-quarters of a cup of cooked rice per person, this is a virtually instant dinner. You can use frozen okra if hard-pressed. A salad, cheese, and bread, and you have a twenty-minute dinner, including setting the table. Start by putting the water on to boil for the rice. Wash the salad. Make a dressing. Make the rice. Make the chicken livers. Assemble and serve. Lots of red wine will help—you and the guests.

• • •

> *2 tablespoons unsalted butter*
> *3 small dried hot peppers, crumbled*
> *1 large clove garlic, peeled and minced*
> *1½ pounds chicken livers, trimmed, finely chopped*
> *1½ teaspoons salt*
> *¼ teaspoon freshly ground black pepper*
> *1 cup liquid from canned tomatoes*
> *1½ cups thinly bias-sliced okra (about 12 medium-*
>   *size pods)*
> *Hot cooked long-grain rice*

In a large skillet, lightly brown the butter over medium-high heat. Sauté the hot peppers and garlic in the butter about 30 seconds, until fragrant. Add the chopped livers, sprinkle with salt and pepper, and stir to separate. Sauté about 2 minutes, until lightly browned.

    Pour in the tomato liquid. Heat to simmering. Reduce the heat to low. Stir in the okra. Simmer until the okra is bright green and tender, about 3 minutes.

    Serve over hot rice.

SERVES 4 TO 6

VENISON STEW

If you hunt or have a friend who hunts, you will be left with lots of meat that, in truth, is not fit to be grilled or roasted. Venison burgers are not the answer; however, this stew is. Cut the meat into neat chunks and freeze in one-pound blocks to use as needed. Alterna-

VENISON STEW, CONTINUED

tively, you can buy imported frozen venison stew meat—it can be bought rather inexpensively—to make a very festive dinner. It does need some forethought, as the meat needs to defrost in the marinade to tenderize and to balance its rich flavor. (Fresh domestic venison can only be sold to restaurants. It's illegal to sell to consumers.)

If venison is anathema, you can make mock venison stew by preparing lamb in the identical way. This dish can be multiplied ad infinitum. It is a surprise at large parties.

• • •

2 pounds 1½-inch cubes frozen venison
3 large carrots, peeled and sliced on the bias into
½-inch-thick slices
2 large onions, cut into 1-inch cubes
12 medium-size cloves garlic, peeled
1 bottle (750 ml) dry red wine, about 3 cups
½ cup red wine vinegar or tarragon vinegar
4 tablespoons vegetable oil
Salt
2 teaspoons minced tarragon leaves or ½ teaspoon
crumbled dried tarragon leaves
Freshly ground black pepper

BEURRE MANIÉ

3 tablespoons unsalted butter
3 tablespoons all-purpose flour

Place the venison cubes, vegetables, and garlic in a deep non-aluminum container. Pour in the red wine and vinegar. Be sure the liquid covers the meat and vegetables. Marinate in the refrigerator at least until the venison is defrosted, about 24 hours, or up to 3 days. Stir from time to time.

Drain the meat and vegetables, reserving the marinade. Pat the meat and vegetables dry thoroughly with paper toweling. (Only proper drying of the venison will give the stew a rich mahogany color.)

In a large, heavy skillet, heat half the oil over high heat. Brown the venison in small batches, stirring occasionally, until all sides are seared. This will take about 5 minutes per batch. As the cubes are browned, remove them with a slotted spoon to a 4-quart non-aluminum Dutch oven or saucepan.

Add the remaining oil to the skillet. Sauté the drained vegetables about 5 minutes, until the pan is deglazed and the vegetables are lightly browned. Set aside.

In another saucepan, bring the reserved marinade to a boil over medium heat. Skim the surface as necessary. Reduce the heat to low and simmer for 5 minutes. Strain it through a sieve lined with cheesecloth. Pour into the venison pot enough of the strained marinade to cover the meat. Bring to a simmer over low heat. Add salt to taste. Simmer, partially covered, about an hour and a half, until the venison is tender. Skim if needed.

After 1 hour add the vegetables and enough of the remaining marinade to cover the contents of the pot. Season with tarragon and salt and pepper to taste.

When the venison and vegetables are tender, make the beurre manié. In a small bowl, beat the butter and flour until smooth. Gradually stir the beurre manié into the stew until it has thickened enough to lightly coat a spoon.

Serve hot with Gorgonzola Polenta (page 263).

SERVES 4 TO 6

SIDE DISHES

• POTATOES AND OTHER SOLID THINGS •

Shoestring Potatoes Fried in Suet

Golden "Turned" Potatoes

Garlic-Roasted Potatoes

Large Potato Pancakes

Mashed Potatoes

Carrot and Potato Purée

Navy-Bean Purée

Kasha

Couscous Risotto

Grits

Creamy Polenta

• SALADS •

Star-Spangled Potato Salad

Cold Mashed-Potato Salad

Bibb Lettuce with Soy-Sesame Vinaigrette

Red-Bean Salad with Red Cabbage

Cucumber Pachadi

Celery Slaw

• VEGETABLES •

Marinated, Roasted Baby Eggplants

Cumin Mushrooms

Sautéed Mushrooms with Lemon and Mustard

Braised Leeks

Melting Tomatoes Provençale

Zucchini Custard

Sautéed Zucchini with Dill

Vegetable Pancakes

Chutney Sorbet

One from Column A . . .
(A general guide to stir-frying)

Side dishes go mainly with main courses, yet every main course does not require a side dish. Indeed, some elegant dishes, complete and sauced, suffer from the intrusion of another presence on the plate. Still others—such as roast meats (pages 165–185)—generally look lonely on the plate without "an attendant lord to swell a scene or two." In this chapter are a few of my favorites.

I generally tend toward habitual pairings or am guided by what I find interesting in the store, in the garden or at the farm stand. When summer is upon the land, a good tomato cut into chunks, salted and combined with onion, basil, salt, pepper, olive oil, and a little lemon juice is perfection. Newly dug potatoes the size of a jacks ball, so thin-skinned that they must be washed carefully lest the skin rub right off, need only be steamed in a little melted butter to be one of the world's great delicacies. Or I'll plunge tiny French string beans into a vast quantity of boiling salted water until they turn tender and a startling green. Then they can be eaten hot with butter and a bit of chopped chervil or thrown into the tomato salad for a feast. And, oh, the stir-fries and vegetable stews that lightly cook and combine almost anything the garden can offer. Unfortunately most of the rest of year we must contrive a little more to obtain such good taste; but it is well worth doing.

Note that some of the dishes that follow would also make good first courses. Use your imagination.

...

POTATOES AND OTHER SOLID THINGS

I don't think this is a meat-and-potatoes country anymore. In fact, it may be a fish-and-vegetable country. Often, I serve neither potatoes nor rice nor noodles with a main course. I almost always provide lots of bread and, if the dish has a good sauce, a spoon.

So, when I serve potatoes or their counterparts with something, it is because the combined tastes are so good or because I crave that particular food. I don't know why, but there is something soothing not only about baked potatoes (page 12) but about all the carbohydrate wonders.

...

SHOESTRING POTATOES FRIED IN SUET

This is not a conceit: people become addicted to these suet-fried potatoes. They go well with any grilled meat, fish, or chicken. Although both are animal fat, suet and lard are essentially different: lard has been rendered, that is, liquefied, filtered, then allowed to solidify, while suet has only been very finely ground. The lard one can buy in neat packages in the supermarket is not worth eating. Suet, on the other hand, is a delight. If you can buy it, get the fat from around the kidney—also called leaf lard. It is white and clean and flaky. Cut it into cubes and process in a food processor until it is like creamed butter. It is at this stage that it can replace other fats in pie crusts to make a flakier, more flavorful product. With at least five pounds of suet you can cook as many, or as few, potatoes as you want.

...

Beef suet
All-purpose (Maine) potatoes
Kosher salt

Chop the suet in a food processor until it is creamed. Cook over medium heat in a heavy pot until completely melted. Strain and discard the solids.

Pour the fat into a broad skillet and heat until smoking.

While the fat heats, peel the potatoes. If you have a julienne disk for a food processor, put some water in the work bowl and grate the potatoes with the disk. Alternatively, use a four-sided hand grater and grate the potatoes into a bowl of water. You want long matchstick pieces.

Have sheets of brown paper ready for draining the potatoes. Sprinkle kosher salt on the paper.

Pat a handful of potatoes dry and drop them in the fat. They are done when they are light brown, about 30 seconds. Drain on the paper and sprinkle with more salt.

Continue cooking the potatoes in batches in this way. Try to resist temptation and keep them long enough to serve.

GOLDEN "TURNED" POTATOES

These potatoes are work; but they are sensationally good.

• • •

18 new white potatoes
8 tablespoons (½ pound) unsalted butter at room
*   temperature*
1¼ cups (about) Meat Stock (page 109) made
*   without salt*
1 tablespoon kosher salt

Heat the oven to 450° F.

Peel the potatoes, then shape them (turn) with a paring knife so you have 10 even facets going lengthwise around. In this way, as the potatoes cook in the butter, they will brown evenly on all sides and not just on the top and bottom.

Heat 4 tablespoons of the butter in a 12-inch skillet. Add the potatoes and cook, turning them often, until they are evenly golden brown all over. Keep the heat low to prevent the butter from burning. The potatoes must be watched carefully to assure an even golden color. The object at this point is just to brown the potatoes, not to cook them.

Place the potatoes in a 9-inch casserole. They should fit in fairly tightly. Pour in the stock; it should come halfway up the sides of the potatoes. Smear the remaining ¼ pound butter on top and bake in the preheated oven until the potatoes are cooked through, about an hour. Serve hot. You may get away with 2 potatoes per person. I can eat 4 myself.

SERVES 6

GARLIC-ROASTED POTATOES

If there is a specialty of the house, it is these potatoes. They are virtually without work. Since they take forty-five minutes in a hot oven, they can be roasted with leg of lamb (page 177) and be ready at the same time. They are best made with white new potatoes though red will do. I serve the garlic cloves as well, encouraging people to put them between their teeth and pull the cooked meat of the garlic out of the skins.

Serve these like baked potatoes—cut them open, scrunch them up, and add butter. They are delicious with their crisp, edible skins. Note that this recipe may be doubled easily.

• • •

> 1 pound new white potatoes, each about 1½ inches
>   long
> 6 large cloves garlic
> 3 tablespoons good olive oil
> ¾ tablespoon kosher salt
> Freshly ground black pepper

Heat the oven to 450° F.

Scrub the potatoes well and dry thoroughly. Place them in a heavy ovenproof casserole, with a tight-fitting lid, that is just large enough to hold them two layers deep. Add the other ingredients and mix well so the potatoes are all coated with the oil. Cover the casserole and bake for 50 minutes, longer if large potatoes. About halfway through the cooking time, lift the cover carefully—watch for steam and fat spatters—and turn the potatoes over with a wooden spoon so they are again covered with oil.

SERVES 4

LARGE POTATO PANCAKES

Miracles of modern science: my potato pancakes are no longer pink—with knuckle blood. The food processor grates the potatoes. Sometimes I add an onion when I grate.

• • •

> *1 pound 10 ounces (about 4 large) boiling*
> *   potatoes, peeled*
> *1 teaspoon kosher salt*
> *Freshly ground white pepper*
> *4 large eggs*
> *Vegetable oil (or rendered chicken fat to make it*
> *   very ethnic)*

Put the potatoes through the grating blade of a food processer, then chop them with the steel blade, until they are creamy but still somewhat gritty to the touch. If they are very watery, pour off some of the water.

Transfer the potatoes to a mixing bowl; stir in the salt and pepper and the eggs, one by one, adding another egg only when the previous one has been absorbed completely. Do not do this step in a food processor.

In an 8-inch omelet pan or any nonstick skillet, heat a small amount of oil until very hot. Stir the potato mixture once, and pour in about ⅓ cup. With a spatula, spread out the mixture to make a thin crêpe. Cook until golden brown on one side, about 2 minutes, regulating the heat so the pancake does not burn. Loosen with a spatula. Turn or flip over and cook until golden on the other side.

Serve hot.

MAKES ABOUT 12   CONTINUED

POTATO PANCAKE HORS D'OEUVRE

Smaller pancakes (a scant tablespoon of batter each) make a delicious hors d'oeuvre served with sour cream or with caviar (page 11) as well. This recipe would make 60 tiny pancakes.

MASHED POTATOES

———————————•———————————

Good mashed potatoes are a delight. They are not difficult but they should be made with care. You can make them less rich if you reduce the butter by half and add one-half cup milk. They are also more French that way. I prefer them indecently voluptuous—with the full allotment of butter—as made below.

•••

> *Kosher salt*
> *2 pounds mealy potatoes, scrubbed, unpeeled*
> *¾ pound unsalted butter, in 1-inch pieces*

Bring 3 quarts of water and 2 tablespoons of salt to a boil. Add the potatoes to the pot and cook over moderate heat just until tender. You should be able to pierce them easily with a sharp skewer. Remove them from the heat and drain.

Peel the potatoes as soon as you can bear to handle them. Do not let them cool. Immediately put them through a ricer or food mill into a mixing bowl. Beat in the butter until smooth. Season to taste with about 1 tablespoon salt.

The potatoes are best if prepared immediately before serving. If you need to prepare them ahead, keep them warm over very low heat (preferably on a flame tamer) until serving time.

SERVES 4 TO 6

CARROT AND POTATO PURÉE

———————————•———————————

This is not only a recipe; it is also a model for countless combined-vegetable purées. Other good combinations are turnip and potato, celery root and potato, beet and potato, broccoli and potato, and cauliflower and potato—vary the seasonings to suit.

• • •

1 pound carrots, coarsely chopped
¾ pound peeled potatoes, coarsely chopped
3 cups water
3 tablespoons sugar
1 tablespoon kosher salt
1 teaspoon ground cumin, optional
6 tablespoons unsalted butter
½ cup heavy cream

Put the carrots and potatoes in a saucepan with the water, sugar, 2 teaspoons salt, and cumin. Simmer over medium heat for 30 minutes, or until tender.

Drain the carrot-potato mixture and place it in the work bowl of a food processor. Process with on-off pulses until the mixture is nearly smooth but small pieces of carrot still show. Add the butter, 1 tablespoon at a time, then beat in the cream and the remaining teaspoon of salt.

SERVES 4 TO 6

NAVY-BEAN PURÉE

———————————•———————————

This is delicious with roast lamb, veal, or pork. If there is any left, dilute it with ample Chicken Stock (page 110) and you have a terrific soup.

• • •

1 pound dried navy beans
1 medium-size head garlic, peeled
¾ cup unsalted butter, softened
2 tablespoons chopped flat-leaf parsley
2 tablespoons olive oil
Kosher salt
½ teaspoon freshly ground black pepper

Pick over the beans. Discard any damaged beans or pieces of stone. Place the beans in a stockpot. Add cold water to cover by 2 inches.

Bring to a boil over high heat, stirring occasionally. Boil 1 minute. Remove the pot from the heat. Let stand 1 hour.

Drain the beans and discard the liquid. Return the beans to the pot and add fresh water to cover. Heat to simmering. Simmer for about 1 hour, until the beans are almost tender. Add the peeled garlic. Simmer an additional 30 minutes, until the beans are very tender.

Drain the beans. Transfer them, along with the garlic, to a large bowl. With a fork, mash the beans and garlic. Incorporate the butter, parsley, oil, salt to taste, and pepper. Continue to mash until the mixture is coarsely puréed.

The bean purée can be served immediately or stored, covered, in the refrigerator until you are ready to use it. Reheat over a low flame.

MAKES 1 QUART, TO SERVE ABOUT 8 PEOPLE

KASHA

———————————•———————————

I find the rich texture and nutty taste of kasha (buckwheat groats) interesting with grilled fish and sensational with Roast Leg of Lamb (page 177).

• • •

2 tablespoons unsalted butter
1 large onion, chopped
2 ribs celery, chopped
½ cup parsley leaves, chopped
1 cup kasha
2 teaspoons kosher salt
Freshly ground black pepper
2 cups water

Melt the butter in a saucepan with a tight-fitting lid. Over medium heat, sauté the onion, stirring occasionally, until it is soft but not brown. Add the celery and the parsley, and continue to cook and stir for 3 minutes. Add the kasha, salt, and pepper, and cook, stirring, for 5 minutes. Add the water, stir, and bring to a boil. Reduce the heat so the liquid simmers; cover and cook for 25 minutes until tender.

SERVES 6

KASHA VARNITCHKES

Follow the recipe for Kasha, stirring in 1 cup cooked bowtie noodles just before serving.

COUSCOUS RISOTTO

———————— • ————————

Overcome by a craving for couscous, I was standing in my kitchen one day with a cardboard box of the stuff in hand and no couscousière. Resolutely experimental, I decided to cook the couscous as if it were risotto. It turned out splendidly and has become one of my staples.

Couscous may be the smallest pasta of them all. It is eaten all over North Africa. The grain is cooked in the bulbous top of a steamer over a rich broth with meats, vegetables, and spices. For many years this delicious grain was unavailable in this country. Today, it can be found in cardboard packages in supermarkets. There are several different kinds: instant and regular in differing textures and sizes. For this recipe it will not matter which couscous you use, though the cooking time will alter slightly as will the amount of chicken stock absorbed.

As with rice and potatoes, it is difficult to say how many this dish serves. Normally, I would think it would make eight portions. Even if I need less, I make a full recipe because it tastes delicious cold or reheated the next day.

• • •

2 small or 1 large yellow onion
5 medium cloves garlic
1½ cups unsalted butter
1 tablespoon cumin
½ teaspoon good curry powder
2 cups instant or regular couscous
5 cups Chicken Stock (page 110)
1½ teaspoons kosher salt
Freshly ground black pepper

Peel the onions and cut them into 1-inch chunks. With a heavy knife or pot smash the garlic cloves and remove the skins. Chop the onions and garlic fine by hand or place together in a food processor and, with on-off pulses, chop fine.

In a 10-inch heavy, deep pot, melt the butter over medium heat. Cook the onion and garlic mixture until transparent but not brown. Add cumin and curry, and continue to cook, stirring constantly, for 2 minutes. Add couscous and cook until all fat and liquid are absorbed.

Begin adding chicken stock in ½-cup increments, stirring and waiting each time until all the stock has been absorbed. Continue until all the chicken stock has been incorporated. Add salt and then pepper to taste. Be careful with the salt if you are using canned stock, as it will probably already contain salt.

When preparing this recipe, you may want to have extra stock on hand, since different kinds of couscous may absorb different amounts of stock. This dish reheats well. To do so, you may need to add a little extra stock so as not to dry it out.

SERVES ABOUT 8

GRITS

In some parts of this country, people have never tasted grits. In others, it is a three-meal-a-day habit. Wherever you are, remember *grits* takes a singular verb—and grits is good.

• • •

4 cups water
2¼ teaspoons kosher salt
1 cup grits (not quick-cooking)
¼ pound unsalted butter, cut into pieces

OPTIONAL
½ teaspoon finely minced garlic
2 fresh jalapeño peppers, or 4 canned, chopped
½ to ¾ cup grated Cheddar cheese

Bring the water and salt to a boil in a saucepan. Stir in the grits. Lower the heat slightly and cook for 25 to 30 minutes, stirring frequently to keep the mixture from sticking. Stir in the butter.

At this point, the grits is neutral. Add sugar for breakfast or the optional ingredients for a spicy accompaniment to anything from eggs to fish to roast chicken.

SERVES 6

CREAMY POLENTA

Somehow, we managed to give away credit for our birthright, cornmeal mush, to the Italians. Let's take it back and eat it.

• • •

6½ cups water
Kosher salt
1 cup yellow cornmeal
¾ to 1 cup heavy cream
6 tablespoons melted unsalted butter
Freshly ground black pepper

Bring 5 cups of water to a boil in a 3-quart pot. Add 2 teaspoons salt. In a large bowl, stir the cornmeal into the remaining cold water. Pour cold water and cornmeal all at once into the boiling water. Stir while boiling approximately 30 minutes. The mixture should pull away from the sides of the pan and be able to hold its shape.

Over low heat, stir in the cream and butter. Continue to stir until the mixture is smooth and creamy. Add pepper and salt to taste.

SERVES ABOUT 6

GORGONZOLA POLENTA

Make the polenta using ½ cup heavy cream. When you stir in the cream and melted butter, add ½ cup crumbled Gorgonzola cheese.

• • •

SALADS

Cooks often come to me to talk about jobs and I tend to ask them what they like to cook. If they are timid, I will prompt them by saying that what I like are stews and soups and sauces; true enough, but still a half truth. As I came to put this chapter together, I realized that above all I like to make salads. Even in years when I have scant courage for a garden, I will have tomatoes, onions, basil, peppers, and fifteen or so kinds of lettuce—not all ready at the same time, of course. These are to fill my salad bowl along with lovage, dill, nasturtiums, chives, burdock, tarragon, burnet, summer savory, mint, and many other herbs from that sunny spot.

• • •

STAR-SPANGLED POTATO SALAD

One of my most popular recipes isn't even mine. I thank Scott Grodnick, who gave it to me—he let me use it and lets me use it again. This is an old-fashioned middle-America taste. Don't overboil the eggs or they will get powdery—about ten minutes in salted water is perfect. Don't boil them in an aluminum pot or they will develop a green, ugly ring between yolk and white. For peeling instructions see page 220.

• • •

5 medium boiling potatoes
Dash white pepper
2 tablespoons chopped scallions
2 tablespoons chopped jarred pimientos
3 hard-boiled eggs, diced
¼ cup diced celery
1¼ cups mayonnaise (commercial, unsweetened)
1 tablespoon kosher salt

Cook the potatoes in boiling water until a knife point slips in easily. Peel and cut into 1-inch dice. In a large bowl, mix the potatoes with the remaining ingredients. Chill at least 2 hours.

MAKES ABOUT 6 CUPS

COLD MASHED-POTATO SALAD

This is an unexpected salad, but good.

• • •

6 cups leftover Mashed Potatoes (page 258)
1½ to 2 cups mayonnaise (see note)
2 tablespoons finely cut chives
½ cup coarsely crumbled crisply-cooked bacon
¼ cup grated onion
¾ teaspoon celery seed
2 teaspoons kosher salt
½ teaspoon freshly ground white pepper

Place the mashed potatoes in a mixing bowl and beat briefly until smooth. Beat in the mayonnaise; blend thoroughly. Add the remaining ingredients and mix until completely blended. You can do the mixing with an electric mixer set at low.

Serve at room temperature.

MAKES ABOUT 7 CUPS

NOTE: It's fine to use commercial mayonnaise for this, but try to find one that's not sweetened.

BIBB LETTUCE WITH SOY-SESAME VINAIGRETTE

———————•———————

This is a knock-off of the salad dressing on Trader Vic's limestone lettuce salad. It's not a perfect reproduction, but it's very good. You can omit the garlic if you prefer.

• • •

SOY-SESAME VINAIGRETTE

1½ tablespoons tarragon vinegar
⅛ teaspoon dry mustard
⅛ teaspoon kosher salt
Freshly ground black pepper
2½ tablespoons Japanese soy sauce
¼ cup olive oil
Scant ⅛ teaspoon oriental sesame oil
¼ teaspoon tightly packed chopped fresh tarragon
*   leaves, if available; otherwise omit*
¼ teaspoon crushed, peeled, finely minced garlic

SALAD

6 heads Bibb lettuce, separated into leaves, washed
*   and dried*

Put the vinegar, mustard, salt, pepper, and soy sauce in a small bowl. Whisk until smooth. Still whisking, pour in the olive oil, then the sesame oil, fresh tarragon, and garlic. At this point, the dressing can keep for an hour—longer and the garlic will get too strong.

Toss with the lettuce leaves and serve immediately.

SERVES 6

RED-BEAN SALAD WITH RED CABBAGE

———————•———————

A good first course, buffet salad, or side salad with cold fish.

• • •

1 cup plus 2 tablespoons vegetable oil
6 tablespoons white wine vinegar
Kosher salt

Freshly ground black pepper
1½ teaspoons dry mustard
3 cups cooked red kidney beans (see note), warm
3 cups red cabbage in 1-by-½-inch strips, blanched
    briefly in boiling water, plunged immediately
    into ice water, and drained well
1 cup diced red onion (about ½-inch dice)

Mix together the oil, vinegar, 1 teaspoon salt, ⅛ teaspoon pepper, and mustard until completely blended. Toss with the still warm beans. Add the cabbage and onion. Stir well to combine and coat with the dressing. Add additional salt and pepper to taste.

Serve at room temperature.

MAKES 7 CUPS

NOTE: If using dried beans (these are preferable), place about 1 cup in a pot and cover with cold water. Bring the water to a boil, then remove from the heat and let rest 1 hour. Drain. Cover with fresh cold water. Bring back to the boil and simmer an additional hour until tender. If using canned beans, rinse them well in warm water.

CUCUMBER PACHADI

———————•———————

This spicy dish is usually served at the beginning of an Indian meal with a hot bread, such as paratha or chapati. It is also a great accompaniment for curry and also for fish, lamb, and chicken simply prepared.

• • •

2 medium cucumbers
1 teaspoon kosher salt
1 onion
1 large fresh ripe tomato
3 small fresh green chilies, stemmed
Bunch of coriander
¾ cup unflavored yogurt

Peel the cucumbers. Trim the ends. Cut in half lengthwise, and with a spoon or knife remove and discard the seeds. Cut the cucumber halves into 1-inch pieces. Fit the work bowl of a food processor with the steel blade. Add the cucumbers and process with 6 or 7 quick on-off pulses. Transfer the coarsely chopped cucumbers to a glass or ceramic bowl. Sprinkle with salt.

Peel and quarter the onion. Place in the work bowl fitted with the steel blade. Peel and seed the tomato. Cut into quarters and add to the work bowl. Cut the chilies in half and add to the work bowl. Wash and dry the coriander. Trim the leaves and place in the work bowl. Process until everything is in small pieces.

Squeeze out the cucumbers by hand or put them in a dish towel and twist to squeeze out the liquid. Put the squeezed cucumbers into a serving bowl. Add the chopped mixture from the work bowl and the yogurt. Mix well. Serve chilled or at room temperature.

SERVES 4 AS A FIRST COURSE, 8 AS AN ACCOMPANIMENT

CELERY SLAW

• • •

This is a variation on coleslaw with some extra crunch. Serve it the way you would coleslaw with anything from hamburgers to simple festive foods.

• • •

¼ cup sour cream
¼ cup plus 2 tablespoons Mayonnaise (page 312)
1 tablespoon red wine vinegar
½ teaspoon kosher salt
⅛ teaspoon freshly ground black pepper
¼ teaspoon sugar
2 drops hot red-pepper sauce
Pinch paprika
3 cups thinly-sliced celery, sliced on the diagonal
3 tablespoons slivered canned pimiento

Mix together all the ingredients except the celery and pimiento. Place the celery and pimiento in a bowl and toss with the dressing.

MAKES ABOUT 3 CUPS

• • •

VEGETABLES

MARINATED, ROASTED BABY EGGPLANTS

These are spectacularly good. The only problem is you have to start them the day before you need them. However, if that's not convenient, you can make them a day or two ahead. They keep well once cooked. Good hot, good cold, good as a first course, good as an hors d'oeuvre, good as a side dish—no problems.

• • •

2 pounds baby eggplants, or small Japanese
  eggplants, or long, thin Chinese eggplants
½ cup fruity olive oil, preferably Californian
⅓ cup soy sauce
¼ cup vegetable oil
6 to 8 medium-size cloves garlic, peeled

Wash the eggplants. Cut each in half lengthwise, leaving the stem attached. With the skin side down, use a paring knife to score the flesh diagonally; criss-cross to form a diamond pattern. Cut as deep as possible without piercing the skin.

In a food processor, blend the olive oil, soy sauce, vegetable oil, and garlic. Pour the marinade into a deep non-aluminum baking dish. Place the eggplants in the baking dish, cut side down. Marinate at least overnight—up to 2 days is fine—in the refrigerator. Before roasting, let the eggplant come to room temperature.

Heat the oven to 250°F. Roast the eggplant in the marinade for 20 minutes. Turn the eggplant over and roast an additional 20 to 25 minutes, until softened.

Let the eggplant cool in the liquid. Remove from the liquid with a slotted spoon and serve at room temperature.

SERVES 8 AS A FIRST COURSE OR SIDE DISH

CUMIN MUSHROOMS

Speared on toothpicks, these make a great cocktail snack. As a vegetable, they go particularly well with fish. Carrots can be prepared the same way.

...

2 pounds firm, white medium-sized mushrooms
½ cup vegetable oil
2 to 2½ teaspoons ground cumin
¼ teaspoon kosher salt, or to taste
Freshly ground black pepper

Wipe the mushrooms clean with the palm of your hand. Cut off the stems and reserve them for another use.

In a skillet large enough to hold all the mushrooms in a single layer, heat the oil over medium heat. If your skillet will not hold all the mushrooms, use two skillets and divide the ingredients equally between them. Set the mushrooms in the pan, cut side down. Sprinkle with 1½ teaspoons cumin, ¼ teaspoon salt, and several grindings of pepper. Reduce the heat to low. Cook the mushrooms uncovered, turning occasionally, about 1½ to 2 hours, until very dark brown.

Five minutes before removing the mushrooms from the heat, stir in ½ teaspoon cumin. Taste and adjust the seasonings. Transfer the mushrooms to a bowl. Cool to room temperature, tossing occasionally. Serve at room temperature.

SERVES 4

SAUTÉED MUSHROOMS WITH
LEMON AND MUSTARD

These are at their best with a thick broiled steak. The steak juices run into the mushrooms to make a sauce.

...

¾ cup (1½ sticks) unsalted butter
2 pounds medium-sized mushrooms, halved
*   through the stems*

4 teaspoons kosher salt
1 teaspoon freshly ground black pepper
2 tablespoons prepared mustard
2 tablespoons fresh lemon juice

Heat the butter in a skillet. Add the mushrooms and cook, stirring, until they are just heated through—about 5 minutes. Add the salt, pepper, mustard, and lemon juice. Cook slightly to reduce the lemon juice and make a sauce.

SERVES 6

BRAISED LEEKS

I love braised leeks. They can be eaten hot or cold, as a first course or as a side dish. Put a thin slice of Virginia or Vermont ham over each portion (three leeks per portion) and a half cup of grated Cheddar over that; place under the broiler until bubbly and you have a light main course.

· · ·

12 small leeks, trimmed and washed well
1½ cups Chicken Stock (page 110), or enough to
 almost cover the leeks
Salt
6 tablespoons unsalted butter

Preheat the oven to 350° F.

Place the leeks in a pan wide enough to hold them flat in layers. Add the stock and salt to taste. (The amount of salt needed will vary according to the saltiness of the stock.) Bring the stock to a boil and cook at a slow boil for 10 minutes.

Butter a baking dish wide enough to hold the leeks flat. Place the leeks in the dish and pour the cooking liquid over them. Dot with the remaining butter. Bake for 30 minutes, or until the leeks are lightly browned and the liquid is almost evaporated.

SERVES 4

NOTE: If you can get only large leeks, cook them longer—about 10 minutes more—on top of the stove. Add ½ cup more stock and continue to cook them in the oven until the liquid evaporates.

MELTING TOMATOES PROVENÇALE

These can be made even in the middle of winter when tomatoes are terrible. The slow cooking drives out the water and intensifies the flavor. I serve them with my omnipresent Roast Leg of Lamb (page 177) and eat any leftovers with eggs. Make the whole recipe even if you have only four guests.

• • •

3 ripe tomatoes, 2 to 3 inches in diameter
1 tablespoon plus 1 scant teaspoon olive oil
2 cloves garlic, minced
6 fresh basil leaves, chopped well
1 teaspoon kosher salt
Freshly ground black pepper
2 tablespoons dried bread crumbs

Cut the tomatoes in half between the stem and the bottom. Cut out the cores. Seed the tomatoes and, with a small spoon, pierce a few holes in the skin side of each half. Put the tomatoes, cut sides down, on absorbent paper to drain for 30 minutes.

Put 1 tablespoon olive oil in a 12-inch skillet. Add the drained tomatoes, cut sides down. Cook them over *very* low heat for 20 minutes. Turn the tomatoes skin side down and cook for 1½ to 2 hours longer, over the lowest possible heat. All cooking is done with pan uncovered.

Heat the broiler.

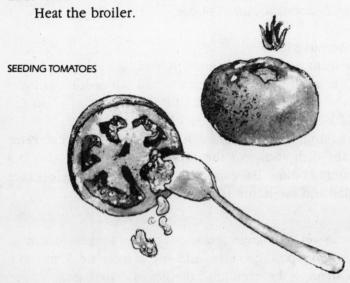

SEEDING TOMATOES

Place the tomatoes, skin side down, on an oiled baking sheet; sprinkle with the garlic, basil, salt, and pepper. Sprinkle the bread crumbs evenly over the tops. Pour the skillet juices over the tops. Put the tomatoes under the preheated broiler for 2 to 3 minutes, or just until they brown and the bread crumbs form a crust.

Serve hot or cold.

SERVES 6

ZUCCHINI CUSTARD

This is one of my all-time bests—a sort of crustless quiche. The quality comes from letting the zucchini drain until there is no liquid left to disrupt the texture of the custard. The peeled zucchini virtually disappear into the custard.

•••

2 pounds small firm zucchini, peeled and cut into
*   2-inch-long, ¼-inch-thick strips*
1½ cups heavy cream
3 large eggs
⅓ to ¾ cup freshly grated Parmesan cheese
Freshly ground black pepper

Bring about 6 quarts of heavily salted water to a boil. Add the zucchini and let the water return to the boil. Boil for 30 seconds, then drain well. Spread the zucchini in a single layer on kitchen towels and let dry for several hours, or all day.

Preheat the oven to 450° F.

Mix the zucchini with the cream, eggs, cheese, and pepper. Pour the mixture into a 9- or 10-inch pie plate or ceramic quiche pan. Place on a baking sheet in the lower third of the preheated oven and bake for 40 minutes, or until puffed, brown, custardy, and set. Serve immediately.

SERVES 8

NOTE: If you prefer individual servings, divide the mixture among 8 six-ounce ceramic quiche pans and bake only 15 to 20 minutes.

SAUTÉED ZUCCHINI WITH DILL

Quick and flavorful, this can be made with yellow summer squash in the fall.

•••

5 tablespoons unsalted butter
2 pounds young zucchini, cut in ¼-inch-thick
  rounds
½ cup chopped fresh dill
Juice of 1 lemon
Kosher salt

Heat the butter in a 12-inch sauté pan. Add the zucchini, dill, and lemon juice. Cook over medium heat, stirring, until the zucchini is cooked but still slightly crisp. Add salt to taste.

SERVES 6 TO 8

VEGETABLE PANCAKES

This is a sort of multicolored potato pancake.

•••

1 medium onion, minced
1 pound carrots, scrubbed and shredded
1 pound zucchini, washed and shredded
1 pound potatoes, peeled and shredded
2 tablespoons minced parsley
½ cup all-purpose flour
2 large eggs
2 teaspoons kosher salt
⅛ teaspoon freshly ground black pepper
Vegetable oil

Put the onion, carrots, zucchini, potatoes, and parsley in a bowl. Stir in the flour, eggs, salt, and pepper.

Heat about ½ inch of vegetable oil in a 12-inch skillet until hot but not smoking. Take about 3 tablespoons of the mixture and put it into the skillet. With a spatula, immediately spread the mixture into a 4-inch circle. Cook for about 3 minutes; turn and cook for 3 minutes on the other side. You can cook about 3 at a time. Remove the cooked pancakes with a slotted spatula and drain on absorbent paper. Keep warm. Repeat until all the batter is cooked. Serve warm.

MAKES ABOUT 14 FOUR-INCH PANCAKES

CHUTNEY SORBET

This is in none of the above categories; but try it with curry or grilled fish.

• • •

2 seventeen-ounce jars Major Grey's chutney
2 cups hot water
2 tablespoons fresh lemon juice

Place the chutney in the work bowl of a food processor and process until smooth. With the machine running, pour in the hot water, then the lemon juice.

Freeze in an ice-cream freezer according to manufacturer's directions or in metal trays in the freezer.

SERVES 6 AS A GARNISH

ONE FROM COLUMN A . . .

This is a general guide to stir-frying vegetables and some suggestions for flavorings. Three cups of vegetables (preferably one cup from each column) makes enough for one main course when served with rice; or for four side dishes. If you want to use all vegetables from one column or two cups from one column and one cup from another, just remember to observe the overall cooking times for each group. The frying and seasoning ingredients are for three cups of vegetables. If changing vegetable quantities, vary frying time and seasoning quantities accordingly. The normal home wok will not hold more than three cups of vegetables comfortably. If you need more vegetables, repeat procedure.

• • •

COLUMN A

Julienne of yellow bell pepper
Julienne of white turnip
Broccoli stems, peeled, cut into coins
Cauliflowerets
Trimmed string beans, cut into 3-inch lengths
Shredded white or red cabbage
Quartered mushrooms
Thin julienne of fennel bulb

COLUMN B

Small broccoli flowerets
Corn kernels
Shredded bok choy
Sliced leek whites
Shelled fresh peas
Thinly-bias-sliced celery
Canned exotic mushrooms
Reconstituted dried shiitake mushrooms or tree
  ears

COLUMN C

Trimmed snow peas
Trimmed sugar snap peas
Tofu
Scallions cut into 3-inch lengths
Shredded lettuces and greens
Canned bamboo shoots or water chestnuts
Celery leaves
Julienne of red or green bell pepper

FOR 3 CUPS VEGETABLES
2 tablespoons peanut oil
1 teaspoon minced fresh ginger
½ teaspoon minced garlic
¼ teaspoon oriental hot oil
2 tablespoons Chicken Stock (page 110)
1 tablespoon soy sauce

Heat the oil in a large wok or skillet over medium-high heat until almost smoking. Add vegetables from Column A. Stir-fry 3 minutes. Add vegetables from Column B. Stir-fry 2 minutes. Add vegetables from Column C, the ginger, garlic, and hot oil. Stir-fry 1 minute. Add the chicken stock and soy sauce. Stir-fry just about 1 minute, until the vegetables are crisp-tender. Serve immediately.

NOTE: Additional seasonings such as 1 teaspoon sesame oil, 1 tablespoon sesame seeds, 1 tablespoon of oyster, plum or hoisin sauces or 2 tablespoons fermented black beans, rinsed and drained, could be added along with vegetables from Column C. One tablespoon black mustard seeds could be added along with vegetables from Column A. Choose your seasonings to complement your choice of vegetables.

DESSERTS

———•———

Papaya Filled with Sour Cream, Glazed with Brown Sugar

Strawberries Tossed in Peppered Vinegar

Macédoine of Fruit

Maple-Syrup–Baked Rome Beauties

Poached Peaches with Raspberries

Poached Pears with Pear Sorbet

Chocolate Sabayon with Fresh Peaches

Clafoutis with Pineapple

Strawberry Bavarian

Chocolate Sorbet

Fresh Pineapple Sorbet

Ginger Ice Cream

Macaroons

Lemon Chiffon Pie

Apple Brioche Tart

Raspberry Bread Pudding

Pâte à Choux and Paris-Brest

Butterscotch Sauce

Chocolate Layer Cake

I must confess that I am not much of a dessert eater and, like an Italian, I am usually happy with fruit and cheese at the end of a meal. Fresh berries with cream; or with raspberry vinegar, sugar, and black pepper; or with lemon juice and sugar are for me a sufficient summer dissipation.

But I have guests and they like dessert. Sometimes what I do will be as simple as hollowing out a ripe papaya, filling the hollow with sour cream, and patting a good layer of brown sugar over the cream (page 282). Left to sit for half an hour, the acid in the cream caramelizes the sugar and we have a delight to eat with a spoon. Sometimes I poach peaches in a fragrant syrup, peel them, and surround them with fresh raspberries, which I then lightly bathe with a reduction of the poaching syrup. Whipped cream would be an almost sinful extra (page 297).

Occasionally a real dessert is required: in this chapter are a few of my living-up-to-the-occasion desserts.

We tend not to have the habit of dessert wine in America. Sometimes a little Champagne will be left from the beginning of a festive meal and it will be served with dessert, but rarely is wine deliberately served. It is a shame since we are beginning to get really excellent dessert wines from California. As a nondessert person, I am often delighted to have a glass or more of a Selected Late Harvest or other botrytisized or sugar-rich wine instead of dessert. The best of these wines tend to be expensive, but small quantities are usually required. A good American Johannisberg riesling that has a fair amount of residual sugar will generally be less costly. I find that a dessert wine always adds a festive note, and in a meal with just a main course and a dessert it gives the opportunity for two wines and two sparkling glasses.

•••

PAPAYA FILLED WITH SOUR CREAM, GLAZED WITH BROWN SUGAR

Quick—start this when you walk in the door or even when you are ready to put the first course on the table. By dessert time it will be ready and the sugar will have caramelized into a slightly runny crust.

•••

4 papayas
1⅓ cups sour cream, approximately
1 cup brown sugar, approximately

Cut the papayas in half and remove the seeds. Fill the cavity with sour cream so it mounds on top. Pat a layer of brown sugar over the sour cream to completely cover it. Refrigerate at least 1 hour before serving. Give each person ½ papaya.

SERVES 8

STRAWBERRIES TOSSED IN PEPPERED VINEGAR

I have often used this recipe in my classes. Students can't believe that it will be good, and it's spectacularly good. Red wine can be substituted for the vinegar. The red wine or vinegar is an Italian touch. The pepper on fruit is a Russian idea. My father used to put it on melon to bring out the sweetness.

•••

½ cup sugar
2 cups raspberry vinegar
1 teaspoon freshly ground black pepper
2 pints strawberries, washed and hulled

Stir the sugar into the vinegar until the sugar dissolves. Add the pepper and stir to mix. Toss with the strawberries.

SERVES 6

MACÉDOINE OF FRUIT

•

You don't need to use all of these fruits nor be limited by this list. Combine fruits by color and texture. The instructions are mainly to give you an idea of the order in which you should combine the fruits. Allow about three-quarters of a cup of fruit per person.

Use the fruits that are in season.

• • •

Oranges
Grapefruit
Kumquats
Blueberries
Melon
Pineapple
Peaches
Pears
Apples
Grapes
Strawberries
Bananas
Fresh mint

Using a serrated knife, peel the oranges and grapefruit until all the white membrane has been removed. Cut on both sides of each sectional membrane and let the fruit slip out into a bowl, removing the seeds. When all the sections have been removed, squeeze the juice out of the remaining pulp over the fruit. Discard the pulp.

Slice the kumquats thin.

Wash, dry, and stem the blueberries. Add to the bowl.

Cut the melon in half and remove the seeds. Peel the melon, and cut it into very thin wedges or cubes. Add to the bowl.

Peel the pineapple by first cutting off the top and the bottom. Stand it flat on the work surface. Cut down the sides with a knife until all the peel is removed. Make sure the "eyes" are removed as well. Turn the pineapple on its side and slice it crosswise into ½-inch-thick slices. Cut out the hard core in each slice with a small knife or a small biscuit cutter. Cut to desired size. Add to the bowl.

Wash and dry the peaches. Cut them in halves; remove the pits, and slice the halves into wedges. If you like, peel with a knife. (Alternatively, before cutting, drop the whole peach in boiling water for

15 seconds to loosen the peel so you can pull it off with your fingers.) Add to the bowl.

Wash and dry the pears and apples. Cut them in halves, and remove the seeds and cores with a paring knife. Cut into even slices lengthwise or crosswise. If desired, peel them before cutting, with a vegetable peeler or small knife. Toss immediately with the other fruits so that the citrus juices keep the pears and apples from turning brown.

Cut the grapes in halves. If the grapes have seeds, remove them. Add the grapes to the bowl with the other fruit.

Just before serving, rinse the strawberries, hull them, and cut in halves. Peel the bananas and slice thin. Toss with the other fruits.

Garnish with mint leaves.

MAPLE-SYRUP–BAKED ROME BEAUTIES

When simple is sophisticated, this is a perfect end to a fall or winter dinner. If Rome Beauties are unavailable, use huge McIntosh apples, Macouns, or Twenty Ounces. Serve in small rim soups or dessert dishes that are fairly deep. Spoon over the pan liquid and pass a pitcher of heavy cream.

• • •

6 Rome Beauty apples
1 tablespoon butter
1 tablespoon dried currants
3 tablespoons chopped walnuts
Grated zest of 1 orange
2 tablespoons orange juice
3 tablespoons lemon juice
¾ cup maple syrup

Heat the oven to 375° F.

Core the apples, leaving about ½ inch core on the bottom of each. Remove about 1½ inches of peel from the top of each apple. Butter a baking pan well. Put in the apples—not touching each other or the sides of the pan.

Divide the currants, walnuts, and orange zest evenly among the apples, filling the cavity with them. Then pour in the juices and maple syrup. Place in the oven and bake for 1 hour, or until soft. Serve warm.

SERVES 6

POACHED PEACHES WITH RASPBERRIES

This not only tastes delicious but also looks beautiful. Choose a large white oval platter that is deep enough to hold the liquid and handsome enough to frame the peaches, which turn a beautiful rosy color from being basted with the raspberries and syrup. Make this at least four hours before dinner so that the flavors and colors have time to blend. If fresh raspberries aren't in season, simply poach the peaches as described below and serve with Raspberry Sauce or Nectarine Sauce (page 287 and page 319).

• • •

8 cups water
2 cups sugar
2 lemons, halved
1 cinnamon stick
1 vanilla bean, split
2 whole cloves
6 large ripe peaches
1 pint raspberries, picked over, rinsed
Heavy cream

In a large, wide pot, combine the water and sugar. Over medium heat, cook until the water is simmering and the sugar is dissolved. Simmer for 5 minutes. Squeeze the lemons into the water and drop in the lemon halves. Add the cinnamon stick, vanilla bean, and cloves. Simmer an additional 5 minutes.

Add the peaches. Reduce the heat until the syrup is just below simmering. Poach the peaches for a half hour or until they are tender when pierced with a knife. Using a slotted spoon, transfer them to a serving platter. Slip off the skins. Sprinkle the raspberries over the platter.

Boil the poaching liquid over high heat until it is reduced by about half. It should be thick enough to lightly coat a spoon. While still warm, strain the syrup and ladle over the peaches and raspberries. Let them stand until serving time, preferably for at least 4 hours, basting occasionally with syrup.

Serve at room temperature with heavy cream.

SERVES 6

POACHED PEARS WITH PEAR SORBET

———————•———————

Another recipe that looks as good as it tastes. The pears become the same translucent color as the sorbet—a kind of trompe l'oeil compliment as well as a nice light ending to a meal. If you don't have time to make a sorbet, you can poach the pears and serve them with a quick raspberry sauce (opposite page) or the Nectarine Sauce on page 319.

•••

2 quarts water
1 cup sugar
2 cloves
1 three-inch piece cinnamon stick
1 vanilla bean
1 lemon, halved
6 ripe but firm pears
Fresh mint sprigs for garnish

Place the water and sugar into a saucepan. Bring the water to a boil and add the cloves, cinnamon and vanilla bean. Squeeze the juice of the lemon into the syrup and add the squeezed halves. Peel, halve and core the pears. Add the pears with the cores and peelings to the pot. The pears should be completely covered with liquid.

Simmer the liquid until the pears are soft through when pierced with a skewer. Cooking time depends on firmness of the pears. Remove the pears with a slotted spoon and set aside to cool. Strain the syrup, discarding the solids. Boil the syrup down to 4 cups.

Purée half the pears in a food processor with the reserved syrup. This will probably have to be done in batches. Freeze the purée in an ice-cream maker according to the manufacturer's directions. If you don't have an ice-cream maker, freeze the mixture in ice-cube trays and then beat it smooth in a food processor.

To serve, place the reserved pear halves, curved side down, on plates and fill with some of the sorbet. Garnish with fresh mint sprigs.

SERVES 6

• POACHED PEARS WITH RASPBERRY SAUCE •

Before poaching, peel the pears, but leave them whole. Use an apple corer or a paring knife to hollow them out from the bottom, leaving the stems intact. Poach according to the recipe above. Cool the pears in the poaching syrup. Meanwhile, defrost two 10½-ounce packages frozen raspberries. Place them in the work bowl of a food processor, fitted with the metal blade. Add the juice of one-half lemon and process until smooth. Remove the purée from the food processor and force it through a strainer to remove the seeds. Serve the poached pears on top of the sauce. (The poaching liquid can be reserved, frozen or refrigerated, for another use. It can also be reduced and frozen for later use in the sorbet.)

If you are desperate for a last-minute dessert and don't have time to poach pears, you can use good-quality canned pears. Slice the pears thinly lengthwise. Arrange the slices in a fan on top of the raspberry sauce.

CHOCOLATE SABAYON WITH
FRESH PEACHES

———————•———————

This unusual combination works. In winter, when peaches are un-available, substitute one and one-half cups peeled sliced pineapple.

• • •

1 ounce unsweetened chocolate
4 large egg yolks
¼ cup sugar
1 tablespoon Kirschwasser
½ cup heavy cream
2 large or 3 medium-size ripe peaches, peeled,
   halved, pitted, and cut into wedges

Melt the chocolate in a saucepan over low heat, stirring often. When melted, remove it from the heat.

Have ready a large stainless-steel bowl that will fit over a sauce-pan so there is a 4- to 6-inch space between the bottom of the pan and the bottom of the bowl. If you have a sabayon pot, certainly use it. Pour 2 inches of water into the pan and bring it to a simmer over moderate heat.

Meanwhile, in the large bowl, beat the egg yolks with the sugar until combined.

Place the bowl over the simmering water and whisk until the yolks are tepid, about 1½ minutes. Stir in the melted chocolate and Kirschwasser, and continue whisking for another 30 to 60 seconds, until the mixture is thick and you can see the bottom of the bowl as you whisk. Pour it immediately into a small cool bowl. Cool for 5 to 10 minutes.

In a separate bowl, whip the cream until soft peaks form. Stir some of the cream into the chocolate mixture to lighten it. Fold in the remaining cream just until mixed. Chill until ready to serve.

To serve, place the peach wedges in a bowl and spoon the sa-bayon over.

SERVES 4

CLAFOUTIS WITH PINEAPPLE

———————————•———————————

I think the surprise of the black pepper, which balances the sweetness of the pineapple, will please you.

• • •

1 twelve-ounce can pineapple chunks in
   unsweetened juice
1 teaspoon unsalted butter
¼ cup plus 1 tablespoon sugar
1½ teaspoons coarsely ground black pepper
3 large eggs
½ cup milk
½ cup heavy cream
⅛ teaspoon kosher salt
½ cup sifted all-purpose flour
1 tablespoon rum
1¼ teaspoons grated lemon rind
Confectioners' sugar

Heat the oven to 350°F.

Drain the pineapple chunks and spread them out on paper towels to dry. Place the juice in a small saucepan over moderate heat. Cook the liquid, stirring occasionally, until reduced to 2 tablespoons. Set aside.

Meanwhile, spread a 9-inch round cake pan with the butter, and sprinkle 1 tablespoon of sugar evenly over the bottom. Sprinkle evenly with ½ teaspoon pepper. Set aside.

With an electric mixer, beat the eggs on medium speed until they begin to foam. Gradually add the remaining ¼ cup of sugar, beating continuously. Combine the milk and cream, and add in a thin stream.

With the mixer set on the lowest speed, add the salt and flour very gradually. When it is all incorporated, increase the speed of the mixer and beat until well combined. Stir in the rum, the reduced pineapple liquid, the remaining teaspoon pepper, and the lemon rind.

Arrange the pineapple chunks over the sugared pan, leaving about ½ inch of space between the pieces. (There may be some pieces left over.) Carefully pour the batter over the pineapple; place the pan in the oven and bake for 35 to 40 minutes. Cover the top of the clafoutis with aluminum foil after 15 to 20 minutes to prevent overbrowning.

Remove the clafoutis from the oven. Allow it to cool for 30 to 40 minutes and then invert it onto a serving plate. Serve it tepid sprinkled with confectioners' sugar.

SERVES 8 TO 10

STRAWBERRY BAVARIAN

———————————— • ————————————

This is always an impressive dessert, gently molded and creamily pink. It slips down the throat easily even after a festive dinner. I rather like the texture of the seeds in this. If you don't, put the strawberry purée through a sieve. Don't heat the strawberries or they will lose their fresh color and taste. The acidity of the berries will be sufficient to dissolve the sugar. If the strawberries aren't fabulous the lemon juice will help.

...

> *3 envelopes unflavored gelatin*
> *½ cup cold water*
> *4 pints strawberries, washed, dried and hulled*
> *1 to 1½ cups sugar*
> *Juice of 1 to 1½ lemons, strained (optional)*
> *2 tablespoons Triple Sec (optional)*
> *3 cups heavy cream, chilled*

Sprinkle the gelatin on the cold water in a measuring cup. Place the cup in a saucepan with water coming halfway up the sides. Place the pan over medium heat until the gelatin dissolves, scraping the sides of the cup occasionally with a spatula.

Meanwhile, add 1 pint of strawberries to the work bowl of a food processor fitted with the steel blade. Process for 1 minute. Add the second pint and process for another minute. When the berries are completely puréed and liquid, transfer them to a stainless steel bowl. Process the remaining strawberries in the same way, combining all the purée in the bowl. If desired, press the purée through a sieve to remove the seeds. Gradually add the sugar to the purée, mixing well and tasting. If additional flavor is desired, add lemon juice and Triple Sec.

Have the strawberry purée at room temperature. If it is too cold, the gelatin will set too fast and become stringy. If the gelatin is completely dissolved, add it to the purée and mix thoroughly. If there are granules that did not dissolve, pour the gelatin through a fine sieve into the strawberry mixture. Place the bowl with the strawberry gelatin mixture into a larger bowl filled with ice. Stir from the sides of the bowl from time to time until the mixture begins to thicken.

Fill a 2½-quart metal ring mold with ice. Place in the refrigerator. Beat the heavy cream until stiff peaks form. Stir about one quarter of the cream into the strawberry mixture. Fold in the remaining cream until thoroughly mixed.

Pour out the ice and dry the mold. Fill the chilled mold with the strawberry mixture. Cover with plastic wrap and chill in the refrigerator for 3 to 4 hours.

If the bavarian is made the day before serving, let it stand at room temperature for about 15 minutes. Before serving, briefly dip the mold in a large bowl containing very hot water. Invert a serving plate over the mold, then turn mold and plate over quickly together. Lift off mold.

Serve with a light Moselle wine and additional whipped cream and strawberries, if desired.

SERVES 10 TO 12

CHOCOLATE SORBET

America did not invent ice cream, but it did invent the ice-cream maker. Our ice-cream maker can today be home to creamless, light sorbets as well as rich, traditional ice creams.

•••

4 ounces unsweetened chocolate, broken into
  chunks
1 quart water
1½ cups sugar

Use a knife or a food processor to chop the chocolate into very small pieces.

Heat the water and sugar together in a heavy saucepan. Add the chocolate and simmer for 20 to 30 minutes, stirring from time to time, until the mixture is very smooth and not grainy. Do not let it boil. Cool thoroughly.

Pour the mixture into an ice-cream maker and freeze according to the manufacturer's directions.

MAKES ABOUT 1 QUART

FRESH PINEAPPLE SORBET

Pineapple sorbet is traditionally hard to make because of the unusual enzymes in this fruit—the same ones that make raw pineapple a disaster in gelatin. Today's stronger, colder electric ice-cream machines solve the problem, and what I get is a lovely, fluffy mixture.

•••

1 cup water
½ cup sugar
1 small ripe Hawaiian pineapple
2 tablespoons lemon juice

Place the water and sugar in a saucepan. Bring to a boil and cook for 1 to 2 minutes, or until the sugar is dissolved. Remove from the heat. Cool and store in a jar in the refrigerator until ready to use.

Peel, core, and cube the pineapple (page 283). Place the cubes in a food processor and process until very smooth and frothy. You should have 2½ cups of purée. Stir in the sugar syrup and lemon juice. Taste and add more syrup if needed.

Pour the mixture into an ice-cream maker and freeze according to the manufacturer's directions.

MAKES ABOUT 1 QUART

GINGER ICE CREAM

Fabulously rich, with the contrast of the fresh ginger bite.

• • •

1¾ cups heavy cream
1½ cups milk
½ cup thinly sliced unpeeled ginger
1 cup sugar
3 large egg yolks

Put the heavy cream, milk, and ginger in a pot and bring to a boil. Reduce the heat and simmer for about 40 minutes. Add the sugar, stir, and let the mixture cook until the ginger is transparent, about 20 minutes longer. Put the mixture through a strainer, pressing on the ginger to release all the liquid. Discard the ginger.

Rinse out the pan and put the strained mixture into it. Off the heat, slowly whisk in the egg yolks, one at a time. Put the pan on low heat and cook, stirring constantly with a spoon, scraping the bottom and edges of the pan, until the mixture thickens enough to coat a spoon.

Remove the pan from the heat and pass the mixture through a very fine sieve into a metal bowl. Set the bowl in a larger bowl half filled with ice. Stir from time to time as the mixture cools.

When it is thoroughly cooled, freeze it in an ice-cream maker according to the manufacturer's directions.

MAKES ABOUT 1 QUART

MACAROONS

These are not crisp Italian or Jewish macaroons. They are French-style, melting and soft. Make many more than you think you need.

• • •

4 ounces almond paste
½ cup sugar
Pinch salt
½ teaspoon almond extract
1 to 1½ egg whites, slightly beaten

Heat the oven to 350°F. Line two baking sheets with parchment paper. Set aside.

Place the almond paste, sugar, salt, and almond extract in the bowl of a food processor fitted with the steel blade. Process with an on-off motion until the almond paste is broken up and the mixture is homogenous. With the machine running, slowly add the egg whites until the mixture is smooth and holds soft peaks. It must not be either too stiff or too runny, or it will not hold the shape of the macaroon.

Place all but 2 tablespoons of the almond mixture in a pastry bag fitted with a ¾-inch tube tip. Pipe the macaroons about 1 inch apart on the prepared baking sheets. Make each macaroon 1 inch in diameter. Bake in the preheated oven for 10 to 12 minutes, or until barely a light brown. Remove them from the oven and let them cool completely on the paper. When cool, remove with a metal spatula. Make sandwich cookies with 2 macaroons apiece, using a tiny amount of the reserved almond mixture to hold them together. The filling should not show but just act as a kind of paste.

MAKES ABOUT 24 FINISHED MACAROONS

NOTE: Store in an airtight container in a cool place for no more than 1 day. Macaroons freeze well.

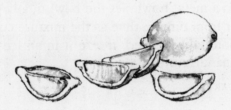

LEMON CHIFFON PIE

———————•———————

This pie, which is straight out of my childhood, is lighter and more elegant than lemon meringue pie. You can substitute lime for the lemon and have what is called Key lime pie, but it's very hard to get real key lime unless you have a tree of your own. The lemon filling is very fragile. If you want something firmer or more secure, sprinkle one envelope of gelatin onto a quarter of a cup of cool water. Add to the warm egg mixture and continue beating.

•••

CRUST

1 cup all-purpose flour
6 tablespoons cold unsalted butter, cut into 4 or 5 pieces
1 tablespoon sugar
½ teaspoon kosher salt
2 tablespoons cold water
1 large egg
1 tablespoon milk

LEMON FILLING

2 large eggs
4 large egg yolks
⅔ cup plus 2 tablespoons sugar
⅔ cup freshly squeezed lemon juice (juice of 4 to 5 lemons), strained
½ cup heavy cream, very cold

WHIPPED CREAM

1 cup heavy cream, very cold
¼ cup sugar

CRUST

Place the flour, butter, sugar, and salt in the work bowl of a food processor fitted with the steel blade. Process, turning on and off rapidly, until the mixture resembles coarse meal. Stop the machine. Add the water and process until a ball of dough forms on top of the blade. Carefully gather the dough together and shape into a disk about 4 inches in diameter. Wrap the dough in wax paper or plastic and refrigerate for 30 minutes.

On a lightly floured work surface, roll the dough into a circle ⅛ inch thick. Fit the dough into a 9-inch glass pie plate, making sure there are no air pockets trapped under the crust. Run a sharp knife around the edge of the crust to trim off the excess dough. Prick the bottom of the crust every ½ inch with the tines of a fork and refrigerate 30 minutes to 1 hour.

Heat the oven to 425° F.

Line the crust with aluminum foil and fill with dry beans or rice. Bake for 12 minutes. Remove from the oven and carefully lift out the foil lining. Beat the egg with the tablespoon milk for a glaze. Brush the bottom, sides, and edge of the crust with the glaze. Return the crust to the oven and bake until nicely colored, about 6 minutes. Turn the pie plate once or twice while baking so the crust browns evenly.

Cool completely before filling.

LEMON FILLING

Mix the eggs, egg yolks, ⅔ cup sugar, and the lemon juice in a large saucepan, and place it over medium heat. Stir, keeping the mixture moving the whole time, until it is warm to the touch.

Tilt the saucepan so the mixture accumulates to one side of the pan. (If cooking with gas, place a flame tamer under the saucepan at this point.) Using a wire whisk, beat the liquid to incorporate air in the same way you beat egg whites. Beat without stopping until the mixture is thick and ribbony and about quadrupled in volume. Place the saucepan flat on the burner and continue beating very hard in a circular motion around the side of the saucepan until the mixture becomes very thick and you see the first signs of steam rising from the surface. Immediately pour the lemon mixture into a clean bowl. Do not scrape the saucepan with a spatula but discard any egg that may have set on the pan. Cover the bowl and set aside to cool to room temperature.

Beat the ½ cup of heavy cream until it holds soft peaks. Add the remaining 2 tablespoons sugar and beat until stiff. Fold the cream into the cooled lemon mixture, and pour into the prebaked and cooled 9-inch crust. Mound the filling slightly higher at the center than the edges to allow for settling.

Refrigerate until set, about 3 hours.

WHIPPED CREAM

Beat the cup of cream until it holds soft peaks. Gradually add the sugar and continue beating until stiff. Spread the whipped cream in a thick, even layer over the lemon filling. Refrigerate an additional 3 hours. Serve chilled. The pie will keep in the refrigerator for up to 2 days.

SERVES 6 TO 8

APPLE BRIOCHE TART

I make adequate apple pie; but I make great apple tart. This is a huge tart, sensational at a party. It is work but the oohs and aahs are worth it. The brioche is not the breakfast-roll type. It is brioche commune.

• • •

BRIOCHE TART DOUGH

1½ teaspoons active dry yeast
3 tablespoons sugar
¼ cup warm milk
1½ cups all-purpose flour
Scant ¾ teaspoon kosher salt
3 ounces unsalted butter, cut into ½-inch pieces
2 large eggs

APPLE FILLING

1 cup sugar
⅛ teaspoon ground cinnamon
Grated rind of 1 lemon
4 cups peeled, cored, and thinly sliced apples,
  approximately
2 to 3 tablespoons unsalted butter

BRIOCHE TART DOUGH

In a small bowl, dissolve the yeast and sugar into the milk. Let sit for 5 minutes, or until foamy. Mix together with ⅓ cup flour. Pour the mixture into a buttered bowl. Cover with plastic wrap and let rest in a warm place until doubled in bulk, about 3 hours.

In the work bowl of a food processor place the remaining flour, the salt, and the butter. Process until the particles are the size of peas. Add the eggs to the bowl and process 10 seconds. Add the yeast-flour mixture and process 20 to 30 seconds longer, or until the dough is smooth. Put the mixture into a buttered bowl and cover tightly with plastic. Let rise 5 to 8 hours, or until tripled in bulk. Punch down. Wrap in plastic and refrigerate at least 2 hours before rolling out.

ASSEMBLING THE TART

Heat the oven to 425°F.

Butter a 12-inch pie plate or similar pan with slanting sides. On a lightly floured surface, roll the dough to ⅛-inch thickness. Fit it into the prepared pan. Prick the bottom heavily with a fork.

Mix the sugar with the cinnamon and lemon rind. Sprinkle about two-thirds of the mixture over the bottom. Arrange the apple slices in overlapping, concentric circles. Sprinkle with the remaining sugar mixture and dot with butter.

Bake in the preheated oven for 10 minutes, reduce the heat to 375°F. and bake 15 to 20 minutes longer. Serve warm immediately or cool on rack.

MAKES ONE 12-INCH BRIOCHE TART, SERVES ABOUT 10

RASPBERRY BREAD PUDDING

———————— • ————————

Best bread pudding I have ever made.

• • •

*12 slices French bread, cut on the diagonal ¾ inch
    wide, dried*
6 tablespoons unsalted butter, softened
1 quart milk
1 one-inch piece vanilla bean, split
8 large eggs
1 cup sugar
*6 tablespoons framboise (raspberry-flavored white
    brandy—not sweet)*
*1 pint fresh raspberries, washed, or 1 ten-ounce
    package frozen raspberries, thawed and drained*

Heat the oven to 350° F.

Spread both sides of the bread with the soft butter. Set aside.

For the custard, put the milk and vanilla bean in a heavy saucepan. Cook over medium heat until the milk is almost boiling. Remove the vanilla bean and scrape the seeds into the milk.

While the milk is heating, in a large bowl whisk the eggs, sugar, and framboise until well blended. Gradually whisk in the hot milk until the mixture is smooth.

In an ungreased 5½-by-9½-by-3-inch loaf pan, make a layer with 4 slices of the bread. Sprinkle half the raspberries over the bread. Pour in one-third of the custard. Repeat with another layer of bread, berries, and custard. Top with the remaining four slices of bread. Pour in the remaining custard.

Cover the pan with aluminum foil. Place it in a large baking dish. Pour hot water into the baking dish so that the water reaches halfway up the sides of the loaf pan. Bake in the preheated oven for 45 minutes.

Remove the pan from the water bath. Return the pan, still covered, to the oven. Bake an additional 30 minutes. Remove the foil and bake 15 minutes longer. The pudding should be set, but will jiggle a bit when shaken. Allow to cool before cutting to serve.

SERVES 8

PÂTE À CHOUX

Pâte à choux is a very versatile dough, used to make the light and elegant Paris-Brest, an extraordinarily celebratory dessert made with pastry cream, whipped cream, and nougat powder. It is also used to make individual cream puffs (both dessert size and miniatures for hors d'oeuvre). It's a simple matter of piping the pâte à choux into different shapes.

• • •

1 cup water
½ cup (1 stick) unsalted butter
½ teaspoon salt
1 cup all-purpose flour
4 large eggs

In a heavy 1-quart saucepan, heat the water, butter, and salt over medium heat until simmering. When the butter has melted, reduce the heat to very low. Add the flour all at once to the simmering liquid. Whisk over low heat until the mixture is smooth, shiny, and forms a ball around the whisk. Remove from the heat.

Beat in the eggs one at a time, making sure each is thoroughly incorporated before adding the next. This mixture is the pâte à choux.

PARIS-BREST

1 recipe pâte à choux
1 egg white
2 tablespoons heavy cream
½ cup sliced blanched almonds

NOUGAT POWDER

½ cup sugar
1½ teaspoons water

1½ *teaspoons lemon juice*
6 *tablespoons toasted blanched almonds, coarsely*
  chopped

PASTRY CREAM

2 *cups milk*
½ *cup sugar*
6 *egg yolks*
3 *tablespoons cornstarch*
¼ *teaspoon almond extract*

• • •

2 *cups heavy cream, whipped*

Heat the oven to 400° F.

Cut a sheet of parchment paper to fit your baking sheet. Trace 2
circles, each 6½ inches in diameter, on the parchment paper. In the
center of each circle draw another circle, 3 inches in diameter.

Begin by spooning the pâte à choux into a pastry bag fitted with
a plain No. 6 tip. With the penciled side up, pipe a small dot of pâte
à choux onto each corner of the parchment. Turn the paper over and
press down the corners to secure it to the baking sheet. Pipe the pâte
à choux onto the parchment between the penciled concentric circles. You will have two rings, each 6½ inches in diameter with a
center hole 3 inches in diameter.

In a small bowl, blend the egg white and heavy cream. Brush
the rings of dough with this mixture. Sprinkle each ring with
blanched almonds. Pat them gently onto the rings.

Bake in the preheated oven for 35 minutes. Remove from the
oven. Pierce the sides of the rings several times with the tines of a
fork to release steam. Replace in the oven and continue to bake
another 10 minutes, or until the rings are medium-dark brown and
feel very light when you pick them up. Cool on a wire rack.

NOUGAT POWDER

Lightly oil a baking sheet.

In a small, heavy skillet, combine the sugar, water, and lemon
juice. Heat over low heat, stirring constantly, until the sugar is
melted and the mixture is a deep amber brown. This will take about
20 minutes. Remove the skillet from the heat. Stir in the almonds.
Immediately pour the mixture onto the lightly oiled baking sheet.

With a spatula, spread the hot nougat into a thin layer. Handle it carefully as it is very hot. Allow the nougat to cool until brittle, about 30 minutes.

When cool, remove it from the baking sheet and wrap it in a clean towel. With a mallet, pound the nougat in the towel to break it into small (½-inch) pieces. Transfer the pieces of nougat to a food processor. Process until it is a very fine powder. Store it tightly covered at room temperature until you are ready to use it. This gives you more powder than you need for this recipe; but it is a delight to have on hand for ice cream topping and other imaginings.

PASTRY CREAM

In a large saucepan, bring the milk to a boil.

In a mixing bowl, beat the sugar and egg yolks until thick and ribbony. Beat in the cornstarch. Gradually pour the boiling milk into the sugar-and-egg mixture. Transfer the mixture back to the saucepan and cook over medium heat, whisking all the time, until it thickens enough to coat a spoon. Continue to cook for another 2 minutes. Remove the pastry cream from the heat and stir in the extract. Pour into a bowl, cover cream with plastic wrap (laying plastic wrap directly on cream), and refrigerate until cold.

TO ASSEMBLE THE PARIS-BREST

Split the rings horizontally with a bread knife. On the bottom half of each ring spread 1 cup Pastry Cream and then 1 cup stiffly whipped heavy cream. Sprinkle cream with 1½ cups nougat powder. Lightly place top of ring on top. Serve at the table—your guests should see this—cutting into sections with a serrated knife.

Each ring of Paris-Brest serves 6–8. You can halve the recipe in order to have just one ring, or you can make the entire amount but fill and serve the second ring another night. (For freezing instructions, see note.)

• CREAM PUFFS •

Heat the oven to 400° F. Lightly grease a baking sheet, or line it with parchment paper. Pipe the pâte à choux onto the baking sheet in twenty-four 1½-inch solid circles. Bake 20 minutes. Remove from the oven. Pierce the sides of each puff two or three times. Return to the oven. Bake another 15 minutes, or until dark brown and very light weight. Cool on a wire rack. Fill with flavored whipped cream (cocoa, vanilla, grated orange rind with Triple Sec, and instant coffee all make good flavorings), Pastry Cream (above) or a mixture of the two. Top with chocolate sauce or Butterscotch Sauce (below).

• MINIATURE PUFFS •

Heat the oven to 400° F. Lightly grease a baking sheet, or line it with parchment paper. Pipe the pâte à choux onto the baking sheet in ⅜-inch mounds. There should be enough to make 96 miniature puffs. Bake 15 to 30 minutes, or until dark brown. Cool on a wire rack. Use for hors d'oeuvre filled with pâté, Curried Chicken Salad (page 199), or even tuna-fish salad.

ENOUGH FOR TWO 8-INCH PARIS-BREST, 24 CREAM PUFFS, OR 96 MINIATURE PUFFS.

NOTE: Once baked, any of the pâte à choux pastries can be frozen. Wrap securely, first in plastic wrap, then in aluminum foil. To defrost, unwrap and place on a baking sheet. Heat the oven to 350° F. Heat the miniature puffs for 5 minutes, the cream puffs for 8 minutes, and the Paris-Brest for 12 to 15 minutes.

BUTTERSCOTCH SAUCE

Flows when hot, then hardens into a semi-glaze as it cools. Use to top Cream Puffs (opposite page) or ice cream.

• • •

> 1 cup brown sugar
> 8 tablespoons unsalted butter
> ½ cup light corn syrup
> 2 tablespoons heavy cream
> ½ teaspoon vanilla extract
> ½ teaspoon kosher salt

Place the brown sugar and 4 tablespoons of the butter in a small, heavy saucepan. Heat over medium heat to boiling. Boil 1 minute.

Whisk in syrup, heavy cream, vanilla, and salt. Boil the syrup until a candy thermometer registers 235° F. Immediately remove the syrup from the heat.

Whisk in the remaining 4 tablespoons butter, one at a time. If you are using the sauce as a glaze, spoon it, while still hot, over individual cream puffs. Allow to cool. For a thin pouring sauce, reheat to simmering just before serving and immediately pour over the cream puffs.

The sauce can be cooled to room temperature then stored, covered, in the refrigerator for up to 4 months.

MAKES 1½ CUPS

CHOCOLATE LAYER CAKE

———————————•———————————

This is another re-creation of a childhood memory. I like American layer cakes. They may be less fashionable than tortes and gâteaux. I prefer them. I like them best for breakfast with a glass of milk. Most people think of them as dessert.

• • •

CHOCOLATE LAYERS

5 ounces unsweetened chocolate
½ cup hot water
1¾ cups sugar
2 cups sifted cake flour
1 teaspoon baking soda
1 teaspoon kosher salt
¼ pound (8 tablespoons) unsalted butter
3 eggs
¾ cup milk
1 teaspoon vanilla extract

CHOCOLATE ICING

4 ounces unsweetened chocolate
1½ cups confectioners' sugar
¼ cup strong brewed coffee
4 eggs, separated

CHOCOLATE LAYERS

Heat the oven to 350° F.

In a saucepan, melt the chocolate with the water over medium heat. Stir until the mixture thickens. Add ½ cup sugar, and cook over low heat for about 1 minute to form a thick, shiny chocolate sauce. Cool to lukewarm.

In a medium-size bowl, combine the flour, soda, and salt. In a separate bowl, cream the butter and 1¼ cups sugar. Add the eggs, one at a time, beating well after each addition. Add the dry ingredients and milk alternately. Then add the chocolate and vanilla. Let rest for 15 minutes.

Butter the bottoms of two 9-inch round cake pans and line with parchment paper. Divide the batter evenly between the two pans. Bake about 30 minutes, or until the batter begins to pull from the sides of the pans and a wooden pick inserted in center is removed clean. Cool in the pans for 10 minutes. Turn the cake out of the pans and cool completely on wire racks. Peel off parchment paper.

CHOCOLATE ICING

Melt the chocolate in the top of a double boiler over hot water. Beat in half the sugar; add the coffee.

In a separate bowl, beat the egg yolks and remaining sugar until smooth. Add the chocolate mixture, stirring well.

Beat the egg whites until stiff but not dry. Fold them into the chocolate mixture. The icing will seem thin at this point. Place in the refrigerator. The icing will thicken as it cools completely.

TO ASSEMBLE CAKE

Place one layer on a serving plate. Frost the top with ⅔ cup of the icing. Top with the second layer. Frost the top and sides of the cake with the remaining icing. You can store the cake at room temperature up to 1 day or refrigerate up to 3 days. Remove from the refrigerator 2 hours before serving.

SERVES 8 TO 12

SAUCES AND DRESSINGS

· GLAZES AND SAUCES ·

Meat or Chicken Glaze

Hollandaise Sauce

Béarnaise

Maltaise

Mayonnaise

Anchovy-Mushroom Sauce

Avgolemono Sauce

· SALAD DRESSINGS ·

Tomato–Celery-Seed Dressing

Yogurt Dressing

Everyday Vinaigrette

· COLD VEGETABLE SAUCES ·

Tomato Frappé

Green-Bean Frappé

· THE LONELY DESSERT SAUCE ·

Nectarine Sauce

GLAZES AND SAUCES

———————•———————

There are sauces through this book that can, if you wish, be used for other things. In the Index you will find not only an alphabetical listing, but also a categorized listing, e.g., Egg-Bound Sauces (Mayonnaise, Hollandaise, and so on).

In addition, everybody needs a few basic sauces that can be varied at will. You will find them in the following pages, along with information about reducing stock to make a glaze, your secret weapon in the customizing of sauces—Chicken Glaze added to a Beurre Blanc (page 53) for Poached Chicken and so forth. The more I cook, the more I am convinced that sauces should be adapted to go with individual dishes of which they then become an integral part.

• • •

MEAT OR CHICKEN GLAZE

———————•———————

This is the prototype for all glazes. It is very simple. The only things to watch out for are, on the one hand, that it gets thick enough and, on the other, that you go very slowly at the end so the glaze doesn't scorch. You can tell that the glaze is thick enough when, as it is tilted from side to side, it has an oceanlike undercurrent. It is still sliding in one direction as you reverse the tilt. Glaze thickens as it cools. Keep it refrigerated if you are going to use it fairly soon. Otherwise freeze it in small portions. As you will see, the yield is very small. You should start with the most profligate amount of stock that you can manage.

If you don't have glaze you can omit it. Don't substitute.

MEAT OR CHICKEN GLAZE, CONTINUED

1 quart meat stock or chicken stock

Pour the stock into a 2-quart saucepan and bring it to a boil. Lower the heat and let it simmer until it is deep brown and syrupy. It may be necessary to transfer the contents to a smaller pot as it reduces. Watch so it does not burn. When the glaze has reduced to about ½ cup, pour it into small containers or an ice-cube tray. Make sure to scrape all the rich, syrupy glaze into the container. Refrigerate or freeze until firm. Then remove the glaze from the container or tray sections and wrap tightly in plastic wrap. Now it can be stored indefinitely in the freezer.

MAKES ½ CUP GLAZE

HOLLANDAISE SAUCE

The classic accompaniment to fresh asparagus, this is wonderful with other vegetables, over fish, and as an essential ingredient for Eggs Benedict. It can be varied as mayonnaise can, with fresh herbs, curry powder, and different glazes.

• • •

1 pound unsalted butter
3 egg yolks
½ teaspoon dry mustard
1 teaspoon kosher salt
¼ teaspoon freshly ground black pepper
2 teaspoons fresh lemon juice

Melt the butter in a saucepan. Keep hot over low heat.

Place the egg yolks, mustard, salt, and pepper in the work bowl of a food processor fitted with the steel blade. Turn the machine on and let it run for 90 seconds.

With the machine still running, slowly but steadily pour the hot butter through the feed tube. The sauce will thicken until it has the consistency of mayonnaise. When all the butter has been added, pour in the lemon juice through the feed tube. Stop the machine.

Scrape the sauce into a serving bowl and serve immediately. If you are not ready to serve, keep the sauce warm in the top of a double boiler over simmering water. Do not let it get too hot or the butter will separate out of the sauce.

MAKES ABOUT 2 CUPS

• BÉARNAISE SAUCE •

The Béarnaise Sauce can be used with red meat, either a grilled sirloin or a freshly-made hamburger. Substitute the following reduction for the lemon juice in the basic Hollandaise sauce.

• • •

6 tablespoons fresh tarragon leaves or 1 tablespoon
　dried
2 large shallots
3 tablespoons dry white wine
⅓ cup tarragon vinegar
¼ teaspoon freshly ground black pepper

Place ¼ cup tarragon leaves in the work bowl of a food processor fitted with the steel blade. Process with 4 or 5 short pulses until the tarragon is chopped. Remove the pusher from the feed tube. Turn the machine on and drop in the shallots one at a time. Run for a few seconds until the shallots are minced.

Place the tarragon and shallots in a saucepan with the wine, vinegar, and pepper. Cook over medium heat until the liquid is reduced to 2 tablespoons. Pour the mixture through a fine sieve, pressing to release all the liquid. Discard the solids and reserve the liquid. Follow the recipe for the Hollandaise Sauce. Stir the reduction into the Hollandaise. Add the remaining 2 tablespoons of tarragon leaves to the finished sauce.

MAKES ABOUT 2 CUPS

• MALTAISE SAUCE •

This is used primarily as a sauce for fish or for asparagus. It is so good I am convinced you will find other uses.

• • •

Juice of 2 oranges
Grated zest of 1 orange
1 recipe Hollandaise Sauce (page 310) without
*   lemon juice*
2 tablespoons grated lemon zest
4 teaspoons lemon juice
⅛ teaspoon ground cumin seed

Combine the orange juice and orange zest in a small saucepan. Boil over medium heat until the juice is reduced to ¼ cup. Strain and reserve the liquid. Proceed as for the Hollandaise Sauce. Add the orange juice reduction and lemon zest to the finished sauce. Stir together the lemon juice and cumin. Stir into the sauce. Let the sauce rest about 15 minutes before serving.

MAKES ABOUT 2 CUPS

MAYONNAISE

Mayonnaise is essentially a cold version of Hollandaise with oil substituted for the butter. If you don't like a heavy taste of olive oil, substitute vegetable oil. This is an adaptable sauce. Add fresh herbs and chopped cooked spinach for a green sauce. Add capers, chopped onion, chopped parsley, and chopped gherkins for tartar sauce. Add some Tomato Purée (page 82) for a pretty, cold sauce for fish. Add some grainy mustard or horseradish to make a spread for cold Roast Beef (page 180) or cold Roast Loin of Pork (page 183).

You can, of course, make a half recipe (or even a third, but, if you have this sauce around, you'll probably find uses for it you never thought of for store-bought mayonnaise.

• • •

6 egg yolks, at room temperature
3 tablespoons fresh lemon juice

1 tablespoon kosher salt
Freshly ground white pepper
2 teaspoons dry mustard
2 cups vegetable oil
2 cups Italian olive oil

Place the egg yolks in the work bowl of the food processor fitted with the steel blade. Turn it on and let it run for 90 seconds. Stop the machine and add the lemon juice, salt, pepper, and mustard. Process with 2 short pulses to mix.

Place the oils in a liquid measuring cup. Remove the pusher and turn on the machine. Beginning very slowly but steadily, pour the oil into the food processor. When about a third of the oil has been added, increase your speed slightly and continue adding the oil until it has all been absorbed. Refrigerate in a closed jar. It will keep a good week.

MAKES ABOUT 1 QUART

ANCHOVY-MUSHROOM SAUCE

———————•———————

This sauce is slightly related to a mayonnaise. It is somewhat mysterious in taste and good with steaks, pork, or lamb chops.

• • •

20 to 24 anchovy fillets, drained
4 medium-size peeled garlic cloves
1½ teaspoons capers, drained
2 egg yolks
2 to 3 tablespoons fresh lemon juice
¾ cup olive oil
¾ cup melted unsalted butter
3 to 4 tablespoons unsalted butter
2 cups thinly sliced mushrooms
1 tablespoon chopped parsley
Pinch cayenne pepper

Place the anchovies, garlic, and capers in the work bowl of a food processor, and process until you have a smooth purée. Add the egg yolks and process 1 minute. Add lemon juice. With the machine on, slowly add the olive oil and melted butter, beginning with droplets and ending in a steady stream. The mixture should be like a mayonnaise in texture.

In a sauté pan, heat 3 or 4 tablespoons butter and add the mushrooms. Sauté just until tender. Stir in the parsley and cayenne pepper. Fold into the sauce.

Serve over grilled meats.

MAKES ABOUT 2¼ CUPS

AVGOLEMONO SAUCE

This is the basic Greek sauce used on fish, chicken, lamb, and vegetables. Add more stock and a little cooked rice and you have soup. Occasionally, dill is added for taste and color.

...

2 cups Chicken Stock (page 110)
3 tablespoons Carolina rice
4 egg yolks
2 tablespoons fresh lemon juice
Kosher salt
Freshly ground black pepper

Bring the stock to a boil, add the rice, cover, and cook until it is tender, about 8 to 10 minutes. Meanwhile, beat the egg yolks and lemon juice together in a large bowl.

When the rice is tender, remove from heat and ladle half of the hot broth slowly onto the yolks in a mixing bowl to heat them gently, beating constantly. Return the egg-yolk mixture to the sauce in the pot and place over low heat, stirring constantly. Cook just long enough to thicken the sauce. The sauce should be thick enough to lightly coat a spoon. Do not boil. Season to taste with salt and freshly ground black pepper.

MAKES ABOUT 1½ CUPS

...

SALAD DRESSINGS

Most of the time, all a salad needs is a clean bowl (not wood, which absorbs the oil and becomes rancid), and good oil, vinegar, salt, and pepper to make a basic vinaigrette. Salad lover that I am, I change dressings particularly when going for a big composed salad that becomes a main course. If you look in the Index you will find several and here are a few more.

• • •

TOMATO–CELERY-SEED DRESSING

Tasting as much as I do, I often need to be on a diet. This is my answer to fattening dressing. It's extremely low in calories. The gelatin gives it a nice texture so that I don't miss more oil.

• • •

> 1 teaspoon unflavored gelatin
> 1½ cups tomato juice
> ⅛ teaspoon minced garlic
> ¾ cup vegetable oil
> 3 tablespoons fresh lemon juice
> 2 teaspoons Worcestershire sauce
> 1 teaspoon celery seed
> 1 teaspoon kosher salt
> 1 teaspoon sugar
> ¼ teaspoon freshly ground black pepper
> ½ teaspoon hot red-pepper sauce

In a small saucepan, combine the gelatin with ½ cup of the tomato juice. Place over moderate heat, stirring until the juice is heated through and the gelatin is dissolved. Cool. Stir in the remaining tomato juice and place in a blender or mixer. Add garlic. Gradually beat in the oil, then the remaining ingredients.

Refrigerate until the mixture thickens. Before using, let it stand a few minutes at room temperature. Whisk if the gelatin has overly thickened it in the refrigerator.

MAKES ABOUT 2¼ CUPS

YOGURT DRESSING

_____·_____

This is a tart and healthful dressing that is low in calories. It is good on fruit salads as well as vegetable salads.

• • •

2 cups plain yogurt
4 tablespoons fresh orange juice
½ teaspoon ground cumin, heated in ½ teaspoon oil
¹⁄₁₆ teaspoon minced garlic
1 teaspoon kosher salt
Pinch freshly ground black pepper

Combine all the ingredients in a blender. Blend on low speed until mixed. Prepare at least a day before using and store covered in the refrigerator.

MAKES ABOUT 2¼ CUPS DRESSING

EVERYDAY VINAIGRETTE

_____·_____

¼ teaspoon Dijon mustard
1 teaspoon kosher salt
⅛ teaspoon freshly ground black pepper
3 tablespoons red wine vinegar (can be part lemon juice)
1 cup light olive oil or vegetable oil, or a mixture of the two

In a small bowl, whisk together all the ingredients. Whisk well each time before using. The sauce can be stored covered in refrigerator up to 2 weeks.

MAKES ABOUT 1¼ CUPS

COLD VEGETABLE SAUCES

These are beautiful and quite wonderful under leftover poached fish, chicken or, if you make them, cold vegetable pâtés.

TOMATO FRAPPÉ

This comes from an idea of the Troisgros. They are great geniuses.

• • •

1¼ pounds fresh ripe tomatoes
1 generous teaspoon tomato paste
4 teaspoons lemon juice
¾ teaspoon kosher salt
Freshly ground black pepper
1½ tablespoons chopped fresh parsley
1 tablespoon coarsely chopped fresh basil
¼ cup olive oil

Peel and seed the tomatoes. Place them in the food processor and process with an on-off motion until the tomatoes are puréed. Press them through a fine sieve. Add the tomato paste, lemon juice, salt, pepper, and herbs. Just before serving, whisk in the oil, a few drops at a time.

MAKES ABOUT 1¾ CUPS

GREEN-BEAN FRAPPÉ

This idea came to me when I had a terrible failure making a string-bean purée. I thought of the Tomato Frappé and improvised this—cool, bright green, and fresh-tasting.

...

1½ pounds string beans
¼ cup olive oil
Salt
Freshly ground black pepper

Trim the beans. Boil in a large pot of salted water until tender, about 8 minutes. Drain in a colander. Refresh the beans under cold running water. Drain thoroughly.

Purée the beans in the food processor, then push through a very fine sieve or a sieve lined with a double thickness of cheesecloth. Beat in the olive oil and salt and pepper to taste. The sauce should be very smooth.

MAKES ABOUT 2 CUPS

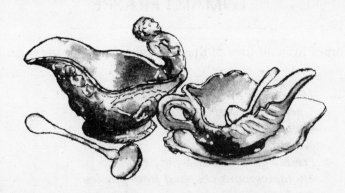

THE LONELY DESSERT SAUCE

True to my lack of interest in desserts, there is but one lonely dessert sauce here. It is unusual, sunset-colored and good. There is also a Butterscotch Sauce following the Paris-Brest (page 303) and a Raspberry Sauce following the recipe for Poached Pears with Pear Sorbet (page 287).

•••

NECTARINE SAUCE

1 slice fresh ginger (about the size of a quarter),
* peeled*
4 nectarines
6 tablespoons fresh lemon juice, or to taste
6 tablespoons brown sugar, or to taste

Place the ginger in the work bowl of a food processor and chop as fine as possible. Peel the nectarines. Cut them into quarters and remove the pits. Add the fruit to the ginger and process until smooth. Add the lemon juice and sugar to taste. Each nectarine will have its own unique balance of acidity and sweetness, so these are only approximate amounts. Taste and correct. Use with sorbets, ice creams, hot sweet fritters, and poached fruits.

MAKES ABOUT 2 CUPS

NOTES ON INGREDIENTS AND EQUIPMENT

The Ingredients

A well-stocked larder is the harried and intelligent cook's best friend. In the Index, you will find a list of recipes that can be made from on-the-shelf ingredients. Take a look at them and see which of them please you, so you can have the ingredients on hand for emergencies. Always have a good brand of canned chicken stock. It can be substituted in recipes calling for stock. Watch when salting; canned chicken stocks already contain salt. Rice and a variety of dry noodles make life easier, as would a few cans of tomatoes. You will need two kinds. Italian plum tomatoes are ideal for some recipes; but, in others, the freshness of ordinary canned tomatoes will be preferable. On the run, omit glazes.

Most of the other ingredients in this book can be gotten just by asking for them at the store. Some may surprise you; but I hope that they will be nice surprises. I am constantly amazed by the wide variety of things available in this country's supermarkets.

When you are using my recipes, there are certain variables such as the intensity of your flame, your pots and pans, your altitude or your ingredients that I can only vaguely discuss with you. There are others such as the use of kosher salt that I can explain.

KOSHER SALT

I use kosher salt because there is nothing in it but salt. I eat enough fish and seafood so that I will never get a goiter. I don't need to add iodine to every meal. I also don't need the chemicals that are added to keep salt free-pouring. If you don't believe me about the difference in taste, put a little of your regular salt and a little kosher salt on a plate. Wet your finger and first taste the kosher salt. Then drink some water and then taste your regular salt. You will taste the kosher salt where the taste receptors for salt are on the tip of your tongue. You will taste the other salt all along your tongue and it will catch you sharply in the back of your throat; that is the taste of the chemicals. Sea salt is very expensive and has a very complex taste of assorted minerals and algae like the sea it comes from. I will sometimes use it when I am cooking fish but not as an everyday thing.

Kosher salt is coarser in texture than most table salt. Therefore, a greater volume is less salty. If you substitute table salt for kosher salt, use much less.

This is not to get into the argument about whether you should use salt or not. You and your doctor know your body. If you want to or should use less salt, do so. These recipes suit my body and my palate. If you are going to cut down on salt or eliminate it, increase the other seasonings, add some lemon juice or some hot red-pepper sauce. The point is to balance the flavors.

PEPPER

Peppercorns are another ingredient to watch out for when cooking. If you put them in your food more than fifteen minutes before serving, it will tend to turn bitter. Ground pepper tastes stronger than whole peppercorns. The flavors of black pepper—and its relative, white—are soluble only in watery liquids. When you cook pepper in hot fat all you can get is the taste of the burning. Conversely, red pepper and other pod peppers release their flavors only in fat and alcohol. That is why paprika recipes always call for sautéeing the paprika—red peppers—with fat and onions before adding the liquid. Too many curries and gumbos taste raw because people neglect this simple rule. Incidentally, some people have a great deal of trouble digesting the skins of pod peppers. These can be removed in two ways. If the peppers are to be used raw, remove the skin with a potato peeler. If you want a smoky taste roast the peppers under the broiler or over an open flame until thoroughly charred. Remove from heat; cover with a damp cloth; after twenty minutes, scrape off the skin with a small knife.

GARLIC

Another very variable element that I use frequently is garlic. Remember that garlic is a live thing like a daffodil bulb. If you plant it, it will grow. The daffodil bulb is poisonous; underground animals will not touch it. Garlic protects itself in a different way. When it is bitten—or cut by your knife—it gives off a sharp and unpleasant odor. When you are not going to cook garlic whole but are going to cut it, smash it sharply first with the flat edge of your knife. This will stop the skunk-type reaction and will also loosen the garlic's skin so that it becomes easy to peel.

As the year progresses, the garlic clove keeps growing until it forms a new green shoot, the beginning of a new plant. This green shoot grows from the central part of the garlic clove, called the germ. The germ is always stronger tasting than the rest of the garlic. Some writers and cooks recommend removing the germ at any season. I don't bother until the germ begins to coarsen and get large and tough or slightly green. When you smash the garlic you will easily be able to see the germ and pick it out if it has gotten heavy.

There is one last thing to remember about garlic. With prolonged cooking it gets smooth, gelatinous and sweet. It will often give body to stocks lacking in bone gelatin. It will lose all sharpness though. I often add a little fresh garlic at the end of cooking to bring the taste forward in the mouth.

LEMON JUICE

I use a great deal of lemon juice in cooking, partly because I love the taste and partly because it is a readily available fresh fruit acid. When fruits are shipped and therefore not picked ripe or cooked for canning they either don't develop or they lose their natural acidity. Without that acidity, all the other good flavors will taste less strong. Lemon juice substitutes for the missing acid.

BUTTER AND CREAM

I like butter. I like cream. For dishes where they are essential ingredients nothing else will do. If you want to limit your fat intake, you can sauté in a nonstick pan, or, better, in a pan lightly sprayed with a light mist of vegetable oil. Remember, if you are going to get your fat really hot, it doesn't matter whether it is a saturated fat to begin with or not as it will break down and turn into a saturated fat in the presence of such heat. Soups can be lightened by not binding them with cream and egg yolks. Increase the amount of stock to compensate for the lessened liquid.

When you use butter and cream, though, make sure that you get the best. Use unsalted butter. Salt in butter holds in water. You get less butter. Salt also disguises any off taste in butter. Salt tends to make meat sautéed in it stick to the pan. It is harder to control the seasoning of foods cooked with salted butter. If you can buy unsalted butter inexpensively, freeze it. It freezes fabulously and defrosts quickly. Cream is a more difficult subject. What you don't want is ultra-pasteurized cream. It tastes more like condensed milk than cream and doesn't beat well. You may have to look in more than one store or ask the manager of your supermarket to get you good cream.

HERBS

I use almost only fresh herbs. Dried herbs don't taste like their fresh counterparts. Either cook things in their right season or substitute the fresh herbs that are available. If you must use dried herbs, use much smaller quantities than you would of the fresh. Steeping them for a bit in hot water, as if you were making tea, sometimes helps refresh them.

VINEGARS AND OILS

The variety of vinegars and oils available has become bewildering. Trial and error is the only true way of finding out how they taste. In general, dark green, first-pressing Italian, Spanish and Greek oils will have a rich fruity taste. Sometimes they will also have an unpleasant acid taste coming from crushed pits. Buy oils in small amounts until you find ones that you like. French olive oils tend to be milder and lighter in taste. American olive oils run the whole gamut. You may find that you want to have a variety of oils on hand for different uses. Don't deep-fat-fry in olive oil unless you are prepared for a very pungent taste and smell.

Vinegars can vary from thin and acid to deep and winy or round and fruity. Acid content alone will not determine how acid a vinegar tastes. A vinegar may have a high acid content but have so much fruit perfume and taste that it is actually perceived as sweet. The same thing happens with wine. When using vinegar, select one that seems to you to go with the dish. Vinegars are not simply interchangeable.

WINE AND LIQUOR

Wine is, for me, an ingredient of every meal. I often serve several wines. I use no more wine and spend no more money by having three different types than by serving a lot of one type. I think it makes for a more festive evening. Food changes the taste of wine just as the right wine makes the food more enjoyable. There is a French wine-trade saying: "Sell on cheese; buy on apples." Fats—butter, cream, olive oil—soften tannin and the other acids of wine, making them more attractive. Bigger, better-balanced wines do better with food. Wines that are lacking in good acidity may taste all right on their own but will taste flabby with food.

If you are not already familiar with wines, buy a few good books and find a merchant who seems to be knowledgeable. Read and ask advice and questions. Buy a couple of wines at a time and use your next meals as a way of comparing them. Keep on tasting and comparing until you have a repertoire of wines that you like. As you go on, you may find that your taste is developing and that the wines that you liked in the beginning are giving way in your favor to more complicated wines. This does not mean that every meal should have a great wine. On the contrary, many of the most enjoyable informal meals would be inappropriate with a major wine. In fact, the strong-tasting foods would kill the wines. Sometimes such foods—the curries and other oriental foods particularly—are best with beer, vodka or a scotch and soda.

Certainly, wines for cooking should not be of the finest. The elegance of many great wines would be totally wasted in cooking even if they were affordable. I generally keep a Côtes-du-Rhône red and a Mâcon on hand to cook with. They are not inferior, just more appropriate. I am perfectly happy drinking them from time to time.

I have gotten very tired of bad white wine instead of drinks. Sometimes, I will serve drinks. More often, I will serve a wine made in the style of Champagne (méthode champenoise). Sometimes, if dinner and I am posh, it will be a genuine Champagne from the Champagne district of France. More often, it will be a wine made the same way from another part of the globe. Memories of thirties' movies ringing brittlely—white tie and British accent, of course—I call these "bubbly."

Most of the liquor called for in the recipes is fairly standard. The one exception is white brandy of one fruit or another. These brandies are usually made in France or Switzerland. They are described as brandy distilled from a fruit other than grapes. Like grape brandies—Cognac, Armagnac, Grappa, Brandy—they come from the still white and therefore are called *alcool blanc*. Unlike most of the grape brandies they are not colored either with caramel or by being placed in charred wooden barrels; they remain white. They should never be sweet. They are marvelous after-dinner drinks in tiny quantities in big snifters. They also add an intense wallop of taste to some dishes.

Some of the sweet brandies, called liqueurs, are useful in dessert cooking. Triple Sec is one I tend to use frequently.

The Tools

The pots and pans you use will vary your results and your timing. I collect heavy copper pots lined with tin—one at each expensive time. I take care that they are relined every few years so that the food doesn't interact with the copper. Copper does the best job of transmitting and diffusing the heat so that it cooks evenly. It also cools swiftly, making it sensitive; sauces don't curdle. If I can't get my hands on copper, I use stainless steel with a heavy aluminum or mild-steel sandwich on the bottom. These handle heat well and are inert in contact with food. They are less sensitive to changes in heat and cold than copper.

I have only one aluminum pot. It is a huge stock pot so large that I would be unable to handle it in another metal. It is coated to make it relatively inert in the presence of food acids; but I feel that I can taste a slight difference between stocks made in this pot and in my other pots. Since stocks don't seem to need such perfect, even cooking, I prefer to use a thin stainless steel.

When it comes to frying, pan-broiling and sautéeing, I often use cast iron—for instance a wok. I don't use cast iron for delicate dishes and sauces because it is porous and retains elements that will discolor and give off tastes. Enamel-coated iron or heavy steel is fine for certain stews and braising. It is not good for searing or pan-frying; the foods won't brown properly.

I never use plain aluminum. The metal interacts with all acids. Almost all foods contain acid, from milk to wine to tomatoes to spinach to vinegar. I have more than once had the experience of giving someone a recipe for my Creamed Sorrel Soup (page 118) only to have them call, practically in tears, because the soup was nasty, black and didn't smell fresh. The first time I was at a loss for an answer. Then, after some detective work, I figured out that my friends had followed my recipe exactly, but they had ignored the sentence saying: "Do not use an aluminum pan." Sorrel is very acid and turns black and nasty when cooked in aluminum. Some dishes can be satisfactorily cooked in coated aluminum; but remember that it is porous and that when you make an intense reduction, such as that for a Beurre Blanc (page 53), as much as half of it may be absorbed by the pan.

Knives must be sharp and of good quality. Carbon steel is easier to sharpen than stainless; but if your sharpening steel or stone is hard enough, you can sharpen stainless knives. High-carbon stainless is the best. You must have some stainless knives for potatoes, onions, apples, lemons, turnips and the like or they will interact with the steel and the food will be discolored. I use a fourteen-inch chef's knife. I am small and I count on the weight of the knife to do most of the work. You can never have too many good paring knives. One non-serrated slicer and a tomato knife are luxuries. A swivel potato peeler and a bread knife are essentials. You will need a variety of sieves—ranging from coarse to very fine—and a colander, wooden spoons, wire whisks, and slotted spoons, a heavy rolling pin in wood and a marble board if you make a lot of pastry (I don't), otherwise a good wooden board to serve for cutting on one side and pastry on the other. A few heavy baking sheets and some stainless steel bowls will complete the list of necessities. If you don't have a food processor—I consider it a necessity by now—then you will need a food mill, a good idea in any case.

Necessity will never limit the avid cook. If you haven't already, you will be led on to amass molds, cake tins, specialty knives and spatulas. Beautiful ceramic bowls and stoneware casseroles increase the aesthetic pleasures of the kitchen. An electric ice-cream maker is a spiffy self-indulgence. You may want to try couscous in a real couscousière. In any case, you will soon want a steamer, although a sieve that fits well into a pot that is slightly deeper will serve. Soon you will want a larger kitchen . . .

• • •

ACKNOWLEDGMENTS

---•---

I learned to cook from cookbooks and from eating wonderfully in homes and restaurants. I owe a debt of gratitude to the authors like Ali Bab, Escoffier, Dione Lucas and James Beard who took the time to spell out the whats and whys of their doings for acolytes. By now, there are so many authors and books that the list of my debts is endless. In an America increasingly interested in good eating, the ideas are all around, particularly among my friends, the writers and restaurateurs. I thank them all.

I particularly thank the wonderful food people who work with me: Christopher Styler, Kathi Long, Lesley Farlow, Susan Frank, and Jane Helsel. Without Lois Bloom I couldn't exist. I send love to Joe Baum, who made me a professional. I thank my boosters and critics: my family, Stephen Spector, and the press. I am very fortunate to have had among them so many good teachers.

328

INDEX

sauces: Vinaigrettes: *(cont.)*
    enriched Vinaigrettes, 32, 197
    Everyday Vinaigrette, 316
    Ravigote Sauce, 44–45
    Soy-Sesame Vinaigrette, 266
  see also salad dressings
sauce supreme, chicken breasts with
    kumquats and, 194–196
sauerkraut, roast pork with, 184
sauerkraut stuffing, roast turkey with,
    170–172
sausages, 16–17
sausages, chicken legs, and bell
    peppers, 203–204
Sautéed Mushrooms with Lemon and
    Mustard, 270–271
Sautéed Zucchini with Dill, 274
Sauté of Chicken Livers with Okra, 247
Scallion and Radish Soup, 123–124
scallops:
    Beurre Blanc with, 52
    with Caviar and Saffron Beurre Blanc,
     56–57
    green pasta with tomato and, 88
    raw, with avocado, 33
    Scallops à la Américaine, 64–65
Scandinavian cold first courses, quick,
    18–19
scrambled eggs, with caviar, 12
scrod, in White Fish Stew, 162–163
seafood, *see* fish; shrimp, etc.
sea salt, 322
sereh powder (from lemon grass), 126
sesame-soy vinaigrette, Bibb lettuce
    with, 266
seviche, scallops, with avocado, 33
shallots, for Beurre Blanc, 52
shellfish:
    Beurre Blanc:
     to serve with, 52
     artichokes and snails with, 54–55
     with scallops and caviar, 56–57
    butters:
     shrimp, 146
     lobster, 146
    pasta, Green Pasta with Tomato and
     Scallops, 88
    salad, Lobster and Chicken Liver
     Salad, 218–219
    in soups:
     Bouillabaisse, 147–149
     Quick Bourride, 135–137
     Oyster Soup with Broth, 129–130
    with striped bass, 156–157
    see also clams, lobster, mussels,
     oysters, scallops, shrimp, snails
Shirred Eggs with Herbs, Tomatoes, and
    Cream, 72–73
Shoestring Potatoes Fried in Suet,
    254–255
short leg of lamb, 179
Short Ribs of Beef, 230–231

shrimp(s):
    Beurre Blanc with, 52
    boiled, spicy, 30–31
    to butterfly, 60
    canned, for quick first course, 18
    Hot Shrimp and Cabbage Slaw, 73–74
    Marinated Shrimp on the Grill, 59–60
    Party Shrimp and Chili Mayonnaise,
     30–31
    in Quick Bourride, 137
    and scallops with caviar and saffron
     Beurre Blanc, 56–57
    shells, to save for shrimp butter, 146
    Shrimp and Chicken Gumbo,
     144–147
    Shrimp Butter, 146–147
     in Beurre Blanc, 52
    Shrimp Quenelles with Watercress
     Sauce, 70–72
shucking of clams, 15–16
shucking of oysters, 16
side dishes, 251–263
    salads, 264–268
    vegetables, 269–277
Simple Potted Mushrooms, 20–21
skinning of smoked trout, 14
slaw, celery, 268
slaw, hot shrimp and cabbage, 73–74
smoked fish, 13–15
    eel, 13–14
    herb-buttered bread for, 14
    salmon, general information, 13; with
     pink peppercorns, 34
    sauces for, Gravlax, 14–15;
     horseradish whipped cream, 14
    to serve, 13–14
    sturgeon, 13
    trout, 13–14
    whitefish, in mousse, 43–44
Smoked Salmon with Pink Peppercorns,
    34
Smoked Whitefish Mousse, 43–44
snails with artichokes and Beurre Blanc,
    54–55
Sole in Pink Wine Sauce, 158–160
Sole Mousse with Grapefruit Sauce,
    57–59
sorbets:
    chocolate, 292
    chutney, 275
    fresh pineapple, 292–293
    pear, 286–287
sorrel, cooked in aluminum, 327
sorrel soup, cream of, 118–119
soups, 105–137
    from lamb stock, 241
    to lower calories, 324
    Navy-Bean Purée, 259
    from stock, 108
    whole-meal soups, 139–151
soy-sesame vinaigrette, Bibb lettuce
    with, 266

tomato(es): *(cont.)*
  Melting Tomatoes Provençale,
    272–273
  Roasted Yellow Peppers and
    Tomatoes, 35–36
  shirred eggs with herbs, cream and,
    72
  tomato purée, homemade, 82
tools, 326–327
tortellini:
  with basil, cream, and chives, 93–94
  Fake Pelmenyi, 141–142
transparent noodles, duck breasts with,
  211–212
trout, smoked, 13–14
  to bone, 14
turkey, roast, with sauerkraut stuffing,
  170–172
turkey stock, 111–112
"turned" potatoes, 255–256
turnip and potato purée, 258

unsalted butter, 324

varnitchkes, kasha, 261
veal:
  breast of, braised with spinach-
    mushroom stuffing, 234–236
  kidneys:
    to grill, 245
    with mustard sauce, 244–245
  Ossobucco, 232–233
  scaloppine with spinach-mushroom
    stuffing, 236
  stew, veal and artichoke-heart, 237
  Veal and Artichoke-Heart Stew, 237
  Veal Kidneys with Mustard Sauce,
    244–245
vegetables, 269–277
  dips for:
    Eggplant Caviar, 28
    Guacamole, 26
    Hummus, 30–31
    Roasted Red Pepper Spread, 19–20
    Tabbouleh, 25
    Tapenade, 24
    Taramasalata with Red Caviar,
      29–30
  mousses, 65–67
  Pot Cheese and Vegetable Salad,
    221–222
  puréed, 258–259
  sauces, cold, 317–318

vegetables *(cont.)*
  sauces for:
    Avgolemono, 314
    Hollandaise, 310–311
    Maltaise, 312
  stir-fried, 275–277
  Warm Vegetable Compote, 36–37
  see also name of vegetable; salads
Venison Stew, 247–249
Very Italian Cappelletti, 94–97
Vinaigrette, 315
  cumin, orange and onion salad with,
    34–35
  enriched, 32, 197
  everyday, 316
  Ravigote Sauce, 44–45
  soy-sesame, Bibb lettuce with, 266
vinegar, strawberries tossed in
  peppered, 282
vinegars, 324–325
vine leaves, stuffed, canned, 18
Volokh, Anne, *Art of Russian Cuisine,*
  12

Warm Vegetable Compote, 36–37
watercress sauce, shrimp quenelles
  with, 70–73
whipped cream, 297
  horseradish whipped cream, 14
White Bean Salad, 22
whitefish, smoked, mousse of, 43–44
White Fish Stew, 162–163
White Noodles, Green Cabbage, String
  Beans, and Cream, 87
white sauces, 90–92
whole-meal soups, 138–151
wine, 325
  in Beurre Blanc, 52
  dessert wines, 281
Winter Chicken, 202–203
Wolfert, Paula, 207
  The Cuisine of South-West France,
    209

yellow bell peppers and tomatoes,
  roasted, 35–36
yellow squash, green gazpacho with
  citrus fruit and, 121–122
Yogurt Dressing, 316

zucchini, sautéed, with dill, 274
Zucchini Custard, 273